EUROPEAN COMPANY LAW
TEXTS

British Institute Studies in International and Comparative Law No. 7

OTHER VOLUMES OF THE BRITISH INSTITUTE STUDIES IN INTERNATIONAL AND COMPARATIVE LAW

AUSTRALIA
The Law Book Company Ltd.
Sydney : Melbourne : Brisbane

GREAT BRITAIN
Stevens & Sons
London

INDIA
N. M. Tripathi Private Ltd.
Bombay

ISRAEL
Steimatzky's Agency Ltd.
Jerusalem : Tel Aviv : Haifa

MALAYSIA : SINGAPORE : BRUNEI
Malayan Law Journal (Pte.) Ltd.
Singapore

NEW ZEALAND
Sweet and Maxwell (N.Z.) Ltd.
Wellington

PAKISTAN
Pakistan Law House
Karachi

U.S.A. AND CANADA
Matthew Bender & Co. Inc.
New York

British Institute Studies in International
and Comparative Law No. 7

EUROPEAN COMPANY LAW
TEXTS

*(including the proposed Regulation on Merger Control and the
Draft Convention on Mergers across the Frontiers)*

Edited and introduced by

PROFESSOR CLIVE SCHMITTHOFF

with a Preface by

PROFESSOR K. R. SIMMONDS

Published under the auspices of
The British Institute of International and Comparative Law

NEW YORK   *LONDON*
MATTHEW BENDER   STEVENS & SONS
1974

Published in Great Britain by
Stevens & Sons of
11 New Fetter Lane, London
Published in the U.S.A. by
Matthew Bender & Co. Inc. of
235 East 45th Street,
New York, New York 10017

Printed in Great Britain by
The Eastern Press Ltd. of
London and Reading

ISBN 0420 444009

Library of Congress Catalog Card No. 73-93426

PREFACE

SINCE the genesis of the modern idea of the European Company (*Societas Europaea*) in 1959, all who are in any way concerned with the progress of the harmonisation and unification of European law, whether inside or outside the territorial boundaries of the European Communities, have followed with the greatest interest the development of proposals designed to bring about a gradual elimination of the major national divergences and differences in the structure and corporate procedures of companies. The Directive issued by the Council of Ministers of the European Economic Community, under Article 54 (2) of the Treaty of Rome, the various Draft Directives submitted to the Council by the Commission, and the Draft Statute prepared by the specialist committee chaired by Professor Pieter Sanders, have in particular attracted wide comment and criticism in recent years.

With the enlargement of the Communities this debate will take on a new impetus and direction. In this volume the principal texts are presented in the best available translation in the English language. They are introduced by a succinct and informative chronological survey, written by an outstanding authority in the field, which sets them in context and points particularly to their features of especial interest to common lawyers. The British Institute of International and Comparative Law is greatly indebted to the work of Professor Schmitthoff which has made this compilation and introduction possible and has enabled its publication at such a timely moment. The present collection of materials is up to date and comprehensive; necessarily, however, it can only present an interim statement of the progress achieved by a unique movement toward international legal co-operation and understanding.

The law is stated as on January 1, 1974.

British Institute of
International and Comparative Law.

K. R. SIMMONDS,
Director

v

CONTENTS

INTRODUCTION

TEXTS

Introduction

Sources of Community measures aiming at harmonisation of European company law

The aim of this introduction is to give a brief account of the sources on which the various measures of the European Community aimed at harmonisation of the company laws of the Member States are founded and to survey these measures. The objects which the Community pursues with its endeavour to achieve company law harmonisation and the philosophy motivating this great task are examined in *The Harmonisation of European Company Law*, published as Volume 1 of the United Kingdom Comparative Law Series.

The measures adopted or proposed by the Community in the field of company law are founded on different provisions of the EEC Treaty. These measures can be arranged into three categories:

1. Directives or Draft Directives;
2. Draft Regulations;
3. Conventions or Draft Conventions.

Directives

The Council Directive of March 9, 1968, and the Draft Directives published by the Commission are founded on Article 54 (3) (*g*) of the EEC Treaty. This Article provides:

> " The Council and the Commission shall carry out the duties evolving upon them under the preceding provisions in particular:
> (g) by co-ordinating to the necessary extent the safeguards which for the protection of the interests of members and others, are required by Member States of companies or firms within the meaning of the second paragraph of Article 58 [1] with a view to making such safeguards equivalent throughout the Community."

According to Article 54 (2) these duties shall be carried out by Council Directives which shall be issued on the proposal of the Commission and after consultation with the Economic and Social Committee and the European Parliament. The first of these Directives has already been approved and enacted by the Council. The others, which are likewise included in this Volume, are Draft Directives,

---

[1] Art. 58 (2): " ' Companies or firms ' means companies or firms constituted under civil or commercial law, including co-operative societies, and other legal persons governed by public or private law, save for those which are non-profit-making."

1

approved by the Commission and submitted to the Council. Considerable alterations may be expected before they will emerge from the Council in their final form and some time will elapse before the compromise on which the Council will be able to agree is reached. There is, however, no doubt that they will be enacted by the Council eventually because the operation of the Common Market is impossible without far-reaching harmonisation of the company laws of the Member States. It is to be hoped that the Council will enact all Draft Directives relating to company law *uno flatu*, so that the Member States can carry out the great reform of their national company laws by a single national enactment.

The Directives and Draft Directives published so far and reproduced in this volume are:

1. The First Council Directive of March 9, 1968, concerning the capacity of the company and its directors, and questions of publicity and nullity of the company.[2]

    By the European Communities Act 1972, which came into operation on January 1, 1973, the United Kingdom gave effect to the obligations undertaken by the Treaty of Accession of January 22, 1972. Section 9 of the Act of 1972, which is reproduced here, is intended to implement the provisions of the First Directive.[3]

2. The Second Draft Directive, concerning the formation of the company and the maintenance of capital, as amended.[4]

3. The Third Draft Directive, concerning mergers between joint stock companies, as amended.[5]

4. The Fourth Draft Directive, concerning the annual accounts of limited liability companies.[6]

5. The Fifth Draft Directive, concerning the structure of the limited liability company.[7]

6. The Sixth Draft Directive concerning groups of companies, which is not yet published.

7. An unnumbered Draft Directive, concerning the content, checking and distribution of the prospectus to be published when

---

2 68/151/EEC; J.O. 1968, L65/8. The First Directive is reproduced in No. 1 A, *post.*

3 s. 9 of the European Communities Act 1972 is reproduced in No. 1 B, *post.*

4 Submitted to the Commission by the Council on March 5, 1970: J.O. 1970, C48/8. The Second Draft Directive is reproduced in No. 2, *post.*

5 Submitted by the Commission to the Council on June 16, 1970: J.O. 1970, C89/20. The Third Draft Directive is reproduced in No. 3, *post.*

6 Submitted to the Commission by the Council on November 10, 1971: J.O. 1972, C7/11. The Fourth Draft Directive is reproduced in No. 4, *post.*

7 Submitted to the Commission by the Council on October 9, 1972: J.O. 1972, C131/49. The Fifth Draft Directive is reproduced in No. 5, *post.*

securities issued by companies are admitted to official stock
exchange quotation.[8]

Regulations

Other measures of company law harmonisation in the Community
will be implemented by way of regulations founded on Article 235
of the EEC Treaty. This Article provides:

> "If action by the Community should prove necessary to attain
> in the course of the operation of the Common Market, one of
> the objectives of the Community and this Treaty has not pro-
> vided the necessary powers, the Council shall, acting unanimously
> on a proposal from the Commission and after consulting the
> Assembly,[9] take the appropriate measures."

Founded on this provision, the Commission has submitted to the
Council the proposed Statute for the European company.[10] The
Commission has further published a Draft Regulation on the control
of mergers.[10a]

Conventions

The EEC Treaty further provides that certain measures relating
to the harmonisation of company law in Europe shall be adopted by
convention. It is surprising that the Treaty which admits the simpler
technique of the Directive for inter-EEC co-operation should refer to
the cumbersome international method of conventions. The explanation is that the measures required to be adopted by convention
necessitate lengthy negotiations between the Member States. These
negotiations are best carried out in the traditional way. As far as
company law is concerned, Article 220 provides:

> "Member States shall, so far as is necessary, enter into nego-
> tiations with each other with a view to securing for the benefit
> of their nationals: . . .
>
> > the mutual recognition of companies or firms within the
> > meaning of the second paragraph of Article 58, the reten-
> > tion of legal personality in the event of transfer of their seat
> > from one country to another, and the possibility of mergers
> > between companies or firms governed by the laws of different
> > countries. . . ."

[8] Submitted by the Commission to the Council on September 26, 1972: J.O. 1972,
C131/61. The Unnumbered Draft Directive is reproduced in No. 6, *post.*
[9] Now the European Parliament.
[10] Submitted by the Commission to the Council on June 30, 1970: J.O. 1970,
C124/1. The proposed Statute of the European Company is reproduced in
No. 7, *post.*
[10a] Submitted by the Commission to the Council on July 18, 1973. The proposed
Regulation is reproduced in No. 9, *post.*

In pursuance of this provision, the original Member States signed on February 29, 1968, the Convention on the Mutual Recognition of Companies and Legal Persons.[11] This Convention is supplemented by the Protocol concerning the Interpretation by the Court of Justice of the Convention, which Protocol was signed on June 3, 1971.[12] By the Act of Accession which forms part of the Treaty of Accession of January 22, 1972, the United Kingdom and the other new Member States have undertaken to accede to this Convention and the Protocol.[13] The United Kingdom has not signed the Convention and the Protocol yet. These measures will come into operation after ratification by all the Member States.

Further, in 1972 a Draft Convention on mergers across the frontiers, prepared by a committee of Government experts, was published.[13a]

The First Council Directive

Aims

The First Council Directive, dated March 9, 1968,[14] concerns three topics: the capacity of the company and its directors, publicity of important information relating to the company and questions of nullity of the company.

Area of application

The Directive applies, in principle, to companies of the public and private type (Art. 1) but, as shall be explained, the important requirement of publication of annual accounts does not apply to companies of the private type; they are, for the time being, exempt therefrom (Art. 2 (1) (*f*)). The companies which are covered by the First Directive are (Art. 1):

— In Germany:
   die Aktiengesellschaft, die Kommanditgesellschaft auf Aktien, die Gesellschaft mit beschränkter Haftung;
— In Belgium:

de naamloze vennootschap	*la société anonyme,*
de commanditaire vennootschap op aandelen	*la société en commandite par actions,*
de personenvennootschap met beperkte aansprakelijkheid;	*la société de personnes à responsabilité limitée;*

— In France:
   la société anonyme, la société en commandite par actions, la société à responsabilité limitée;

---

[11] The Convention is reproduced in No. 8 A, *post.*
[12] The Protocol is reproduced in No. 8 B, *post.*
[13a] Draft Convention reproduced in No. 10, *post.*
[13] Act of Accession, Art. 3 (2).
[14] n. 2, *ante*; p. 51, *post.*

— In Italy:

la società per azioni, società in accommadità per azioni, società a responsabilità limitata;

— In Luxembourg:

la société anonyme, la société en commandite par actions, la société à responsabilité limitée;

— In the Netherlands:

de naamloze vennootschap, de commanditaire vennootschap op aandelen, de besloten vennootschap.

In the United Kingdom, section 9 of the European Communities Act 1972 which seeks to implement the First Directive, states in subsection (8) that " this section shall be construed as one with the Companies Act 1948." The 1948 Act provides in section 455 that " ' company ' means a company formed and registered under this Act or an existing company." It follows that the First Directive, as applied in the United Kingdom, extends in principle to all public or private companies, whether companies limited by shares, limited by guarantee or unlimited companies. The extension to unlimited companies goes beyond the ambit of the First Directive which, as far as the original Member States are concerned, applies only to limited companies. It is, of course, possible that, having regard to Article 1 of the Directive, English courts will interpret section 9 as applying only to limited companies. Such an interpretation would, it is thought, be justified.

Arrangement

The First Directive is divided into four sections:

I. Disclosure. This section comprises the articles dealing with the various publicity requirements;
II. Validity of obligations entered into by a company;
III. Nullity of the company; and
IV. General provisions.

Publicity

As regards the first of these topics, subsections (3) to (7) of section 9 of the United Kingdom European Communities Act 1972 seek to give effect to Articles 2 to 6 of Section I of the First Directive. Thus, the requirement of public notification in subsection (3)—a new concept in British company law—is necessary to comply with Article 3 (4), according to which the disclosure of the documents and particulars required by the Directive shall be effected by publication in the national gazette, *inter alia* by a reference to the document which has been deposited in the file or entered in the register. On occasion the provisions of the Directive are expressed in clearer terminology than the corresponding provisions of section 9. This is, in particular true of the provisions explaining the effect of official notification before the expiration of fifteen days of grace after its publication in the official gazette. While the wording of subsection (4) of section 9 is somewhat obscure, it is clear from Article 3 (5) of the Directive, that the company may rely on the documents and particulars in question even before the official notification becomes effective if it can prove that the third party had knowledge of it.[15] In other instances the Directive gives no clue to the solution of controversial issues in English law. It is, for example, doubtful what an " order form " is which, according to subsection (7) of section 9 must state the place of registration, registration number and other particulars required by the subsection. Some argue that that means only supply orders, *i.e.*, orders on standardised forms emanating from the company and addressed to its suppliers. Others hold that the phrase includes purchase forms, *i.e.*, order forms of a standardised nature which the company issues to the purchasers of its goods. The Directive, in Article 4, uses the ambiguous phrase " order forms " (*notes de commande*). It is believed that the wider interpretation of this term is correct.

Unfortunately the differences in the registration of information in the register relating to companies are so great in the continental Member States that the First Directive could not prescribe the publication in a central register. It provides in Article 3 that—

" In each Member State a file shall be opened in a central register, commercial register, or companies register, for each of the companies registered therein."

The companies regulation of the United Kingdom applies the principle of central registration. There exist three Registrars of Companies: one in London for companies registered in England and Wales, another in Edinburgh for companies registered in Scotland and the third in Belfast for companies registered in Northern Ireland.[16] In West Germany, on the other hand, the principle of decentralised registration is applied. The particulars relating to companies are registered in the commercial registers kept by the county courts (*Amtsgerichte*), and in the Federal Republic there are 776 of these courts.[17]

---

[15] See Robert Drury in [1973] J.B.L. 98.

[16] Northern Ireland has its own Companies Act. The British Companies Acts 1948 and 1967 do not extend to Northern Ireland (1948 Act, s. 461).

[17] Wolfgang Heyde, *The Administration of Justice in the Federal Republic of Germany*, p. 61. But not all *Amtsgerichte* keep commercial registers.

Validity of obligations entered into by a company

Here the Directive introduces the broad principle that a third party who contracts with the company may rely on the act being within the objects of the company, provided that the act is done by " the organs " of the company. The term " organs " is rendered in section 9 (1) of the European Communities Act as " directors," meaning evidently the board of directors (Art. 9 (1) and s. 9 (1)). The Directive authorises Member States to provide " that the company shall not be bound where such acts are outside the objects of the company, if it proves that the third party knew that the act was outside those objects or could not in view of the circumstances have been unaware of it " (Art. 9 (1)). The United Kingdom has made use of this authorisation, but the European Communities Act 1972 has substituted for the precise terms of the Directive the nebulous phrase of " good faith " (s. 9 (1)). It is clear from the wording of Article 9 (1) of the Directive that a party does not act in good faith if he is put on inquiry by the circumstances surrounding the transaction. Constructive notice, as such, does not impute knowledge to the third party.

This section of the Directive also contains provisions aiming at the protection of third parties in two other cases: where a director who has been appointed irregularly has acted on behalf of the company (Art. 8), and where a contract has been concluded in the name of the company prior to its registration (Art. 7).

The provisions of Article 9 (1) and (2) of the Directive made it necessary to carry out a most incisive change in British company law. That is the restriction of the *ultra vires* doctrine which is provided for by section 9 (1) of the European Communities Act.

As against a third party, a company can no longer plead that a transaction decided on by its board of directors is not within its objects, provided that the third party acted in good faith. Internally, *i.e.*, in the relationship of the company to its shareholders and directors, the *ultra vires* doctrine is still operative. It is, *e.g.*, possible for the shareholder to obtain an injunction preventing the directors from acting outside the objects of the company.[18] Further, the third party can apparently still plead against the company that it acted *ultra vires*.

Nullity of the company

The First Directive contains in Section III, provisions regulating a problem which has caused difficulty in some continental countries but is fortunately unknown in the United Kingdom. In English law,

---

[18] See Fifth Cumulative Supplement to Palmer's *Company Law* (21st ed., 1973), note to p. 82.

the grant of the certificate of incorporation is regarded as an act of delegated legislation [19] which derives its authority from the sovereign power of Parliament. It is a constituent act: it " creates " the company as a body corporate.[20] Consequently, it is not surprising that the certificate of incorporation is treated as conclusive evidence that the company has been duly formed [21]; this prevents the reopening of matters prior and contemporaneous to the registration and essential to it, and it places the existence of the company as a legal person beyond doubt.[22] The question of nullity or invalidity of the company owing to a defect in its formation cannot arise in English law.

In continental European company law the situation is different or at least was different before effect was given to the First Directive in the continental Member States. The doctrinal difference is that particularly in France the contractual theory is adopted. The company is regarded as founded on a contract between the incorporators and is, therefore, subject to the same grounds of invalidity as every other contract, for example, in case of fraud or relevant mistake. In Germany, on the other hand, as in the United Kingdom, the institutional theory prevails. In striking contrast with the French pattern, . . . the idea of the company as a contract has been done away with [23]; and the invalidity based on contractual grounds has been abolished. According to Professor Eric Stein [24]—

> " [German law] offers other remedies designed to protect those interests that deserve protection, without impairing the existence of the company. This has also been the solution in Belgium and Luxembourg. Paradoxically, however, the German (and Italian) law has retained action for invalidity on a number of grounds based on more or less formal defects, such as omission of certain received information from the charter [25]; yet no action is available on these grounds in French law."

The doctrinal difference of continental jurisprudence on the nature of the company has led to a different attitude in the procedure of registration. In Germany, Italy and the Netherlands the preventive method of registration is used but in France the registration is purely declaratory. Under the preventive method the documents sought to be registered are examined with respect to their formal and substantial validity. Under the declaratory system the registrar has to

---

[19] Palmer's *Company Law*, 21st ed., p. 119.
[20] Companies Act 1948, s. 13 (2).
[21] *Ibid.* s. 15 (1).
[22] Palmer's *Company Law*, 21st ed., p. 121.
[23] Eric Stein, *Harmonisation of European Company Laws* (Indianapolis: Bobbs-Merrill Co., 1971), p. 306.
[24] *Ibid.* pp. 306–307, footnotes omitted.
[25] In the English terminology " the memorandum," in French " *le statut*," in German " *die Satzung*."

accept them if the formal requirements are satisfied, and to register them. In Germany and Italy the preventive function is performed by a judge, in the Netherlands by the Ministry of Justice. In France, the company documents are registered by a clerk (*greffier*).

Faced with the divergencies of doctrine in the original member countries, Section III of the First Directive has adopted a compromise solution. It provides that in all countries which have not adopted preventive control, administrative or judicial, the company statutes and any amendments shall be drawn up and certified in due legal form (Art. 10). Both types of registration, the preventive and declaratory, are thus admitted. The Directive then goes on to restrict the claim for nullity of the company considerably. Nullity can be ordered only by a decision of the court and only on a few narrowly defined grounds (Art. 11). Further, public notification of the court decision pronouncing for nullity of the company is required if it is intended to rely on it against a third party who has acted in good faith (Art. 12). Two further provisions have to be mentioned: nullity shall not of itself affect the validity of any commitment entered into by or with the company (Art. 12 (3)), and the shareholders remain liable for the unpaid amount due on their shares, in spite of the nullity of the company, to the extent that commitments entered into with the creditors so require (Art. 12 (5)).

Since English law does not know the concept of nullity of the company, once it is registered, Section III of the First Directive did not necessitate an alteration of English company law.

The European Communities Act 1972, s. 9

The object of this section is to give effect in the United Kingdom to the provisions of the First Directive.[25a] As far as English law was at variance with the principles of that Directive, it had to be altered. The main provisions of section 9 are:

(1) the *ultra vires* doctrine is restricted (s. 9 (1));

(2) the law relating to the powers of the directors to act for the company is affected (s. 9 (1));

(3) pre-registration contracts are regulated (s. 9 (2));

(4) official notification of the issue or receipt of specified documents is introduced (s. 9 (3));

(5) the latest version of the memorandum and articles must be made available to the public in an easily accessible form (s. 9 (5) and (6)); and

(6) certain particulars must be stated on business letters and order forms (s. 9 (7)).

Comparative reference to some of the provisions of section 9 is

[25a] s. 9 is reproduced at p. 58, *post*.

made in the preceding discussion of the First Directive. A detailed
treatment of section 9 and its effect on English company law is out of
place here; it is contained in the Fifth and following Cumulative
Supplements to Palmer's *Company Law*, 21st edition.

The Second Draft Directive

Aims

The Second Draft Directive [26] is reproduced in this volume in a
version showing the amendments adopted by the Commission following the accession of the three new Member States to the Community.

The aims of the Second Draft Directive are to provide minimum
requirements for the formation of the company, the maintenance,
increase and reduction of capital.

Area of application

The Draft Directive applies only to companies of the public
type. They are defined in the amended version as follows (Art. 1 (1));

— in Germany: *die Aktiengesellschaft*;
— in Belgium : *la société anonyme, de naamloze vennootschap*;
— in France: *la société anonyme*;
— in Italy: *la società per azioni*;
— in Luxembourg: *la société anonyme*;
— in the Netherlands: *de naamloze vennootschap*;
— in the United Kingdom: companies incorporated with limited
   liability;
— in Ireland: companies incorporated with limited liability;
— in Denmark: *Aktieselskab*.

It should be noted that, as far as the United Kingdom and
Ireland are concerned, the amended Second Draft Directive refers
to " companies incorporated with limited liability " and not to public
companies [27] although the Draft Directive does not extend to the
société à responsabilité limitée and the *Gesellschaft mit beschränkter
Haftung*. The reason for this remarkable regulation is that the Commission does not consider the United Kingdom private company as
equivalent to the French SARL and the German GmbH but treats
it as a company of the *société anonyme* type which has not obtained
—and cannot obtain—quotation at the stock exchange. On the other
hand, the Netherlands *besloten vennootschap* is treated as equivalent
to the French and German form of private company; it is not

---

[26] Submitted by the Commission to the Council on March 5, 1970; J.O. 1970,
C48/8; reproduced in No. 2, *post*.
[27] The expression " public company " is used in the Companies Act 1948, *viz*., in
s. 181 (5) (c) and the heading of the Third Schedule; see Palmer's *Company
Law*, 21st ed., p. 33, n. 8.

included in the catalogue of Article 1 (1). To achieve equivalence, an alteration of the law relating to private companies would be necessary in the United Kingdom. It would be necessary to provide by statute that a private company must indicate its character in its name, for example, by adding the word " private " or an abbreviation of it, and that the transfer of shares, on principle, be restricted to existing members or, if the transfer is intended to an outsider, shall require the consent of the board of directors for its validity. Such a statutory alteration of the present law relating to private companies would be desirable. It would make it unnecessary to prescribe a minimum capital for companies of that type.

The Second Draft Directive authorises the Member States to exempt from its application investment companies (Art. 1 (2)). They are defined as companies—

— whose sole object is to invest their funds in a variety of stocks and shares with the single aim of spreading investment risks and giving their shareholders the benefit of the results of the management of the investment portfolio;

— which invite the public to invest in their own shares; and

— whose statutes provide that within the limits of a minimum and a maximum capital the shares may at any time be issued, redeemed or resold.

If the companies are exempted by national legislation from complying with the requirements of the Second Draft Directive, they must show the words " investment company " on all documents in respect of which there exists an obligation of disclosure and on all business papers (Art. 1 (2)).

Arrangement

The Second Draft Directive is arranged in five sections:

I. Formation of the company.
II. Maintenance of the integrity of the company's capital.
III. Increase of capital.
IV. Reduction of capital.
V. Final provision.

Formation of company

The provisions relating to the formation of the company are described by Dr. H. C. Ficker thus [28]:

" As far as formation is concerned, Articles 2 and 3 require minimum standards for the memorandum and articles and the

[28] *The Harmonisation of European Company Law*, ed. by Clive M. Schmitthoff, 1973, p. 76.

formation act, if any. The required indications are the classical information about the company, such as the corporate form, the commercial name, legal seat, company's objects, the amount of share capital, the different kinds of shares and the composition and competence of the different corporate organs."

The Second Draft Directive further provides that, where a national company law requires a minimum number of shareholders, the fact that their number has fallen below the legal minimum, shall not lead to the automatic dissolution of the company (Art. 5). This is in harmony with the law of the United Kingdom (Companies Act 1948, s. 31). The Draft Directive also lays down that where a company may be " dissolved " in these circumstances by order of the court, it must be possible for the competent court to give the company a period of grace of at least six months to regularise the position. That is again similar to the provisions of English law (1948 Act, ss. 31 and 222 (*d*)). This regulation of the Draft Directive appears to oblige Member States to abolish the French doctrine of *simulation* for companies to which the Draft Directive applies,[29] if they subscribe to that theory. According to that doctrine, if all the shares of a company are held by one shareholder, the company is a *société fictive*, ceases to be a company automatically, and the one man who holds all the shares is personally liable without limitation of liability.

The most important provision in this section of the Second Draft Directive is that requiring a minimum capital of 25,000 units of account [30] (approximately £10,000 [31]) on subscription for a company covered by that Draft Directive, but that amount may be raised or lowered by 10 per cent. for purposes of conversion into national currency (Art. 6 (I)). Higher amounts may be required by national legislation as a condition for quotation on a stock exchange or if the company engages in special kinds of business, for example, banking or insurance (Art. 6 (II) (2)). As far as the United Kingdom and Ireland are concerned, a lower minimum capital is admitted for private companies. These companies can be formed with a minimum capital of 4,000 units of account (approximately £2,000) if they satisfy the following conditions (Art. 6 (II) (1)) :

  (a) they cannot issue bearer shares, bearer certificates relating to registered shares, or debentures;
  (b) their shares cannot be quoted on a stock exchange;
  (c) the statutes restrict the right to transfer the shares;
  (d) the name of the company must include the word " private."

---

[29] See R. Rodière, *Droit commercial, Groupements commerciaux* (7th ed., 1971), para. 12.
[30] One unit of account is equivalent to one U.S. dollar at the pre-devaluation rate of exchange, *i.e.*, prior to 1972.   [31] Position on July 1, 1973.

These conditions differ from those imposed by section 28 of the Companies Act 1948:

1. The Companies Act only prescribes that the conditions must be laid down in the articles, but apart from (c) above the Draft Directive appears to require its conditions to be an obligatory statutory provision.
2. The Draft Directive requires the name of the company to contain the word " private." No such condition is imposed by section 28.
3. The section postulates, on principle, a maximum number of fifty shareholders, but no maximum number is provided by the Draft Directive.
4. The Draft Directive requires a statutory prohibition preventing the shares from being quoted on a stock exchange, whereas the section requires a prohibition in the articles preventing the company from issuing a prospectus whether the shares are quoted on the stock exchange or not.

The requirement of a minimum capital poses a problem. All national laws in the European Community, except those of the Netherlands, Ireland and the United Kingdom, require a minimum capital for companies of the public and private type. The introduction of a minimum capital of 25,000 units of account for public companies would cause no difficulty in the United Kingdom because most public companies have such a capital. On the other hand, the requirement of a minimum capital of 10,000 units of account for private companies would be unfortunate. Many private companies may be unable to satisfy this requirement. That would be a serious threat to the economic structure of Great Britain which in 1971 had 560,551 private companies, as compared with 100,690 GmbHs in West Germany at the end of 1972.[32] It is to be hoped, as already indicated,[33] that the equalisation of the British private company with the French SARL and the German GmbH can be achieved and the imposition of the requirement of a minimum capital for the private company can be avoided. The difference between British law and the regulation proposed by the Second Draft Directive does not extend to the area of publicity of accounts because in British law a private limited company has to publish its accounts in like manner as a public company.[34]

If on formation the shares are issued against cash they must be paid up to at least 25 per cent. (Art. 7). If they are issued in con-

---

[32] For Great Britain: *Companies in 1971*, published by H.M.S.O. in 1972. For West Germany: *Frankfurter Allgemeine Zeitung*, April 14, 1973.
[33] See p. 11, *ante.*
[34] Companies Act 1967, s. 2.

sideration of assets other than cash, a valuation of these assets and
the shares issued against them by an independent expert must be
carried out and official notification has to be given of the report of
the expert (Art. 8). Similar rules apply to shares issued on an
increase of capital (Arts. 21 and 23).

Maintenance of the integrity of the company's capital

Of the detailed provisions of section II of the Second Draft
Directive, the following deserve to be mentioned.

Dividends shall only be paid out of " clear profits " which would
include realised profits on sale of capital assets (Art. 13). The company is not allowed to acquire its own shares by subscription (Art. 17).
The Draft Directive does not prohibit the purchase of its own shares
by the company because, unlike the position in English law,[35] the
company can acquire its own shares in Germany freely,[36] in the
Netherlands fully paid up shares can be acquired by the company
usually up to 50 per cent. of the capital [37] and in France shares may
be purchased, subject to certain conditions, up to 10 per cent.[38] The
Draft Directive contains, however, strict rules regulating the purchase
of its own shares by the company (Arts. 18–20). It provides in
particular that if a national law permits a company to include its
own shares into its assets, the following safeguards must be prescribed:

  (a) the voting rights of the shares shall be suspended;
  (b) where the shares are included into the balance sheet as assets,
      a non-distributable reserve—a quasi-capital fund—shall be
      shown of the same amount on the liabilities-side; and
  (c) the directors' report must give full publicity relating to those
      shares (Art. 20).

The British capital structure and particularly the concept of the
authorised capital are unknown on the continent of Europe. The
Draft Directive naturally adopts the continental capital structure
but it allows the general meetings to authorise the " competent
organs " of the company—presumably the managing board—to
increase the subscribed capital up to a fixed amount. This authority
may be given for a maximum of five years but may be renewed from
time to time for like periods (Art. 22 (2)).

---

[35] *Trevor* v. *Whitworth* (1887) 12 App.Cas. 409.
[36] See German Companies Act of 1965, ss. 215 and 237 (1).
[37] *Wetboek van Koophandel*, Arts. 41*a* and 41*b*.
[38] The French Regulation is complicated: see Professor André Tunc in *The
Harmonisation of European Company Law*, ed. C. M. Schmitthoff, 1973, p. 35.

Increase and reduction of capital

The increase of capital must be voted by the general meeting, subject to the five-years' authority to the directors which has just been discussed (Art. 22). Where on increase there is a cash issue of shares, the existing shareholders have a proportionate right of pre-emption (Art. 25 (1)) but this right may be restricted or withdrawn if the articles so provide, by the general meeting or by an organ of the company acting under authority of the general meeting (Art. 25 (2) and (3)); convertible bondholders have the same rights (Art. 25 (4)). If the company makes a bonus or rights issue, it may use the legal reserve only in so far as it exceeds 10 per cent. of the capital (Art. 26).

The reduction of capital is likewise decided upon by the general meeting, but it may also be authorised by it. This presumably means that the capital can be reduced by the board of directors with the authority of the general meeting (Art. 27). The Draft Directive contains the usual provisions aimed at the protection of creditors and classes of shares but, unlike English law (1948 Act, s. 66), does not require the confirmation of the court for the contemplated reduction of capital (Arts. 27–34). The Draft Directive contains, however, two important provisions which should be mentioned here. First, the national laws shall prescribe that in the case of serious loss of the subscribed capital a general meeting must be called for the purpose of " taking the necessary measures or considering whether the company should be dissolved "; a " serious loss " is the loss of 50 per cent. of the subscribed capital but the national laws may prescribe a lower figure (Art. 16). Secondly, where Member States' laws authorise the redemption of shares with or without reduction of the company's capital, several conditions must be observed, one of which is that " the procedure adopted for the transaction complies with the principle of equal treatment of shareholders " (Art. 34 (*a*)).

The Third Draft Directive
Aims

The aims of the Third Draft Directive [39] are to secure a minimum degree of co-ordination in the provisions dealing with internal mergers in the company laws of the Member States. At present the national regulation varies considerably. One of the reasons why harmonisation is necessary in this area is that without it it is hardly possible for the Member States to conclude a convention on mergers across the frontiers, as demanded by Article 220.[40] The amended Draft Directive is already aligned on the proposed draft convention.

---

[39] Submitted by the Commission to the Council on June 16, 1970, and published in J.O. 1970, C89/20. The Third Draft Directive is reproduced in No. 3, p. 74, *post*, in the form amended after the accession of the three new Member States.

[40] See pp. 3 and 4, *ante*. The Draft Convention on mergers across the frontiers is reproduced in No. 10, *post*.

Area of application

The Third Draft Directive applies only to companies of the public type which are defined as follows (Art. 1 (1)) :

— in Germany: *die Aktiengesellschaft*;
— in Belgium: *la société anonyme, de naamloze vennootschap*;
— in France: *la société anonyme*;
— in Italy: *la società per azioni*;
— in Luxembourg: *la société anonyme*;
— in the Netherlands: *de naamloze vennootschap.*
— in Denmark: *Aktieselskab*;
— in Ireland: companies incorporated with limited liability:
— in the United Kingdom : companies incorporated with limited
   liability.

Arrangement

The Third Draft Directive is arranged in six chapters:

    I. Merger by take-over of one company by another and merger by formation of a new company.
    II. Merger by take-over.
    III. Merger by formation of a new company.
    IV. Take-over of one company by another which is its sole shareholder.
    V. Other operations.
    VI. General and final provisions.

The meaning of " merger "

A merger within the meaning of the Draft Directive takes place when by a universal act of succession the whole of the assets and liabilities of the company to be absorbed is transferred to the absorbing company, the former is wound up and, without going through the winding up procedure, ceases to exist, and the shareholders of the absorbed company are allotted shares in the absorbing company. Various types of merger are admitted by the Draft Directive, as we shall see, but the features here explained are common to all of them; without them there would be no merger within the meaning of the Draft Directive.

Comparison with British take-over procedure

The procedure envisaged by the Draft Directive can be carried out in English law but does not correspond to the take-over procedure customary in the United Kingdom. It can be carried out here by virtue of sections 206 and 208 of the Companies Act 1948, and possibly also under section 287. The sanction of the court is required by the former two sections and the court has power to sanction the transfer to the absorbing company " of the whole or any part of the undertaking and of the property or liabilities " of the absorbed company [41] and the issue of shares of the former company to the shareholders of the latter.

The customary British take-over procedure does not, as such, fall under the Third Draft Directive. Under the customary British procedure the absorbing company purchases directly the shares in the absorbed company from the shareholders of the latter, and neither a universal transfer of assets and liabilities from the absorbed to the absorbing company nor the winding up of the absorbed company is required. On the contrary, more often than not, after a successful take-over, the absorbed company remains operative as a wholly-owned subsidiary of the absorbing company. Only if, after the take-over is carried out successfully, the absorbing company contemplates the universal transfer of the assets and liabilities of the absorbed company, the winding up of the latter and its cessation without going through the winding up procedure, would the case fall under the Third Draft Directive because the situation is covered by Chapter IV (Art. 20). Nor can it be said that the customary British take-over is a transaction akin to a merger within Chapter V of the Draft Directive because the absorbed company does not transfer to the absorbing company " the whole or part of its assets." All that takes place is that the shareholders of the absorbed company, in consideration of cash or paper (shares in the absorbing company) or both, sell and transfer their shares in the absorbed company to the absorbing company.

Difficulties encountered by the draftsmen of the Third Draft Directive

The draftsmen of the Third Draft Directive encountered serious difficulties because the legal requirements prescribed in the national laws of the original Member States varied considerably. These difficulties are described in the explanatory memorandum to the Draft Directive as follows [42]:

> " Although the way in which mergers are prepared and implemented is much the same in all Member States, there are serious divergences in the legal classification of the various transactions.

---

[41] There is, however, the difference that in English law the act of universal transfer does not operate as a transfer of a contract of service from the old to the new employer, because that type of contract is personal and cannot be transferred without consent of the employee (*Nokes* v. *Doncaster Amalgamated Collieries* [1940] A.C. 1014), whereas continental law does not know this qualification.
[42] Comment to Art. 3.

In some Member States the managements are required to conclude a merger contract before the general meetings rule on the matter. Under other legal systems the agreement between the managements is not subject to special conditions and all that the law does is to give the general meetings the power to decide on the merger. Finally, in other Member States, a merger contract may not be concluded by the managements until the merger has been approved by the general meetings of the companies involved."

The Commission saw no need completely to eliminate these divergences and considered it sufficient to ensure compliance with certain minimum requirements. The most important of them are that the merger should be approved by the general meetings of both merging companies. A two-thirds majority of the votes attaching to the shares represented at the meeting or of the company capital represented at the meeting (Art. 4 (1)) is prescribed, but the national company laws of the Member States may require a higher majority (*ibid.*). This should be compared with the three-quarters majority required by section 206 (2) of the 1948 Act. Secondly, before the general meetings decide whether to approve or reject the proposed merger, the directors must prepare a " merger plan " which must contain at least the particulars listed in Article 3 (2). The merger plan must be made available to the shareholders of each of the merging companies at least two months before the general meeting and official notification must be given of it (Art. 5 (3)). In addition, the directors of each of the merging companies must present a detailed report explaining and justifying the merger and valuations by experts have to be produced (Art. 5). Further, the directors must present a report to the staffs of each of the merging companies and their report must explain the legal, economic and social effects which the merger will have on the staff. This report must be discussed with the works council (*comité d'entreprise, Betriebsrat*) before the general meeting takes place and the council may express its opinion in writing; that opinion must be available at the general meeting voting on the merger (Art. 6). When the merger becomes effective, the absorbed company ceases to exist (Art. 15 (1) (*c*)).

Kinds of mergers

The Draft Directive admits three types of merger:

(1) merger by take-over (*fusion par absorption*);

(2) merger by formation of a new company (*fusion par constitution d'une société nouvelle*);

(3) take-over of one company by another company which is its sole shareholder (*absorption d'une société par une autre possédant la totalité des actions de la première*).

The merger by take-over (Arts. 3–18) is the pure form of merger: company A acquires all assets and liabilities of company B by a single act of universal transfer, company B is wound up and disappears without going through the winding up procedure, and the former shareholders of B are given shares in A. A merger by formation of a new company (Art. 19) is carried out by companies A and B transferring their assets and liabilities by universal transfer to the newly formed company C, companies A and B disappear and their shareholders become shareholders in C. This is a kind of merger which is not essentially different from the pure merger. In the third kind of merger, the acquisition of a company by another holding all shares in it (Art. 20), a wholly owned subsidiary disappears without going through the winding up procedure and its assets and liabilities are transferred by a single act to the holding company.

The essential requirements prescribed by the Draft Directive for merger and discussed in the preceding section apply to all types of merger but there are variations in detail. Thus, in the last-mentioned kind of merger the report of the directors to the shareholders and the valuation by experts (Art. 5 (1), (2)) are not required (Art. 20 (1)).

The Fourth Draft Directive
Aims

The Fourth Draft Directive on the Annual Accounts of Limited Liability Companies [43] aims at establishing in the Community " equivalent legal requirements as regards the extent of the financial information that should be made available to the public by companies." [44] To that end, the Draft Directive prescribes numerous obligatory items for the balance sheet and profit and loss account. Further, in the view of the Commission, the different methods permitted in the Member States for the valuation of assets and liabilities require co-ordination. The establishment of uniform minimum standards for the accounts of companies is one of the key subjects of company law harmonisation in the Community.

Area of application

The Fourth Draft Directive applies to companies of the public and private type but different measures of co-ordination are prescribed for these companies (Art. 1).

[43] Submitted to the Commission by the Council on November 10, 1971, and published in J.O. 1972, C7/11; reproduced in No. 4, *post.*
[44] Preamble to the Fourth Draft Directive.

Articles 2 to 47 apply to companies of the public type, *viz.*:

— in Germany: *die Aktiengesellschaft, the Kommanditgesell-schaft auf Aktien*;

— in Belgium: *la société anonyme, de naamloze vennoot-schap*; *la société en commandite par actions, de commanditaire vennootschap op aandelen*;

— in France: *la société anonyme, la société en commandite par actions*;

— in Italy: *la società per azioni, la società in accomandita per azioni*;

— in Luxembourg: *la société anonyme, la société en commandite par actions*;

— in the Netherlands: *de naamloze vennootschap, de commanditaire vennootschap op aandelen.*

Articles 48 to 50 contain special provisions applying to companies of the private type, *viz.*:

— in Germany: *die Gesellschaft mit beschränkter Haftung*;

— in Belgium: *la société de personnes à responsabilité limitée, de personenvennootschap met beperkte aansprakelijkheid*;

— in France: *la société à responsabilité limitée*;

— in Italy: *la società a responsabilità limitata*;

— in Luxembourg: *la société à responsabilité limitée*;

— in the Netherlands: *de besloten vennootschap met beperkte aanspakelijkheid.*

As regards companies of the private type, the Draft Directive establishes three categories (Arts. 49 and 50).

1. The lowest category comprises small private companies. They must satisfy at the date of the balance sheet all of the following requirements:

(a) the balance sheet total must not exceed 100,000 units of account;

(b) the net turnover must not exceed 200,000 units of account; and

(c) the average number of employees during the year must not have exceeded twenty.

The Member States may allow these companies to publish only an abridged balance sheet (Art. 50 (2) (*b*)) and abridged notes on the accounts (Art. 50 (2) (*b*)).

2. The next category includes medium-sized companies. They must satisfy the following conditions at the date of the balance sheet:

(a) the balance sheet total must not exceed 1,000,000 units of account;

(b) the net turnover must not exceed 2,000,000 units of account; and

(c) the average number of employees during the year must not have exceeded 100.

The Member States may permit these companies to publish an abridged profit and loss account but they must publish the balance sheet and notes on the accounts in full (Art. 50 (2) (*a*)).

3. The third category includes large private companies which do not fall into the preceding categories. They must, on principle, publish their accounts in full, like companies of the public type (Art. 48).

The Member States are authorised not to apply the provisions of the Draft Directive to banks and insurance companies until the requirements for these types of business are co-ordinated (Art. 1 (2)).

Arrangement

The Fourth Draft Directive is arranged in twelve sections:

1. General requirements.
2. Lay-out of the annual accounts.
3. Balance sheet lay-out.
4. Special provisions relating to certain items in the balance sheet.
5. Lay-out of the profit and loss account.
6. Special provisions relating to certain items in the profit and loss account.
7. Valuation rules.
8. Contents of the notes on the accounts.
9. Contents of the annual report.
10. Publication.
11. Special provisions relating to the *société à responsabilité limitée, the Gesellschaft mit beschränkter Haftung, the società a responsabilità limitata and the Vennootschap met beperkte aansprakelijkheid.*
12. Final provisions.

The accounts

The accounts required by the Draft Directive are:

(1) the balance sheet;
(2) the profit and loss account; and
(3) the notes on the accounts.

These documents shall constitute a composite whole (Art. 2 (1)). The annual accounts must be audited [45] and adopted by the general meeting but the national laws of the Member States may provide that they may be adopted by the management organ and the supervisory organ unless those two organs decide otherwise or fail to agree.[46]

The Fourth Draft Directive also contains provisions on the annual report. That report " shall contain a detailed review of the development of the company's business and of its position " (Art. 43 (1)). The report shall also contain particulars of—

(a) any important events that have occurred since the close of the business year;

(b) the company's likely future developments (Art. 43 (2)).

The annual report has to be made by the organs of the company. The Draft Directive refrains from requiring an annual report as part of or in combination with the annual accounts because in some Member States no distinction is drawn between the notes on the accounts and the annual report. In those countries the information to be given in the annual report must be given in the notes.

The notes on accounts which form part of the annual accounts must be published in full in the national gazette (Art. 44 (2)), but the annual report need only be deposited with the register of companies and official notification has to be given of it (Art. 44 (3)). The auditor's certificate must likewise be published in full (Art. 45). Together with the published account the allocation of the results must be published where the accounts do not show how the results are to be used (Art. 47).

The balance sheet

For presentation of the balance sheet the Member States are to allow companies to choose between the horizontal and the narrative forms, of which Articles 8 and 9 contain the respective lay-outs. In the former case, the asset items and liability items are arranged on opposite sides, the asset items appearing on the debit side and the liability items on the credit side. In the narrative form, the asset items and the liability items are set out in columnar form. The choice of the one method of presentation or the other does not materially affect the making of comparisons between different companies.

Presentation in the horizontal form is the more widespread in practice. The narrative form, already in use in one of the original Member States, is offered as an alternative, in view of possible future

---

[45] The provisions on the audit, including the qualifications required of the auditor, are contained in the Fifth Draft Directive, Arts. 48 to 63. They are discussed on p. 31, *post.*

[46] Fifth Draft Directive, Art. 48.

developments.[47] For both forms of the balance sheet long lists of compulsory items are prescribed (Arts. 8 and 9); an omission of some of these items is admitted in the case of small private companies (Art. 50 (2) (*b*)).[48]

Both forms of the balance sheet contain as an obligatory item a position for a " legal reserve." The Fifth Draft Directive which applies to companies of the public type requires the formation of a legal reserve of not less than 10 per cent. of the capital.[49] In so far the proposals of the Commission follow German law.[50]

The profit and loss account

For presentation of the profit and loss account, the Member States must introduce into their law one of the four different lay-outs provided for in Articles 20 to 23. These lay-outs differ first as to their external form (horizontal or narrative) and secondly as to the method of treating and distributing charges and earnings. In the lay-outs given in Articles 20 and 21, there are on the one hand the total charges for the year classified according to their nature, and on the other hand the products sold (turnover), plus the production effected during the year but not yet sold, less the production sold during the year but produced in a previous year. In the lay-out set out in Articles 22 and 23 the operating charges are classified essentially according to their function, and the charges corresponding to the production sold are shown opposite the amount of the turnover. Freedom of choice between several lay-outs is necessary because from the business point of view the different principles governing the profit and loss account all have their advantages and disadvantages.[51]

Valuation rules

According to Dr. H. C. Ficker[52] " perhaps the most important part of the Directive consists in the harmonisation of the provisions concerning valuation (Sect. 7). Annual accounts which are not established on the same basis of valuation are without any indicatory effect."

The principles which guided the Commission in its proposals are set out in the explanatory memorandum thus[53]:

[47] Statement of Grounds (Explanatory Memorandum) of the Fourth Draft Directive, comment on Article 7.
[48] See p. 20, *ante.*
[49] Fifth Draft Directive, Art. 49; see p. 31, *post.*
[50] German *Aktiengesetz* of 1965, s. 150.
[51] Statement of Grounds, p. 47.
[52] *The Harmonisation of European Company Law*, ed. Clive M. Schmitthoff, 1973, p. 80.
[53] Statement of Grounds, pp. 51–52.

" Valuation in the annual accounts can at present be effected in principle by two methods: the purchase price method and the replacement value method.

In favour of the use of the purchase price method it can basically be said that the historical value can be ascertained precisely, whereas values that are determined by taking account of fluctuations in the value of money or changes in replacement prices due to any other causes are difficult to calculate accurately. Even if the annual profit calculated on a purchase price basis may include adventitious amounts, this profit need not necessarily be distributed. On the contrary, it is open to the company's administrative organs when they decide on the allocation of the profit to apply the principle of conservation of the capital in real terms or of maintenance of the company's substance by appropriating the necessary amounts to a reserve opened for that purpose.

On the other hand, it can be argued in favour of a method of valuation that takes account of the fluctuations in the value of money or changes in replacement prices due to other causes, that the annual profit can be calculated more accurately. This method makes it possible to apply the principle of conservation of the capital in real terms or of maintenance of the company's substance when the profit is being calculated, and so makes it possible to determine more accurately what charges are required for this purpose. At all events, a wide margin of discretion is left in this case to the administration of the undertaking as regards the calculation of values, as the criteria in this field are less precise than those for ascertaining purchase prices or production costs.

In accordance with the existing regulations and the practice obtaining so far in the majority of the Member States, the provisions of the Directive are based on the purchase price or production cost principle, the essential rules for the application of which are contained in Articles 32 to 39. However, to take account also of the practice in one of the Member States and so as not to prevent the development and adaptation of the rules of valuation for the purpose of taking into consideration fluctuations in the value of money or changes in replacement prices due to any other causes, an exception in respect of the requirements of Articles 32 to 39, which allows the Member States to provide for valuation on a replacement value basis, has been introduced in Article 30. In addition, Article 31 authorizes the Member States under certain conditions to permit revaluation, which also constitutes a derogation from the purchase price or production cost principle."

Accounting principles of the Fourth Draft Directive and British company law

A comparison of the accounting principles underlying the Fourth Draft Directive and the United Kingdom Companies Acts shows considerable differences in fundamental attitudes. It is true that both policies aim at what the Fourth Draft Directive states in this manner:

> "[The annual accounts] shall be drawn up clearly and, in the context of the provisions regarding the valuation of assets and liabilities and the lay-out of accounts, shall reflect as accurately as possible the company's assets, liabilities, financial position and results " (Art. 2 (3)).

There are, however, several ways of achieving this objective. The overriding principle of British company law is that the accounts should give a true and fair view of the company's affairs at the end of the financial year.[54] The provisions of Schedule 8 to the Companies Act 1948 [55] and the Statements of Standard Accounting Practice published by the Institute of Chartered Accountants in England and Wales [56] are sufficiently flexible to allow this principle to prevail. The Fourth Draft Directive, on the other hand, is founded on the belief that strict compliance with a list of obligatory items which must be shown in the accounts will best reflect the true financial position of the company.[57] It appears that a compromise between these two opposing views has been reached in negotiations between the leading accounting bodies of the Member States. It is reported [58] that the accounting bodies have agreed to accept the British principle of the true and fair view of company accounts. If the Commission agrees to these proposals, some amendments to the Fourth Draft Directive will become necessary.

The Fifth Draft Directive

Aims

The Fifth Draft Directive concerning the structure of the limited liability company [59] is probably the most important and, as far as the

[54] Companies Act 1948, s. 149 (1).
[55] In the form of Schedule 2 to the Companies Act 1967.
[56] See Fifth Cumulative Supplement to Palmer's *Company Law*, 1973, Appendices 3.19 to 3.21.
[57] In Art. 40 (which deals with the contents of the notes on the accounts) the Fourth Draft Directive refers to the true and fair view.
[58] *The Times*, July 14, 1972.
[59] Submitted by the Commission to the Council on October 9, 1972, and published in J.O. 1972, C 131/49. The Fifth Draft Directive is reproduced in No. 5, *post*.

United Kingdom is concerned, the most controversial harmonisation measure promoted by the Community. The aim is to co-ordinate the national laws of the Member States relating to the structure of companies of the public type and the powers and obligations of their organs.

Area of application

The Fifth Draft Directive applies only to companies of the public type which are defined as follows (Art. 1 (1)):

— in Germany: *die Aktiengesellschaft*;
— in Belgium: *de naamloze vennootschap, la société anonyme*;
— in France: *la société anonyme*;
— in Italy: *la società per azioni*;
— in Luxembourg: *la société anonyme*;
— in the Netherlands: *de naamloze vennootschap.*

Here again, as in the case of the Third Draft Directive,[60] the Member States are authorised to exempt from the operation of the Directive the co-operative societies whose legal form is that of one of the types of company indicated above (Art. 1 (2)).

Arrangement

The Draft Directive is arranged into five chapters.
    I. Structure of the company.
    II. The management organ and the supervisory organ.
    III. General meeting.
    IV. The adoption and audit of the annual accounts.
    V. General provisions.

Structure of the company

The Draft Directive requires the Member States to prescribe that every company of the public type shall have not less than three organs (Art. 2 (2)):

(a) a managing board " responsible for managing and representing the company ";

(b) a supervisory board " responsible for controlling the management organ ";

(c) the general meeting of shareholders.

In addition, the company must have (Art. 2 (2)):
(d) an auditor.

The Draft Directive thus demands the introduction of the two-tier system of the board into the constitution of companies of the public type as an obligatory item. This, together with the requirement of

---

[60] Third Draft Directive, Art. 1 (2).

employee participation in the management of the company's affairs for larger companies, would constitute profound changes in the company law of the United Kingdom, if eventually accepted. Indeed, the principle of employee participation presupposes the obligatory two-tier structure of the board because one of the forms of that participation is that some members of the supervisory board shall be elected or co-opted with the approval of the employees.

The two-tier system shall, according to the explanatory memorandum,[61] apply to all undertakings, irrespective of size, which are incorporated in the form of a company of public type. That form is intended principally for medium or large undertakings. Smaller undertakings can adopt the form of the company of private type.

The managing board

The Draft Directive [62] regards it as a feature of the two-tier system that the members of the managing board should always be appointed by the supervisory board (Art. 3 (1)). The Explanatory Memorandum to the Draft Directive gives as reason that "the supervisory board, with its, generally speaking, smaller membership, is better suited than the general meeting of all the shareholders to choose the persons to whom the management and representation of the undertaking are to be entrusted. The dismissal of the members of the managing board is likewise entrusted to the supervisory board " (Art. 13 (1)).

It is further provided that where the managing board consists of more than one member, the supervisory board shall designate one member of the managing board as personnel director, so that the employees always know which member of the board is specifically responsible for their affairs (Art. 3 (2)).

Only natural persons can be appointed as members of the managing board (Art. 5 (1)). As far as the supervisory board is concerned, legal persons may serve on it, subject to certain restrictions (Art. 5 (2)). A person cannot be a member of the managing and the supervisory board of a company at the same time (Art. 6). The appointment to membership of either board must not exceed six years but the appointment is renewable (Art. 7). A natural person shall not hold more than ten supervisory directorships (Art. 9 (3)).

The managing board must send a report on the progress of the company's affairs to the supervisory board every three months (Art. 11 (1)). The supervisory board may at any time ask for special reports (Art. 11 (3)), and is entitled to obtain from the management

[61] Explanatory Memorandum, Introduction.
[62] *Ibid.* note to Art. 3.

all information which it requires; a similar power is given to one-third of the supervisory board (Art. 11 (4)).

The managing board must obtain the authorisation of the supervisory board to the following measures (Art. 12 (1)):

(a) the closure or transfer of the undertaking or of substantial parts thereof;

(b) substantial curtailment or extension of the activities of the undertaking;

(c) substantial organisational changes within the undertaking;

(d) establishment of long-term co-operation with other undertakings or the termination thereof.

The national legislation or the articles of the company may add to this list but cannot reduce it (Art. 12 (2)).

The Draft Directive further prescribes detailed rules relating to the civil liability of members of the managing and supervisory board for breaches of law or the articles or for wrongful acts committed by them in carrying out their duties (Arts. 14–21).

The supervisory board

The members of the supervisory board are appointed by the general meeting, subject to what is stated in the following (Art. 4 (2)). It has already been observed [63] that they need not be natural persons but that, if legal persons are appointed, certain conditions have to be observed (Art. 4 (2)).

The Draft Directive prescribes detailed rules with respect to employees' participation on the supervisory board but draws here a distinction between smaller and larger companies. Smaller companies are those having less than 500 employees, larger companies those having 500 or more employees.

In the case of smaller companies employees' participation is not an obligatory requirement and the members of the supervisory board may be appointed solely by the general meeting (Art. 4 (4)). A scheme of employees' participation may, of course, be adopted by the company voluntarily or a national legislation may prescribe a lower figure—or other requirements—for the obligatory provision of such a scheme.

If the company is a larger company within the meaning defined earlier, the national legislations must require employees' participation on the supervisory board as an obligatory provision (Art. 4 (1)).

As regards details, the explanatory memorandum states [64] that " the forms taken by such participation need not necessarily be

[63] See p. 27, *ante.*
[64] Explanatory Memorandum, note to Art. 4.

identical throughout the Community. The Member States may be left to choose from among several examples which are considered as equivalent." In fact, the Draft Directive gives the Member States the choice of two alternatives, *viz.*, either to adopt the German system of one-third participation or the Dutch system of co-optation.[65]

If the German system is adopted, the legislation of the Member States must obviously provide that the number of members of the supervisory board must be three or a multiple of it. The Draft Directive states here (Art. 4 (2)):

> " Not less than one-third of the members of the supervisory organ shall be appointed by the workers or their representatives or upon proposal by the workers or their representatives."

It should be noted that the Draft Directive does not prescribe a particular method of appointment of the employees' members of the supervisory board; it leaves this to the national legislations. They can determine, in particular, whether those members shall be elected directly by the employees or indirectly by the works councils or the trade unions represented in the undertaking. Further, the national legislations may provide that some members of the supervisory council may be appointed neither by the general meeting nor by the employees, for example, they may be representatives of the public interest appointed by the state or a consumer organisation (Art. 4 (2), para. 3).

If the Dutch system is adopted, the members of the supervisory board are appointed by that organ itself (co-optation; Art. 4 (3)). The general meeting or the representatives of the employees may object to the appointment—

> " on the ground either that [the appointee] lacks the ability to carry out his duties or that if he were appointed there would, having regard to the interests of the company, the shareholders or the workers, be imbalance in the composition of the supervisory organ."

If use is made of the veto, " an independent body existing under public law " shall decide whether its exercise was justified (Art. 4 (3)).

The responsibilities of the supervising body are limited to the control of the managing board.[66] That, however, does not exclude that certain managerial activities of major importance which are listed earlier,[67] require the authorisation of the supervisory board (Art. 12 (1)).

---

[65] See C. M. Schmitthoff in *The Harmonisation of European Company Law*, ed. Schmitthoff, pp. 26–27.
[66] Explanatory Memorandum, comment to Art. 12.
[67] See p. 28, *ante.*

The members of the supervisory board may be dismissed at any time by the organs or persons who appointed them, such as the general meeting or the employees or their representatives; the same procedure should be used for their dismissal as for their appointment (Art. 13 (2)). Where the members were co-opted under the Dutch procedure, they can only be dismissed where proper grounds for dismissal are found to exist by a court in proceedings brought by the supervisory board, the general meeting or the employees' representatives (Art. 13 (2), second sentence).

The general meeting
The general meeting which is convened by the managing board shall meet once each year (Art. 22). Shareholders who hold—
   (a) 5 per cent. of the subscribed capital or more; or
   (b) shares amounting to at least 100,000 units of account
may request the company to convene a general meeting and if the company should fail to do so within one month, the court must be given power to convene a meeting (Art. 23). This is the same minority which can request proceedings on behalf of the company to be commenced in order to enforce the liability of a member of the managing or supervisory board for breach of law or the articles or another wrongful act (Art. 16).

The shareholder's right to vote shall be proportional to his participation in the capital, but it may be restricted or excluded in certain circumstances, particularly if the shares are preference shares carrying special financial advantages (Art. 33). Shares carrying plural votes disproportionate to the participation in the capital are not admitted. The shareholder may appoint a proxy but the national laws must require the invitation to appoint a proxy to include a request for instructions concerning the exercise of the vote and an indication how the vote will be exercised in the absence of the shareholder giving such instructions (two-way proxies; Art. 28 (1) (*d*) (*dd*) and (*ee*)). Voting agreements are void if they oblige a shareholder to vote always on the instructions of the company or one of its organs or to vote in a specific manner in consideration of special advantages (Art. 35).

The national legislations shall provide that the right to alter the articles shall be reserved to the general meeting which may pass a resolution for alteration with not less than a two-thirds majority (Art. 39). Where the capital of the company is divided into several classes, a resolution detrimental to the holders of a class must be approved by a separate vote of at least each class so affected (Art. 40). Such a vote is of course subject to the majority requirements laid down in Article 39.

The Draft Directive further regulates in detail the conditions under which a decision of the general meeting can be declared void (Arts. 42 to 45).

The annual accounts and their audit

Some of the provisions relating to the adoption and audit of the annual accounts contained in the Fifth Draft Directive have been discussed already in the note on the Fourth Draft Directive which deals with the annual accounts.[68] The auditors must be " persons independent of the company . . . who are nominated or approved by a judicial or administrative authority " of a Member State (Art. 52). In no circumstances must the auditors be persons who are members of the managing or supervisory board or staff of the company or were in that position during the last three years; partners of such persons are likewise excluded (Art. 53). Nor must the auditors or their partners become members of these boards or employees of the company for three years following the audit (Art. 54). The auditors are appointed by the general meeting (Art. 55); they shall hold their appointment for not less than three years and not more than six years (Art. 56). The remuneration of the auditor shall be fixed by the general meeting for the whole of their period of office before that period commences (Art. 57). The auditor shall not be dismissed by the general meeting before the end of his period of office, except where proper grounds exist (Art. 61).

The Draft Directive thus goes to great lengths to safeguard the absolute independence of the auditor. Many of these provisions obviously follow the pattern of the United Kingdom Companies Acts.

The Draft Directive concerning prospectuses

Aims

The unnumbered Draft Directive concerning the content, checking and distribution of the prospectus to be published when securities issued by companies are admitted to official stock exchange quotation [69] deals, properly speaking, with the law of investor protection and not with company law. However, since the Companies Act 1948, following previous companies legislation in the United Kingdom, includes this subject, at least in outline, in its ambit,[70] the Draft Directive is included in this collection of texts.

---

[68] See pp. 19, 22–23, *ante*.

[69] Submitted by the Commission to the Council on September 26, 1972: J.O. 1972, C131/61. This Draft Directive is reproduced in No. 6 A, *post*.

[70] The detailed regulation is contained in *Admission of Securities to Listing*, issued by authority of the Stock Exchange (revision of March 1973).

The aims of this Draft Directive are indicated in its explanatory memorandum [71]:

> "At present the requirement to provide information when securities are admitted to stock exchange quotation sometimes differs considerably in content and in legal basis from one Member State to another. Consequently, issuers provide information which varies markedly both in quality and quantity and the protection afforded to the investor in this respect is not everywhere the same. . . .
>
> It appears to be necessary to establish minimum requirements for the information to be provided at the time of a grant of quotation in order to avoid undermining the confidence of holders of various European securities by differing information and to provide effective protection for holders irrespective of where the security is quoted."

Area of application

The Draft Directive applies to securities admitted to or introduced for official quotation on a stock exchange situated within the territory of a Member State (Art. 1 (1)). Securities means here shares, stock, convertible and other debentures. Unit trust certificates are exempt from the operation of the Draft Directive (Art. 1 (2)). Further, securities issued by the States or their local authorities are excluded from its application (Art. 1 (3)) but it is intended to cover these securities by a proposed Council Recommendation.[72]

The Draft Directive obliges the Member States to introduce into their national law provisions ensuring that before securities are admitted to or introduced for official quotation on a stock exchange a prospectus examined by an authority appointed for this purpose is published or made available to the public (Art. 1 (1)). Presumably, in order to comply with this provision if it is adopted by the Council, the United Kingdom Stock Exchange or its Council or its Quotations Department would have to be recognised by an enactment and to be given statutory authority which it does not possess at present.

Arrangement

The Draft Directive is divided into five sections:

I. General rules and field of application.

II. Content of the prospectus in special cases.

III. Arrangements for enforcing the prospectus requirements and for making it publicly available.

---

[71] Explanatory Memorandum, Introducton No. 1, p. 47.
[72] The Draft Recommendation is reproduced in No. 6 B, *post*.

IV. Procedure for co-operation between Member States in the application of the Directive.

V. Final provisions.

Appended to this Draft Directive are three schedules which contain schemes of presentation for prospectuses for the admission to stock exchange quotations, *viz.*

    (a) of shares,

    (b) of debentures issued by industrial or commercial undertakings,

    (c) of certificates representing shares.[73]

Contact group

The provisions of this Draft Directive are too detailed to admit brief explanation. Only one interesting feature may be mentioned, namely, the formation of a contact group (Art. 19).

The contact group will be set up by the Commission and be composed of representatives of the Member States and the Commission (Art. 19 (1) and (2)). Its task will be threefold, *viz.,*

    (a) to facilitate harmonised application of the Directive throughout the Community territory;

    (b) to facilitate a concerted approach to supplements and improvement of the proposed schemes; and

    (c) to assist the Commission in drawing up new proposals for the amendment of the Directive.

The proposal of the Draft Directive for the constitution of a permanent contact group is wise, in view of the complexity of the subject-matter and the fact that the practical application of the proposed schemes of prospectuses may disclose loopholes which will have to be stopped by amendment of the existing regulation.

The proposed European Company

History [74]

The ambitious project of the European Company was first launched in 1959 almost simultaneously by the Dutch professor Pieter

---

[73] Certificates representing shares and admitted to quotation are known at some stock exchanges when foreign securities do not conform to the requirements for stock exchange quotation, or where the delivery time for the original securities is too long, or where multiples or fractions of the denominations of the original securities are traded; see Explanatory Memorandum, note to Art. 11, p. 58.

[74] The historical survey is founded on Clive M. Schmitthoff, " The Role of the Multinational Enterprise in an enlarged European Community," in *Legal Problems of an Enlarged European Community*, ed. by M. E. Bathurst, K. R. Simmonds, N. March Hunnings and Jane Welch (Stevens, 1972), p. 224.

Sanders and the French notary M. Thibierge.[75] In 1965 the French Government addressed a note to the Council of Ministers expressing itself strongly in favour of creating a European Company. In 1966 the Commission of the EEC charged a group of experts under the chairmanship of Professor Sanders to examine the problems involved and to publish a Draft Statute of the European Company. In 1967 the Council constituted a working party, again under the chairmanship of Professor Sanders, and that party submitted its reports in 1967 and 1968. The Commission then examined the matter and on June 30, 1970, submitted a proposed Statute for the European Company (*Societas Europaea, société anonyme européenne*, SE) to the Council.[76] There the matter rests at present. The move from project to Draft Statute before the Council has been relatively quick, as international legal affairs go. It is reported that at the summit meeting between President Pompidou and Prime Minister Heath in 1972 it was decided that progress should be given to the project of the SE.

Aims

The object of the proposed Statute for the European Company is to create, by virtue of Community law, a form of company which has the status of a national company in the territory of each Member State. Article 1 (4) provides unambiguously:

> " The SE has legal personality. In each Member State and subject to the express provisions of this Statute it shall be treated in all respects concerning its rights and powers as a *société anonyme* [77] incorporated under national law."

The SE is thus not in the position of a national company registered in one of the Community countries. It need not claim recognition in the other Community countries under the Convention on the Mutual Recognition of Companies and Bodies Corporate of February 29, 1968, because, by virtue of Community law, it enjoys automatically and *ipso facto* the status of a national company in each Community country.

The object of the proposed admission of the SE is to enable at least two companies of different nationality in the Community to

---

[75] Pieter Sanders, " Structure and Progress of the European Company," in *The Harmonisation of European Company Law*, ed. by Clive M. Schmitthoff, 1973, pp. 83 *et seq.*; Pieter Sanders, " The European Company " [1968] J.B.L. 184; Michel Vasseur, " A Company of European Type " [1964] J.B.L. 358 and [1965] J.B.L. 73; Hans Claudius Ficker, " A Project for a European Corporation " [1970] J.B.L. 156 and [1971] J.B.L. 167.

[76] Submitted to the Commission by the Council on June 30, 1970: J.O. 1970, C124/1. The proposed Statute of the European Company is reproduced in No. 7, *post*.

[77] This means a company of the public type.

merge wholly or partly without one company being absorbed by the other. It is true that Article 220 of the EEC Treaty envisages that the Member States will conclude a convention admitting mergers across the frontiers and that the draft of such a convention already exists.[77a] But the effect of such a merger would be that the absorbed company in one Member State disappears and the absorbing company in the other Member State survives. The parties may not always desire that solution as it may arouse national susceptibilities. These possible complications are avoided if, instead of engaging on a merger across the frontiers, the parties choose the supranational form of the SE.

Area of application

An SE can only be formed by companies of the public type but not by those of the private type. Further, it cannot be formed by natural persons.

The founder companies, of which there must be at least two, must be subject to different national laws in the Community. Article 2 of the proposed Statute states that companies of the public type—

" incorporated under the law of a Member State and of which not less than two are subject to different national laws may establish an SE by merger or by formation of a holding company or a joint subsidiary."

But an SE already in existence may form another SE, either on its own by forming a subsidiary or in combination with other SE or national companies of public type (Art. 3).

Arrangement

The proposed Statute for the SE is arranged in fourteen titles:

1. General provisions.
2. Formation.
3. Capital; shares and the rights of shareholders; debentures.
4. Administrative organs.
5. Representation of employees in the SE.
6. Preparation of the annual accounts.
7. Groups of companies.
8. Alteration of the statutes.
9. Winding up, liquidation, insolvency and similar procedures.
10. Conversion.
11. Merger.
12. Taxation.
13. Offences.
14. Final provisions.

[77a] This draft convention is reproduced in No. 10, *post.*

Added to the Draft is an Annex which contains a list of offences in relation to the SE. The Statute itself does not include penal provisions, probably because the Community would have no possibility of enforcing them directly but Article 282 of the Statute of the SE requires the Member States to introduce into their law appropriate offences which are listed in the Annex.

The proposed Statute of the SE is very different in character from the Directives founded on Article 54 (3) (*g*) of the EEC Treaty. It represents a self-contained regulation of company law which is complete in itself; it does not deal only with segments of company law, as do the Directives. In fact, the proposed Statute is a modern code of company law, drafted with great skill and competence.

Formation

The SE comes into existence by registration in the European Commercial Register which will be kept by the European Court in Luxembourg (Art. 8 (1)). The court shall examine whether the application for registration satisfies the legal requirements (Art. 17); the proposed Statute thus adopts the theory of preventive judicial control.[78] The SE has legal personality from the date of publication of its registration in the official gazette of the Community (Art. 19 (1)).

The minimum capital of the SE shall be not less than:

    (a) 500,000 units of account for mergers or the creation of holding companies;

    (b) 250,000 units of account for the formation of a subsidiary by two or more companies; and

    (c) 100,000 units of account for the formation of a subsidiary by one SE (Art. 4).

These amounts are high. They reveal the intention of the Commission to make available the form of the SE only to large multinational enterprises but not to small or medium-sized undertakings. This attitude of the Commission has been criticised, particularly by Professor Michel Vasseur.[79]

The proposed Statute does not require the national companies promoting an SE to be of indigenous character. Two subsidiaries of an American enterprise situate in different Community countries can form an SE. This liberal attitude is to be welcomed. The SE may have one or several registered offices which must be situate within the Community (Art. 5). The recognition of several registered

---

[78] See p. 8, *ante*.
[79] Michel Vasseur, " Towards a European Company—II," in *The Round Table*, January 1973, p. 119.

offices of the SE may create legal difficulties which are described thus [80] :

> " For an SE, the fact of having more than one registered office may create difficulties in the matter of legal jurisdiction in cases where this is determined by the location of the registered office. . . . It may be necessary to consider the signing of a supplementary protocol giving exclusive jurisdiction, in certain types of action, to the court first seized thereof, to the exclusion of other courts which, by reference to the location of the registered office, would also have jurisdiction."

The capital of the SE

The capital of the SE must be expressed either in European units of account or in the currency of one of the Member States (Art. 40). The proposed Statute admits the creation, by increase of capital, of " approved capital " which is similar in nature to the authorised but not issued capital of English law. Where the general meeting creates approved capital, such capital must not exceed one half of the capital fixed in the articles (Art. 41 (3)) and the managing board has to report each year, in an annex to the annual accounts, how it has been employed (Art. 43 (1)).

Where the capital is increased by subscription of new capital, the existing shareholders have a proportionate right to subscribe to the new shares (Art. 42 (1)) but this right does not exist where the new shares are issued wholly or in part for a consideration consisting in kind (Art. 42 (3)).

The Statute not only prohibits the SE from acquiring its own shares directly or through nominees but enjoins it to dispose of shares in undertakings controlled by it within one year (Art. 46). Further, reciprocal shareholdings are prohibited if one of the undertakings is an SE (Art. 47 (1)). Reciprocal shareholdings are deemed to exist where each company holds, directly or indirectly, more than 10 per cent. of the capital of the other (Art. 47 (2)).

Shares and debentures

The shares of the SE may be bearer or registered shares (Art. 50). Non-voting shares may be issued subject to certain conditions (Art. 49 (2)) but the issue of shares carrying multiple voting rights is prohibited (Art. 49 (3)).

Debentures may be issued by the managing board with the approval of the supervisory board (Art. 54). An interesting provision of the proposed Statute is that the holders of the debentures of the

[80] Notes to Art. 5, p. 12.

same public issue shall automatically constitute a body which, however, does not have legal personality (Art. 56). The company shall appoint a person to act as representative of the body of debenture holders and that person must be independent of the company (Art. 57). Meetings of debenture holders deciding by a three-quarter majority can bind all debenture holders (Art. 58 (3)).

The organs of the SE

The proposed Statute of the SE adopts the German system of the two-tier board. The notes to the Statute give as reason that " this system makes for more continuous and for more effective supervision and control." [81]

The overall structure of the SE presents the following picture:

I. *The administrative organs of the company*
1. The managing board (Arts. 62 to 72).
2. The supervisory board (Arts. 73 to 82).
3. The general meeting (Arts. 83 to 96).

II. *Other organs of the SE*
4. The auditor (Art. 203).
5. The European works council (Arts. 100 to 129).

III. *Exceptional measures*
6. Special commissioners appointed by the court in case of serious disturbance in the usual operation of the company (Art. 97).

The managing board

The members of the managing board are appointed and dismissed by the supervisory board (Art. 63 (1) and (7)). Dismissal is possible if there are serious grounds to justify such action (Art. 63 (7)). Only natural persons can be members of the managing board (Art. 63 (2)). Where the managing board consists of one or two members, he or they must be nationals of a Member State; where it consists of more members, their majority must satisfy that test (Art. 63 (3)). Nobody can be a member of the managing and the supervisory board at the same time (Art. 69 (1)).

In the following cases the managing board requires the prior authorisation by the supervisory board (Art. 66):

(a) closure or transfer of the undertaking or of substantial parts thereof;
(b) substantial curtailment or extension of the activities of the undertaking;
(c) substantial organisational changes within the undertaking;

[81] Notes to Title IV, p. 55.

(d) establishment of long-term co-operation with other undertakings or the termination thereof.

The supervisory board

The number of members of the supervisory board must be divisible by three. Where an SE has permanent establishment in several Member States, the minimum number of the board is to be twelve (Art. 74 (1)). One-third of the members represents the employees of the SE on the supervisory board (Art. 137 (1)), unless the employees of the SE decide by a two-thirds majority that there shall be no employee representation on the board (Art. 138 (1)). The articles of the SE may provide for a higher participation of employees than one-third (Art. 137 (1)). The Statute of the SE thus adopts the German system of employees' participation.

The members of the supervisory board who represent the shareholders are appointed by the general meeting for not more than five years (Art. 74 (3)); they may be re-elected (Art. 75 (1)); they may be dismissed by the general meeting at any time. The members of the supervisory board who represent the employees are not elected by the latter directly but are elected by the European works council (Art. 139).[82] They hold office for the same period as the other members of the supervisory board (Art. 144) but cease to be members when their contract of employment is terminated or the mandate of the works council expires or they resign (Art. 108). The representatives of the employees have the same rights and duties as the other members of the supervisory board (Art. 145).

The members of the supervisory board must be natural persons (Art. 74 (2)). No nationality requirement exists for them and it would be possible for all of them to be nationals of a non-Member State.

It is the function of the supervisory board to exercise permanent control over the management of the company by the managing board which must report to the supervisory board at least every quarter (Art. 73 (1)). In certain matters of major importance, listed earlier,[83] the managing board requires the prior authorisation of the supervisory board.

The special commissioners

When there are firm grounds for believing that the managing or supervisory board has committed a serious breach of its obligations, or a member of these boards has done so, or the boards are no longer in a position to perform their functions, and where there is con-

[82] See p. 41, *post.*
[83] See pp. 38–39, *ante.*

sequent risk that the SE may thereby suffer substantial loss, special commissioners to investigate the complaint and to report on it may be appointed by the court (Arts. 97 to 99). This feature of the Statute of the SE is clearly founded on the provisions of English company law which enable the Board of Trade to appoint inspectors charged with the investigation of the company's affairs.[84]

The court which has jurisdiction to appoint the special commissioners is the national court in whose jurisdiction the registered office of the SE is situate (Art. 97). If the company has several registered offices in different Member States, presumably several national courts have concurrent jurisdiction, a phenomenon not unusual in private international law. The Member States may specially designate a court for hearing such applications (Art. 97).

An application for the appointment of special commissioners may be made by—

(a) shareholders owning between them 10 per cent. of the capital or shares to the value of 200,000 units of account;

(b) the representative of the body of debenture holders; or

(c) the European works council.

On receipt of the report, the court may—

(i) suspend from office one or more members of the managing or supervisory board;

(ii) dismiss them;

(iii) appoint new members to these bodies on a temporary basis (Art. 99 (2)).

The court retains the power to control the action initiated by it (Art. 99 (3)).

Representation of employees in the SE

The proposed Statute is founded on the assumption that " it is generally accepted nowadays in the Member States that an employee has both a *de facto* and *de jure* relationship to the undertaking. He is a member of the unit constituted by the undertaking and brought into being by orderly co-operation in the process of production, a unit expressed in a single management and organisational authority." [85] Few will quarrel with this fundamental assumption.

Founded on these premises, the proposed Statute provides legal machinery on three levels for regulating the representation of employees within the undertaking and for facilitating the regulation of conditions of employment and remuneration within the SE:

---

[84] Companies Act 1948, ss. 164–171, as altered by the Companies Act 1967, ss. 36–42 and 50 (a).
[85] Notes to Title V, p. 87.

(1) the European works council, representing the employees in each establishment of the SE;

(2) the representation of employees on the supervisory board; and

(3) the possibility of concluding collective agreements between the SE and the unions represented within the undertaking.

The form of representation of employees on the supervisory board has already been considered.[86] A few observations have to be made on the European works council.

The European works council

Every SE having establishments in several Member States must have a European works council (Art. 100).

The Statute proposes to respect, as far as possible, the national autonomy of the laws of the Member States in this sphere. For that reason the representative bodies of the employees required by national law are left unaffected in every establishment of the SE, *e.g.*, the *comités d'entreprise* in the French establishments and the *Betriebsräte* in those situate in Germany (Arts. 101 and 102). But in addition, a European works council has to be elected by direct election of the employees in each of the individual establishments of the SE, according to the rules applying to the election of the local works council in the establishment (Arts. 103 and 104). The Statute rejects the system of direct election by all the employees of the SE because " this system would carry the risk of employees of small establishments being outnumbered by those of larger establishments." [87] An additional reason for the rejection of that system are the difficulties of language which may arise in the presentation of candidates.

The number of members of the European works council is determined by the number of establishments in the SE and the number of their employees.

The following key is provided:

from 200 to 999 employees: 2 representatives;

from 1,000 to 2,999 employees: 3 representatives;

from 3,000 to 4,999 employees: 4 representatives;

where there are more than 5,000 employees, 1 representative for each additional 5,000 employees (Art. 105).

Apparently, establishments below 200 employees are not entitled to send any representatives to the European works council.

The members of the council are elected for three years and membership to the local *comité d'entreprise* is no objection to the simultaneous membership to the European council (Art. 107). Here

[86] See p. 39, *ante*.
[87] Notes to Art. 103, p. 91.

again the membership ceases with the termination of the contract of employment, if a member resigns or if he ceases to be eligible for membership (Art. 108).

The members of the European works council are under a strict obligation to observe professional secrecy (Art. 114). This is a corollary to the extensive obligation of the managerial board to keep the council informed. The management must send the council a detailed report every quarter (Art. 120).

The Statute contains catalogues of matters pertaining to industrial relations which can be decided on by the managerial board only with the agreement of the council or after consultation with it; a decision of the board which disregards these provisions would be void (Arts. 123 and 124). The managerial board must also consult the council on the matters which require the prior authorisation of the supervisory board (Art. 125).[88]

Where the SE is the controlling company in a group having establishments in a number of Member States or whose dependent undertakings have establishments in a number of Member States, a group works council has to be formed (Arts. 130–136).

Minority shareholders

The proposed Statute contains provisions aimed at the protection of minority shareholders—described as outside shareholders—in a dependent company having its registered office in one of the Member States where the controlling company is an SE or is incorporated under national law (Art. 228).

In this case the controlling company has an alternative: either it may offer to purchase the shares of the minority shareholders for cash at a fair price (Art. 229) or it may offer to exchange the shares of those shareholders for shares in the controlling company (Art. 230). A third option which is a variant of the cash offer is to offer the shareholders of the dependent company payment of an annuity in compensation for the shares (Art. 231). These provisions are designed to give minority shareholders protection. They follow the German regulation for connected companies (*Konzerne*)[89] and differ from the British regulation of section 209 of the Companies Act 1948 in many important respects; in particular, they are not restricted to the situation of a take-over and do not require the controlling company to have a numerically expressed overwhelming majority in the dependent company.

The proposed cash offer or share exchange must be put to the vote

---

[88] See pp. 38–39, *ante*.
[89] Sections 304 and 305 of the German *Aktiengesetz* of 1965; see Marcus Lutter, " The Konzern in German Company Law " [1973] J.B.L. 278.

of the general meeting of the dependent company, after an opinion by an expert concerning the fairness of the offer has been obtained (Arts. 232–237). Eventually a national court would have to decide whether the offer is fair. These provisions likewise apply where the dependent company is of the private type (Art. 238).

Taxation

The leading principle of the provisions of the Statute on taxation is that special tax advantages for the SE must be ruled out. Such tax advantages—

"would not only run counter to the principles of modern tax law, which tend to attach more importance to the function and business structure of undertakings than to its legal form; it would also deliberately create new sources of distortion and discrimination detrimental to free and effective competition and inconsistent with fiscal neutrality. Accordingly, the tax regulations now prevailing must apply to SEs just as to other companies." [90]

The proposed Statute contains provisions dealing with the following aspects of taxation:

1. The formation of the SE (Art. 275).
2. Tax domicile (Arts. 276–277).
3. Permanent establishments and subsidiaries (Arts. 278–281).

Two provisions may be mentioned here. For the purposes of taxation, the SE has its tax domicile in the Member State in which the centre of its effective management is located (Art. 276). Further, where an SE whose tax domicile is in a Member State has a permanent establishment in another Member State, only the latter has the right to charge to tax the profit of that establishment (Art. 278 (1)), but a loss made by the establishments in one Member State may be deducted from the taxable profits of the SE in the country of its tax domicile (Art. 278 (2)). By these provisions the proposed Statute seeks to avoid the incidence of double taxation.

Interpretation of the proposed Statute

There is considerable danger that the Statute may be interpreted differently in the Member States. This danger is particularly great as questions of interpretation will arise in the first line in the jurisdiction of the national courts. Two measures are devised to minimise that danger.

First, the national courts are enjoined not to interpret according

[90] See Note on Title XII—Taxation, p. 215.

to national law matters governed by the Statute, except if the Statute expressly so provides. Article 7 (1) states:

" A matter not expressly dealt with herein shall be resolved:

    (a) in accordance with the general principles upon which this statute is based:

    (b) if those general principles do not provide a solution to the problem, in accordance with the rules or general principles common to the laws of the Member States."

This attempt at making the Statute an autonomous legal regulation, *i.e.*, a legal regulation not founded on national law, is based on Article 17 of the Hague Convention of July 1, 1964 on the Uniform Law on the International Sale of Goods to which effect is given in the United Kingdom by the Uniform Laws on International Sales Act 1967.

Secondly, since the Statute will be issued in the form of a Regulation founded on Article 235 of the EEC Treaty, the national courts may, and if they are courts of final jurisdiction must, state a preliminary question on the interpretation of the Statute for the decision of the European Court in Luxembourg under Article 177 of the Treaty.

There thus exists machinery to safeguard the uniform interpretation of the Statute.

The Convention on the Mutual Recognition of Companies

Aims

The Convention on the Mutual Recognition of Companies and Bodies Corporate,[91] signed at Brussels by representatives of the six original Member States on February 29, 1968, was concluded in pursuance of Article 220 of the EEC Treaty and will have to be acceded to by the new members.[92] The Convention has not been ratified by the signatories and is not in force yet.[93]

The aim of the Convention is to ensure that companies established in a Member State are granted recognition in the other Member States. The Convention thus deals with a topic pertaining to private international law.

The Convention attempts to reconcile two principles applied to the problem of corporate recognition, *viz.*, the principle that a company duly *incorporated* in one country can claim recognition in other

---

[91] Signed on February 29, 1968. The Convention is reproduced in No. 8 A, *post.* The translation of this Convention, as reproduced, is the official translation of the EEC. It is capable of improvement.

[92] See p. 4, *ante.*

[93] It will come into force three months after the deposit of the last instrument or ratification. Each Member State must ratify.

countries (incorporation theory) and the theory adopting as the decisive test for recognition the situation of the seat of central management in the territory of the country in question (*siège réel* theory). To give an illustration: if a company incorporated in country A has its seat of central management in country B, which is the law determining the domicile of the company, that of A or that of B? As the recognition of the company is founded on the domicile of the company, this is no empty question.[94] It is particularly important if country A is a member of the Community and country B is not, or vice versa.

The Convention attempts to solve this difficulty by adopting as guiding principle the incorporation theory but has admitted important exceptions some of which are founded on the *siège réel* theory. The resulting compromise does not always present a happy solution.

Area of application

The Convention applies to companies under civil or commercial law, including co-operative societies, established in accordance with the law of a signatory State to the Convention and having its statutory registered office in one of those States (Art. 1). In brief, it applies to all companies incorporated in any of the signatory States. It applies also to bodies corporate under public or private law which satisfy these conditions and engage in economic activity, such as the nationalised undertakings (Art. 2).

It is further provided that " the capacity, rights and powers of a company recognised by virtue of the Convention may not be denied or restricted for the sole reason that the law in accordance with which it was established does not grant it the legal status of a body corporate " (Art. 8).

Thus, the following which are commercial associations but are not bodies corporate, appear to be entitled to mutual recognition of their capacity, rights and powers under the Convention: an English partnership,[95] a French *société en participation*[96] and a German *Gesellschaft des bürgerlichen Rechts*,[97] *offene Handelsgesellschaft, Kommanditgesellschaft, and Stille Gesellschaft.*[98]

By a Joint Declaration No. 1, appended to the Convention, it has been declared that the Convention extends to the *società semplice* in Italian law and the *vennootschap onder firma* in Dutch law.

---

[94] See G. K. Morse, " Mutual Recognition of Companies in England and the EEC " in [1972] J.B.L. 195.

[95] See G. K. Morse, *loc. cit.*, p. 200, n. 94.

[96] *Code de Commerce*, arts. 42–45; R. Rodière, *Droit commercial, Groupements commerciaux*, 7th ed., para. 295.

[97] *Bürgerliches Gesetzbuch*, ss. 705–740.

[98] *Handelsgesetzbuch*, paras. 105–160, 161–177, 335–342; J. von Gierke, *Handelsrecht und Schiffahrtsrecht*, 8th ed., p. 183.

Arrangement

The Convention is arranged in four chapters:

    I. Recognition: scope and conditions.

    II. Recognition: effects.

    III. Public policy.

    IV. Final provisions.

Appended to the Convention is a Protocol containing three Joint Declarations. Joint Declaration No. 1 has already been mentioned. Joint Declaration No. 2 states the willingness of the signatories to extend the benefit of the Convention to associated States of the Community. Joint Declaration No. 3 expresses the willingness of the signatories to enter into negotiations with a view to conferring certain powers on the European Court concerning the interpretation of the Convention by the court; in pursuance of this Joint Declaration a Protocol was signed at Luxembourg on June 3, 1971.[99]

The scheme of the Convention

The fundamental principle underlying the Convention is, as already observed, that a company incorporated in one of the Convention countries and having its statutory registered office in a Convention country shall be entitled to recognition in the other Convention countries as of right (Art. 1). It should be noted that according to the Convention the two conditions for recognition need not coincide territorially. At present this situation cannot arise in English law. A company incorporated in England must always have its statutory registered office in England or Wales. But Article 220 of the EEC Treaty envisages the conclusion of a convention for the transfer of the registered office from one country to another. It is therefore possible, if such a convention is signed and given the force of law, for an English company to transfer its registered office to France. Such a company could claim recognition under the present Convention.

The Convention admits the following exceptions:

1. A contracting State may refuse recognition under the Convention if the company has its " real registered office " outside the Convention territory and has " no genuine link with the economy of one of the said territories " (Art. 3). " Real registered office " is defined as the place where the company's central administration is established (Art. 5). This is a notable concession to the *siège réel* theory.

2. A contracting State need not apply the Convention if a company claiming recognition contravenes by its object, purpose or

[99] The Protocol is reproduced in No. 8 B, *post.*

activity the public policy of that State (Art. 9). The fact that the company is a genuine one-man company, *i.e.*, has only one shareholder, must not be regarded as contravening public policy (Art. 9, 2nd para.). The exception in favour of public policy is germane to all national systems of private international law.

3. A contracting State may further declare that mandatory provisions of its own law shall be applied to a company claiming recognition under the Convention and having its real registered office in its—the State's—territory (Art. 4).[1]

The non-mandatory provisions of the guest State may be made applicable " if the company's constitutional documents do not contain a reference to its own law under which it was formed, or if the company is unable to show that it has in fact conducted its activity during ' a reasonable time ' in the state of its formation " (Art. 4, 2nd para.).[2]

The qualification of Article 4, like that of Article 3, is a concession to the *siège réel* theory. Its weakness is that it is difficult to define what rules of the guest State are mandatory and what are optional. Professor Eric Stein rightly observes[3] :

" The practical effects are uncertain and could vary from State to State. The formula has all the disadvantages of complexity and ambiguity that characterise a laborious compromise."

Effect of recognition

On principle a company recognised by virtue of the Convention has the capacity accorded to it by its law of incorporation in all other Convention countries (Art. 6).

However, this principle is subject to two exceptions. First, it operates only subject to the qualification of Article 4 which has been discussed under No. 3, above (Art. 6). In other words, a contracting State may declare that the mandatory provisions of its own law shall apply to a company claiming recognition by virtue of the Convention and having its central place of management in that State.

Secondly, the guest State may refuse companies claiming recognition by virtue of the Convention any rights and powers which it does not grant to companies of a similar type governed by its own law (Art. 7). Thus, if after the accession of the United Kingdom to the Convention an insurance company incorporated in one of the Con-

---

[1] A similar problem arises in the application of the Hague Convention on the Uniform Laws on International Sales under the Uniform Laws of International Sales Act 1967: see Supply of Goods (Implied Terms) Act 1973, s. 5 (2).
[2] Eric Stein, *op. cit.* n. 23, p. 411.
[3] *Ibid.* p. 411.

vention countries which has less stringent laws regulating these companies than the United Kingdom claims recognition in the United Kingdom by virtue of the Convention, it would be subject to Part II of the Companies Act 1967 which amends the law with respect to insurance companies.[4]

Comparison with English private international law

The principle of the Convention of recognising companies incorporated in a foreign country does not cause difficulty in the English jurisdiction. It has always been the rule of English private international law that a company incorporated under the law of a foreign State that is recognised by the United Kingdom should be recognised as a legal person here. Dicey and Morris state this rule thus[5]:

> " The existence or dissolution of a foreign corporation duly created or dissolved under the law of a foreign country is recognised by the court."

The incorporation theory is thus the common basis of the English rule and the Convention.

Further, the rules of the Convention relating to the capacity of the company to transact business are not fundamentally different from those of English private international law.[6] But in a particular issue the regulation of the Convention, with its distinction between mandatory and non-mandatory rules, may lead to a different result from that obtaining under the present rules of English private international law; here an amendment of English law will be required in order to bring it in line with the provisions of the Convention.

Further, the extension of the provisions of the Convention to commercial associations that are not legal persons (Art. 8) would require an alteration of English law. The best way of overcoming this difficulty would be to amend the Partnership Act 1890, s. 4 (1), by according an English partnership legal personality. This would not be a far-reaching alteration of the law because by virtue of the Rules of the Supreme Court, Order 81, an English partnership is practically treated for procedural purposes as if it were a legal person. It would mean the transfer of this procedural rule to the substantive level which would not be harmful, considering that the Scottish partnership has always been a legal person, by virtue of the Partnership Act 1890, s. 4 (2).

[4] G. K. Morse, *loc. cit.*, p. 202, n. 94.
[5] Dicey and Morris, *The Conflict of Laws* (Stevens, 8th ed., 1967), Rule 70, p. 479.
[6] See Dicey and Morris, *loc. cit.*, in n. 5 to Rule 73, pp. 484–485.

Interpretation of the Convention

By the Protocol of June 3, 1971,[7] the contracting States have agreed that the European Court in Luxembourg shall have jurisdiction to give preliminary rulings concerning the Convention (Art. 1 of the Protocol). The procedure laid down in Article 2 of the Protocol corresponds to that of Article 177 of the EEC Treaty.

Draft Regulation on Merger Control; Draft Convention on International Mergers

These measures, reproduced in Texts Nos. 9[8] and 10,[9] were received too late to be commented on.

---

[7] See p. 46, *ante*. The Protocol is reproduced in No. 8 B, *post*.
[8] See p. 283, *post*.
[9] See p. 295, *post*.

Texts

Text 1

A. *First Council Directive of March* 9, 1968 (*No.* 68/151/ *EEC*), *concerning the capacity of the company and its directors, and questions of publicity and nullity of the company*

The Council of the European Communities

Having regard to the Treaty establishing the European Economic Community, and in particular Article 54 (3) (*g*) thereof;

Having regard to the General Programme for the abolition of restrictions on freedom of establishment,[1] and in particular Title VI thereof;

Having regard to the proposal from the Commission;

Having regard to the Opinion of the European Parliament [2];

Having regard to the Opinion of the Economic and Social Committee [3];

Whereas the co-ordination provided for in Article 54 (3) (*g*) and in the General Programme for the abolition of restrictions on freedom of establishment is a matter of urgency, especially in regard to companies limited by shares or otherwise having limited liability, since the activities of such companies often extend beyond the frontiers of national territories;

Whereas the co-ordination of national provisions concerning disclosure, the validity of obligations entered into by, and the nullity of, such companies is of special importance, particularly for the purpose of protecting the interests of third parties;

Whereas in these matters Community provisions must be adopted in respect of such companies simultaneously, since the only safeguards they offer to third parties are their assets;

Whereas the basic documents of the company should be disclosed in order that third parties may be able to ascertain their contents and other information concerning the company, especially particulars of the persons who are authorized to bind the company;

Whereas the protection of third parties must be ensured by pro-

---

[1] J.O. 1962, 36.
[2] J.O. 1966, 1519.
[3] J.O. 1964, 3248.

51

visions which restrict to the greatest possible extent the grounds on which obligations entered into in the name of the company are not valid;

Whereas it is necessary, in order to ensure certainty in the law as regards relations between the company and third parties, and also between members, to limit the cases in which nullity can arise and the retroactive effect of a declaration of nullity, and to fix a short time limit within which third parties may enter objection to any such declaration;

Has adopted this Directive :

Article 1

The co-ordination measures prescribed by this Directive shall apply to the laws, regulations and administrative provisions of the Member States relating to the following types of company:

— *In Germany*:

die Aktiengesellschaft, die Kommanditgesellschaft auf Aktien, die Gesellschaft mit beschränkter Haftung;

— *In Belgium*:

de naamloze vennootschap,	la société anonyme,
de commanditaire vennoot-schap op aandelen,	la société en commandite par actions,
de personenvennootschap met beperkte aansprakelijk-heid;	la société de personnes à responsabilité limitée;

— *In France*:

la société anonyme, la société en commandite par actions, la société à responsabilité limitée;

— *In Italy*:

società per azioni, società in accomandita per azioni, società a responsabilità limitata;

— *In Luxembourg*:

la société anonyme, la société en commandite par actions, la société à responsabilité limitée;

— *In the Netherlands*:

de naamloze vennootschap, de commanditaire vennootschap op aandelen.

SECTION I: DISCLOSURE

Article 2

1. Member States shall take the measures required to ensure compulsory disclosure by companies of at least the following documents and particulars:

(a) The instrument of constitution, and the statutes if they are contained in a separate instrument;

(b) Any amendments to the instruments mentioned in (a), including any extension of the duration of the company;

(c) After every amendment of the instrument of constitution or of the statutes, the complete text of the instrument or statutes as amended to date;

(d) The appointment, termination of office and particulars of the persons who either as a body constituted pursuant to law or as members of any such body:

> (i) are authorized to represent the company in dealings with third parties and in legal proceedings,
>
> (ii) take part in the administration, supervision or control of the company.

It must appear from the disclosure whether the persons authorized to represent the company may do so alone or must act jointly;

(e) At least once a year, the amount of the capital subscribed, where the instrument of constitution or the statutes mention an authorized capital, unless any increase in the capital subscribed necessitates an amendment of the statutes;

(f) The balance sheet and the profit and loss account for each financial year. The document containing the balance sheet shall give particulars of the persons who are required by law to certify it. However, in respect of the Gesellschaft mit beschränkter Haftung, société de personnes à responsabilité limitée, personenvennootschap met beperkte aansprakelijkheid, société à responsabilité limitée and società a responsabilità limitata under German, Belgian, French, Italian or Luxembourg law, referred to in Article 1, and the besloten naamloze vennootschap under Netherlands law, the compulsory application of this provision shall be postponed until the date of implementation of a Directive concerning co-ordination of the contents of balance sheets and of profit and loss accounts and concerning exemption of such of those companies whose balance sheet total is less than that specified in the Directive from the obligation to make disclosure, in full or in part, of the said documents. The Council will adopt such a Directive within two years following the adoption of the present Directive;

(g) Any transfer of the seat of the company;

(h) The winding up of the company;

(i) Any declaration of nullity of the company by the courts;

(*j*) The appointment of liquidators, particulars concerning them, and their respective powers, unless such powers are expressly and exclusively derived from law or from the statutes of the company;

(*k*) The termination of the liquidation and, in Member States where striking off the register entails legal consequences, the fact of any such striking off.

2. For the purposes of paragraph 1 (*f*), companies which fulfil the following conditions shall be considered as besloten naamloze vennootschappen:

(*a*) They cannot issue bearer shares;

(*b*) No bearer certificate of registered shares within the meaning of Article 42c of the Netherlands Commercial Code can be issued by any person whatsoever;

(*c*) Their shares cannot be quoted on a stock exchange;

(*d*) Their statutes contain a clause requiring approval by the company before the transfer of shares to third parties, except in the case of transfer in the event of death and, if the statutes so provide, in the case of transfer to a spouse, forebears or issue; transfers shall not be in blank, but otherwise each transfer shall be in writing under hand, signed by the transferor and transferee or by notarial act;

(*e*) Their statutes specify that the company is a besloten naamloze vennootschap; the name of the company includes the words " Besloten Naamloze Vennootschap " or the initials " BNV."

Article 3

1. In each Member State a file shall be opened in a central register, commercial register or companies register, for each of the companies registered therein.

2. All documents and particulars which must be disclosed in pursuance of Article 2 shall be kept in the file or entered in the register; the subject matter of the entries in the register must in every case appear in the file.

3. A copy of the whole or any part of the documents or particulars referred to in Article 2 must be obtainable by application in writing at a price not exceeding the administrative cost thereof.

Copies supplied shall be certified as " true copies ", unless the applicant dispenses with such certification.

4. Disclosure of the documents and particulars referred to in paragraph 2 shall be effected by publication in the national gazette appointed for that purpose by the Member State, either of the full

or partial text, or by means of a reference to the document which has been deposited in the file or entered in the register.

5. The documents and particulars may be relied on by the company as against third parties only after they have been published in accordance with paragraph 4, unless the company proves that the third parties had knowledge thereof. However, with regard to transactions taking place before the sixteenth day following the publication, the documents and particulars shall not be relied on as against third parties who prove that it was impossible for them to have had knowledge thereof.

6. Member States shall take the necessary measures to avoid any discrepancy between what is disclosed by publication in the press and what appears in the register or file.

However, in cases of discrepancy, the text published in the press may not be relied on as against third parties; the latter may nevertheless rely thereon, unless the company proves that they had knowledge of the texts deposited in the file or entered in the register.

7. Third parties may, moreover, always rely on any documents and particulars in respect of which the disclosure formalities have not yet been completed, save where non-disclosure causes them not to have effect.

Article 4

Member States shall prescribe that letters and order forms shall state the following particulars:

— the register in which the file mentioned in Article 3 is kept, together with the number of the company in that register;
— the legal form of the company, the location of its seat and, where appropriate, the fact that the company is being wound up.

Where in these documents mention is made of the capital of the company, the reference shall be to the capital subscribed and paid up.

Article 5

Each Member State shall determine by which persons the disclosure formalities are to be carried out.

Article 6

Member States shall provide for appropriate penalties in case of:

— failure to disclose the balance sheet and profit and loss account as required by Article 2 (1) (*f*);
— omission from commercial documents of the compulsory particulars provided for in Article 4.

SECTION II: VALIDITY OF OBLIGATIONS ENTERED INTO BY A COMPANY

Article 7

If, before a company being formed has acquired legal personality, action has been carried out in its name and the company does not assume the obligations arising from such action, the persons who acted shall, without limit, be jointly and severally liable therefor, unless otherwise agreed.

Article 8

Completion of the formalities of disclosure of the particulars concerning the persons who, as an organ of the company, are authorised to represent it shall constitute a bar to any irregularity in their appointment being relied upon as against third parties unless the company proves that such third parties had knowledge thereof.

Article 9

1. Acts done by the organs of the company shall be binding upon it even if those acts are not within the objects of the company, unless such acts exceed the powers that the law confers or allows to be conferred on those organs.

However, Member States may provide that the company shall not be bound where such acts are outside the objects of the company, if it proves that the third party knew that the act was outside those objects or could not in view of the circumstances have been unaware of it; disclosure of the statutes shall not of itself be sufficient proof thereof.

2. The limits on the powers of the organs of the company, arising under the statutes or from a decision of the competent organs, may never be relied on as against third parties, even if they have been disclosed.

3. If the national law provides that authority to represent a company may, in derogation from the legal rules governing the subject, be conferred by the statutes on a single person or on several persons acting jointly, that law may provide that such a provision in the statutes may be relied on as against third parties on condition that it relates to the general power of representation; the question whether such a provision in the statutes can be relied on as against third parties shall be governed by Article 3.

SECTION III: NULLITY OF THE COMPANY

Article 10

In all Member States whose laws do not provide for preventive control, administrative or judicial, at the time of formation of a company, the instrument of constitution, the company statutes and any amendments to those documents shall be drawn up and certified in due legal form.

Article 11

The laws of the Member States may not provide for the nullity of companies otherwise than in accordance with the following provisions:

1. Nullity must be ordered by a decision of a court of law;
2. Nullity may be ordered only on the following grounds:
   (*a*) that no instrument of constitution was executed or that the rules of preventive control or the requisite legal formalities were not complied with;
   (*b*) that the objects of the company are unlawful or contrary to public policy;
   (*c*) that the instrument of constitution or the statutes do not state the name of the company, the amount of the individual subscriptions of capital, the total amount of the capital subscribed or the objects of the company;
   (*d*) failure to comply with the provisions of the national law concerning the minimum amount of capital to be paid up;
   (*e*) the incapacity of all the founder members;
   (*f*) that, contrary to the national law governing the company the number of founder members is less than two.

Apart from the foregoing grounds of nullity, a company shall not be subject to any cause of non-existence, nullity absolute, nullity relative or declaration of nullity.

Article 12

1. The question whether a decision of nullity pronounced by a court of law may be relied on as against third parties shall be governed by Article 3. Where the national law entitles a third party to challenge the decision, he may do so only within six months of the public notice of the decision of the court being given.
2. Nullity shall entail the winding up of the company, as may dissolution.
3. Nullity shall not of itself affect the validity of any commitments entered into by or with the company, without prejudice to the consequences of the company's being wound up.
4. The laws of each Member State may make provision for the consequences of nullity as between members of the company.
5. Holders of shares in the capital shall remain obliged to pay up

the capital agreed to be subscribed by them but which has not been paid up, to the extent that commitments entered into with creditors so require.

SECTION IV: GENERAL PROVISIONS

Article 13

Member States shall put into force, within eighteen months following notification of this Directive, all amendments to their laws, regulations or administrative provisions required in order to comply with the provisions of this Directive and shall forthwith inform the Commission thereof.

The obligation of disclosure provided for in Article 2 (1) (*f*) shall not enter into force until thirty months after notification of this Directive in respect of naamloze vennootschappen under Netherlands law other than those referred to in the present Article 42 (c) of the Netherlands Commercial Code.

Member States may provide that initial disclosure of the full text of the statutes as amended since the formation of the company shall not be required until the statutes are next amended or until 31 December 1970, whichever shall be the earlier.

Member States shall ensure that they communicate to the Commission the text of the main provisions of national law which they adopt in the field covered by this Directive.

Article 14

This Directive is addressed to the Member States.
Done at Brussels, March 9, 1968
For the Council
The President
M. COUVE DE MURVILLE

B. *European Communities Act* 1972 (1972 *c.* 68), *section* 9

Companies

9.—(1) In favour of a person dealing with a company in good faith, any transaction decided on by the directors shall be deemed to be one which it is within the capacity of the company to enter into, and the power of the directors to bind the company shall be deemed to be free of any limitation under the memorandum or articles of association; and a party to a transaction so decided on shall not be bound to enquire as to the capacity of the company to enter into it or as to any such limitation on the powers of the directors, and shall be presumed to have acted in good faith unless the contrary is proved.

(2) Where a contract purports to be made by a company, or by a person as agent for a company, at a time when the company has not been formed, then subject to any agreement to the contrary the contract shall have effect as a contract entered into by the person purporting to act for the company or as agent for it, and he shall be personally liable on the contract accordingly.

(3) The registrar of companies shall cause to be published in the Gazette notice of the issue or receipt by him of documents of any of the following descriptions (stating in the notice the name of the company, the description of document and the date of issue or receipt), that is to say—

(*a*) any certificate of incorporation of a company;

(*b*) any document making or evidencing an alteration in the memorandum or articles of association of a company;

(*c*) any return relating to a company's register of directors, or notification of a change among its directors;

(*d*) a company's annual return;

(*e*) any notice of the situation of a company's registered office, or of any change therein;

(*f*) any copy of a winding-up order in respect of a company;

(*g*) any order for the dissolution of a company on a winding up;

(*h*) any return by a liquidator of the final meeting of a company on a winding up;

and in the following provisions of this section " official notification " means, in relation to anything stated in a document of any of the above descriptions, the notification of that document in the Gazette under this section and, in relation to the appointment of a liquidator in a voluntary winding up, the notification thereof in the Gazette under section 305 of the Companies Act 1948, and " officially notified " shall be construed accordingly.

(4) A company shall not be entitled to rely against other persons on the happening of any of the following events, that is to say—

(*a*) the making of a winding-up order in respect of the company, or the appointment of a liquidator in a voluntary winding up of the company; or

(*b*) any alteration of the company's memorandum or articles of association; or

(*c*) any change among the company's directors; or

(*d*) (as regards service of any document on the company) any change in the situation of the company's registered office;

if the event had not been officially notified at the material time and is not shown by the company to have been known at that time to the person concerned, or if the material time fell on or before the fifteenth day after the date of official notification (or, where the fifteenth day was a non-business day, on or before the next day that was not) and it is shown that the person concerned was unavoidably prevented from knowing of the event at that time.

For this purpose " non-business day " means a Saturday or Sunday, Christmas Day, Good Friday and any other day which, in the part of Great Britain where the company is registered, is a bank holiday under the Banking and Financial Dealings Act 1971.

(5) Where any alteration is made in a company's memorandum or articles of association by any statutory provision, whether contained in an Act of Parliament or in an instrument made under an Act, a printed copy of the Act or instrument shall not later than fifteen days after that provision comes into force be forwarded to the registrar of companies and recorded by him; and where a company is required by this section or otherwise to send to the registrar any document making or evidencing an alteration in the company's memorandum or articles of association (other than a special resolution under section 5 of the Companies Act 1948), the company shall send with it a printed copy of the memorandum or articles as altered.

If a company fails to comply with this subsection, the company and any officer of the company who is in default shall be liable to a default fine.

(6) Where before the coming into force of this subsection—

(*a*) an alteration has been made in a company's memorandum or articles of association by any statutory provision, and a printed copy of the relevant Act or instrument has not been sent to the registrar of companies; or

(*b*) an alteration has been made in a company's memorandum or articles of association in any manner, and a printed copy of the memorandum or articles as altered has not been sent to him;

such a copy shall be sent to him within one month after the coming into force of this subsection.

If a company fails to comply with this subsection, the company and any officer of the company who is in default shall be liable to a default fine.

(7) Every company shall have the following particulars mentioned in legible characters in all business letters and order forms of the company, that is to say,—

(*a*) the place of registration of the company, and the number with which it is registered;

(*b*) the address of its registered office; and

(*c*) in the case of a limited company exempt from the obligation

to use the word " limited " as part of its name, the fact that
it is a limited company;

and, if in the case of a company having a share capital there is on
the stationery used for any such letters or on the order forms a
reference to the amount of the share capital, the reference shall be
to paid-up share capital.

If a company fails to comply with this subsection, the company
shall be liable to a fine not exceeding £50; and if an officer of a
company or any person on its behalf issues or authorises the issue of
any business letter or order form not complying with this subsection,
he shall be liable to a fine not exceeding £50.

(8) This section shall be construed as one with the Companies
Act 1948; and section 435 of that Act (which enables certain provisions of it to be extended to unregistered companies) shall have effect
as if this section were among those mentioned in Schedule 14 to that
Act with an entry in column 3 of that Schedule to the effect that this
section is to apply so far only as may be specified by regulations
under section 435 and to such bodies corporate as may be so specified,
and as if sections 107 (registered office) and 437 (service of documents)
were so mentioned (and section 437 were not included in the last
entry in the Schedule).

The modifications of this section that may be made by regulations
under section 435 shall include the extension of subsections (3), (5)
and (6) to additional matters (and in particular to the instruments
constituting or regulating a company as well as to alterations thereof).

(9) This section shall not come into force until the entry date
(except to authorise the making with effect from that date of
regulations by virtue of subsection (8) above).

Text 2

Second Draft Directive, submitted by the Commission to the Council on March 5, 1970, concerning the formation of the company and the maintenance of capital (as amended)

The Council of the European Communities,

Having regard to the Treaty establishing the European Economic Community, and in particular Article 54 (3) (*g*) thereof;

Having regard to the proposal from the Commission;

Having regard to the Opinion of the European Parliament;

Having regard to the Opinion of the Economic and Social Committee;

Whereas the co-ordination provided for in Article 54 (3) (*g*) and in the General Programme for the abolition of restrictions on freedom of establishment, which was begun by Directive No. 68/151/EEC of 9 March, 1968, is especially important in relation to public limited liability companies, because their activities frequently extend beyond their national boundaries;

Whereas co-ordination of national provisions relating to formation of public limited liability companies and to the increase or reduction of their capital is particularly important in order to ensure equivalent protection both for shareholders and for creditors of such companies;

Whereas the statutes of a public limited liability company must make it possible for any interested person inside the common market to acquaint himself with the basic particulars of the company at the time of formation and with the composition of its capital;

Whereas Community provisions must be adopted for maintenance of the capital, which constitutes the creditors' security, in particular by prohibiting any diminution thereof by unauthorized distribution to shareholders and by restricting the Company's right to acquire its own shares;

Whereas it is important, having regard to the objectives of Article 54 (3) (*g*), that the Member States' laws relating to increase or reduction of capital ensure that the principles of equal treatment of shareholders and of protection of creditors whose claims exist prior to the decision for reduction are observed and uniformly applied;

Has adopted this Directive:

Article 1

1. The co-ordination measures prescribed by this Directive shall apply to the laws, regulations and administrative provisions of the Member States relating to the following types of company:

— In Germany: *die Aktiengesellschaft*
— in Belgium: *la société anonyme*
                 de naamloze vennootschap
— in France: *le société anonyme*
— in Italy: *la società per azioni*
— in Luxemburg: *la société anonyme*
— in the Netherlands: *de naamloze vennootschap*
— in the United Kingdom: companies incorporated with limited liability
— in Ireland: companies incorporated with limited liability
— in Denmark: *Aktieselskab*

2. Pending co-ordination at a later date of the guarantees required from investment companies, it shall be permissible for the Member States not to apply the provisions of this Directive to them. The expression " investment companies " means exclusively companies limited by shares:

— whose sole object is to invest their funds in a variety of stocks and shares with the single aim of spreading investment risks and giving their shareholders the benefit of the results of the management of the investment portfolio;
— which invite the public to invest in their own shares;
— whose statutes provide that within the limits of a minimum and a maximum capital the shares may at any time be issued, redeemed or resold.

If the national laws do not apply the provisions of this Directive to the companies specified in the previous paragraph, they shall require such companies to include the words " investment company " in all documents in respect of which there exists an obligation of disclosure and on all business papers of those companies.

SECTION I: FORMATION OF THE COMPANY

Article 2

The Member States shall stipulate that company statutes shall contain at least the following details:

(a) the form and name of the company;
(b) the registered office;
(c) the nature of the company's business;
(d) the amount of the capital and whether it is subscribed or authorised;

(e) the categories of shares where there are several of these; the number of shares subscribed or to be issued in each category and the rights attached to each category, also,
- the nominal value of the shares;
- the number of shares without nominal value, where such shares may be issued under the national law;
- the special conditions limiting the right to transfer shares;

(f) the form of the shares, whether registered or bearer, and any provisions relating to the conversion of shares, unless the procedure for this is laid down by law;

(g) the rules, in so far as they are not legally determined, governing the composition and function of the organs responsible for representation, management, supervision or auditing of the company;

(h) the duration of the company, except where this is indefinite.

Article 3

The following information must be contained in the statutes or the deed of incorporation if this is embodied in a separate instrument:

(a) the identity of the promoters. The promoters are deemed to be the natural or legal persons who have signed the statutes or the deeds of incorporation, or, where the formation of the company is not simultaneous, have signed the draft statutes or deeds of incorporation;

(b) the amount of capital initially paid in;

(c) the number and value of the shares allotted against each investment not made in cash;

(d) the approximate amount of the formation expenses legally payable by the company or chargeable to it by agreement;

(e) any privilege or consideration granted to any person who has participated in the formation of the company.

Article 4

The duration of the company shall be indefinite unless otherwise specified by the statutes.

Article 5

1. In any Member State where, by law, a number of persons must combine to form a company, the fact that all the shares are held by one individual or that the number of members has fallen below the legal minimum after the formation of the company shall not lead to the automatic dissolution of the company.

2. If the law of a Member State permits such a company to be

dissolved by order of the court, it must be possible for the competent court to give the company a period of not less than 6 months to regularise its position.

3. Where a company is dissolved in this way, it shall go into liquidation.

Article 6

I. The laws of the Member States shall require that a minimum capital of 25,000 units of account be subscribed for formation of the company. This amount may be raised or lowered by not more than 10 per cent. for purposes of conversion into national currency.

II. Notwithstanding the provisions of the foregoing paragraph:

1. The minimum amount aforesaid may be reduced to 4,000 units of account for companies governed by United Kingdom or Irish law which satisfy the following conditions:
   (a) they cannot issue bearer shares, bearer certificates relating to registered shares, or debentures;
   (b) their shares cannot be quoted on a Stock Exchange;
   (c) the statutes restrict the right to transfer the shares;
   (d) the name of the company must include the word " private ".
2. Amounts exceeding 25,000 units of account may be required:
   (a) as a condition for quotation of the shares on a Stock Exchange;
   (b) pending co-ordination at a later date for the carrying on of activities whose special nature makes special provisions necessary.

Article 7

The shares issued against cash brought in must be paid up to not less than 25 per cent. of their nominal value or accountable par.

Shares allotted against investment not made in cash must be entirely paid up.

Article 8

A report on any acquired assets brought in other than cash shall be drawn up prior to the formation of the company by one or more independent persons appointed or approved by an administrative or judicial authority.

This report must inform future shareholders of the prospective assets, their value and the value of the shares to be issued against them.

At least the conclusions of the experts contained in this report must be published in the manner laid down by the law of each Member State, in accordance with the provisions of Directive No. 68/151 of 9 March, 1968.

Article 9

If, during the two years following its formation, the company acquires any asset from a founder or shareholder for a consideration of not less than one-tenth of the subscribed capital, the acquisition shall be examined and published in manner provided in Article 8 and shall be submitted for approval to the general meeting of shareholders. The provisions of this Article do not apply to acquisitions made in the normal course of business of the company.

Article 10

The subscribed capital shall not be made up of unrealisable assets such as, in particular, an undertaking to perform work or supply services.

Article 11

Subject to the provisions relating to the reduction of capital, the shareholders may not be exempted from their obligations to pay in their contribution.

SECTION II: MAINTENANCE OF THE INTEGRITY OF THE COMPANY'S CAPITAL

Article 12

Where the net assets of a company fall below the amount of the subscribed capital plus the unavailable reserves, no distribution may be made to the shareholders except as specified by this directive.

Article 13

The dividends, and where appropriate the interim dividends, may only be taken from the clear profits.

Article 14

Dividends and interim dividends distributed contrary to the preceding Article 13 shall be returned to the company by shareholders who have received them other than in good faith.

Article 15

No interest may be paid to shareholders in the absence of profits. The legislations of those Member States, which, however, permit the distribution of interim interest in the absence of profits during the period of winding up the company shall require the statutes or the deed to provide for—

(a) the possibility of distributing such interest;

(b) the maximum period for each distribution, which may not exceed four years;

(c) the rate of such interest, which may not exceed 4 per cent.

Article 16

In the case of serious loss of the subscribed capital, a meeting of shareholders must be called within a period laid down by law in the Member States, for the purpose of taking the necessary measures or considering whether the company should be dissolved.

The extent of a loss deemed to be serious for the purposes of the first paragraph shall not be placed by the laws of the Member States at a figure higher than half the subscribed capital.

Article 17

The shares of a company may not be subscribed by the company itself.

If the shares of a company have been subscribed by a person acting in his own name but on behalf of the company, the subscriber shall be deemed to have subscribed the shares for his own account.

In any case, the directors of the issuing company shall be personally responsible for paying up irregularly subscribed shares.

Article 18

1. Where the laws of the Member States permit companies to acquire their own shares, those laws shall impose at least the following conditions:

(a) each transaction must be specially approved by the general meeting, which shall settle the terms and in so doing apply the principle of equality of shareholders;

(b) the acquisition must not have the effect of reducing the net assets below the amount of the subscribed capital plus the non-distributable reserves;

(c) acquisition must relate only to fully paid up shares;

(d) the nominal value or proportionate value of shares acquired, together with own shares previously acquired by the company and held in its portfolio, must not exceed 25 per cent. of the subscribed capital.

2. The conditions set out above may be waived where acquisition of the company's own shares is essential to prevent serious detriment to the company. In such case:

(*a*) the acquisition must not have the effect that the amount of the net assets falls below the amount of subscribed capital;

(*b*) the nominal value or proportionate value of the shares acquired, together with own shares previously acquired by the company and held in its portfolio, must not exceed 10 per cent. of the subscribed capital.

3. The provisions of paragraph 2 (*a*) and (*b*) above shall apply to fully paid up shares acquired for distribution to the company's employees.

4. The foregoing provisions, with the exception of those contained in paragraph 1 (*c*) shall not apply to acquisition of shares for no payment.

Article 19

Article 18 shall not apply to:

(*a*) shares acquired as a result of a regular decision to reduce capital or in consequence of compulsory depreciation;

(*b*) shares coming into the company's possession following a merger or the transfer of a branch of activity.

(*c*) fully paid shares coming into a company's possession following a transfer of property in full.

Article 20

The laws of those Member States which permit companies to include their own shares among their assets shall impose the following requirements for so long as such inclusion takes place:

(*a*) the right to vote attached to each share shall in every case be suspended;

(*b*) where such shares are included in the balance sheet as assets, a non-distributable reserve of like amount shall be shown on the liabilities side;

(*c*) the directors' management report shall state at least:
 — the proportion of share capital acquired during the last financial year;
 — the purchase price of the shares;
 — the proportion of share capital acquired prior to the last financial year.

SECTION III: INCREASE OF CAPITAL

Article 21

1. Where the capital is increased by the acquirement of assets in cash, the shares already issued must first be paid up.

2. However, national laws may provide for exceptions to this

principle. They shall lay down these exceptions, restricting them to cases where a company's needs have to be met, and this could not be done by paying up existing shares. Where such exceptions are made, the percentage of the payments required from new shareholders may not be higher than that of the payments made by existing shareholders.

3. Shares issued following an increase of capital must be paid up to at least 25 per cent. of their nominal value or accountable par and, where appropriate, the total share premium must be paid.

Article 22

1. Any increase of capital must be voted by the general meeting by a decision taken in each case under the publication, quorum and majority conditions required for any amendment of the statutes.

2. Nevertheless, the statutes or the general meeting voting under the quorum and majority conditions specified above may authorize the increase of the subscribed capital up to a stipulated maximum amount. Any increase of subscribed capital up to that amount shall then be decided by the competent organ of the company. The competence of the organ shall last for a maximum of five years and may be renewed on one or more occasions by the general meeting for a period not exceeding five years on any one occasion.

3. Where there are several categories of shares, the validity of an increase of capital or authorization to increase capital as specified in the preceding paragraph shall be subject to a separate vote for each category at least where the transaction is detrimental to the holders of shares in these categories.

4. The preceding paragraphs shall apply to the issue of bonds convertible into shares, but not to the conversion of these.

Article 23

Where the capital is increased by the transfer of assets not in cash, the shares allotted in consideration of such transfers must be fully paid.

The valuation of such transfers must be examined in the manner required upon the formation of the company.

A report as specified in Article 8 of this Directive must be drawn up in such case either by one or more independent persons appointed or approved by an administrative or judicial authority, or by the person or persons responsible for auditing the company's accounts.

Article 24

Where an increase of capital by subscription in cash is not fully subscribed within the stipulated period, the subscribers shall cease to be bound only if the resolution for increase of the capital expressly so provided.

Article 25

1. Whenever the capital is increased by the acquisition of assets in cash, the shares must be offered first to the shareholders according to the proportion of the capital represented by their shares.

2. This preferential right may not be restricted or withdrawn by the statutes. This may be done, however, by decision of the general meeting when debating the increase under the conditions laid down for any amendment of the statutes. The company directors shall be required to submit a written report to such meeting pointing out the reasons for restricting or withdrawing the preferential right, and accounting for the proposed issue price.

3. The general meeting, under the conditions laid down for any amendment to the statutes, may also empower any organ nominated by it to restrict or withdraw this preferential right.

4. The preceding paragraphs shall apply to the issue of bonds convertible into shares, but not to the conversion of these.

Article 26

Where an increase of the subscribed capital occurs as a result of the incorporation of reserves, the legal reserve, if available for this purpose, may be utilized only in so far as it exceeds 10 per cent. of the capital.

SECTION IV: REDUCTION OF CAPITAL

Article 27

Any reduction of capital, except in the case of redemption or compulsory withdrawal in the meaning of Articles 32 and 33, must be decided or authorized by the general meeting, voting in each case under the publication, quorum and majority conditions laid down for any amendment to the statutes.

The notice convening the meeting must at least specify the reasons for the reduction and the procedure to be followed in achieving it.

Article 28

Where there are several categories of shares, the validity of a reduction of capital shall be subject to a separate vote for each category at least where the transaction is detrimental to the holders of shares in these categories.

Article 29

1. In the case of reduction of capital, the laws of the Member

States shall recognize the right of creditors with claims ante-dating the publication of the decision to make the reduction, to be paid off or obtain security. They shall lay down the conditions for the exercise of this right. They may not set aside this right unless the creditor has some other security or unless no guarantee to the creditor is necessary.

2. They shall also stipulate, either that the reduction shall be void, or that no payment may be made for the benefit of the shareholders until the creditors have been satisfied or the court has decided that their demands need not be met.

3. The same rules shall apply whether the reduction of capital comes about through the total or partial waiving of the payment of the balance of the shareholders' contributions, or whether the reduction of capital has led to the building up of reserves which are subsequently distributed.

Article 30

The provisions of Article 29 shall not apply to a reduction of capital for the purpose of making the subscribed capital correspond with company assets which have fallen in consequence of losses. The laws of the Member States shall lay down the necessary measures to ensure that the shareholders are not able to profit from any surplus of assets over liabilities resulting from a reduction of capital.

Article 31

Where a general meeting decides to reduce the subscribed capital to a figure below the minimum legal capital, it must at the same time decide either to increase the capital to an amount not falling below the legal minimum or to change the corporate status of the company.

Article 32

Where the laws of the Member States authorize redemption without reduction of the company's capital, they shall ensure that the following conditions are observed:

- (a) the redemption must be expressly provided for or authorized by the statutes. Where the statutes authorize redemption it may be decided upon by the general meeting voting under the usual conditions of attendance and majority; the general meeting shall determine the procedure to be adopted;
- (b) the redemption may take place only with the aid of reserves built up for this purpose, free reserves or profits;
- (c) shareholders whose shares are paid off shall return their rights in the company, with the exception of repayment of their

investment and participation in the distribution of a first dividend.

Article 33

Where the laws of the Member States authorize the compulsory withdrawal of shares with reduction of share capital, they shall ensure that the following conditions are observed:

(a) the transaction must have been provided for or authorized by the statutes before the issue of the shares concerned;

(b) where the statutes merely authorize the transaction, it may be decided upon by the general meeting under the ordinary conditions of attendance and majority. The general meeting shall determine the procedure to be adopted and in particular the amount to be paid to shareholders whose shares are withdrawn;

(c) the rules on the ordinary reduction of the share capital must be complied with in respect of the protection of creditors.

Nevertheless, these rules may be set aside where the shares are allotted to the company free of charge, or where the sums distributed to the shareholders are taken out of reserves built up specially for this purpose or out of profits or free reserves.

In this case, an amount equal to the total nominal value of the withdrawn shares shall be paid into a reserve which can only be disposed of under the conditions required for a reduction of capital.

Article 34

In the cases covered by Articles 32 and 33, the legislation of the Member States shall also take the necessary measures to ensure that:

(a) the procedure adopted for the transaction complies with the principle of equal treatment of shareholders;

(b) where there are several categories of shares and the transaction may be detrimental to the holders of shares in one of these categories, the validity of any decision of the general meeting shall be subject to a separate vote for each category.

SECTION V: FINAL PROVISIONS

Article 35

The Member States shall put into force within 18 months following notification of this Directive such amendments to their laws, regulations and administrative provisions as may be necessary to comply with the provisions of this Directive and shall forthwith inform the Commission thereof.

The Member States may provide that the amendments referred to in paragraph 1 :

— which are made in pursuance of Articles 2, 4, 6, 7, 12, 13, 14 and 15 of this Directive shall not apply to companies existing at the date of entry into force of this Directive until 18 months after that date;

— which are made in pursuance of Article 3 shall not apply to such companies.

The Governments of the Member States shall communicate to the Commission the texts of the draft laws and regulations in the field governed by this Directive, together with the grounds on which they are based. The same shall be communicated not later than six months before the proposed date of entry into force.

Article 36
This Directive is addressed to the Member States.

Text 3

Third Draft Directive, submitted by the Commission to the Council on June 16, 1970, concerning mergers between joint stock companies (as amended)

The Council of the European Communities,

Having regard to the Treaty establishing the European Economic Community, and in particular Article 54, paragraph 3 (g) thereof;

Having regard to the proposal of the Commission;

Having regard to the Opinion of the European Parliament;

Having regard to the Opinion of the Economic and Social Committee;

Whereas the co-ordination provided for in Article 54, paragraph 3 (g) and in the general programme for the removal of restrictions on freedom of establishment was begun with Directive No. 68/151/EEC of 9 March 1968 [1];

Whereas this co-ordination was continued with Directive No. ... of ...[2] harmonizing the rules adopted by the various Member States concerning the formation of a joint-stock company and the maintenance and alteration of its capital;

Whereas to protect the interests of members and other parties it is imperative to co-ordinate the laws of the Member States on mergers between joint-stock companies and to require the Member States which so far have no legislation on mergers to introduce it;

Whereas in the framework of this co-ordination it is particularly important for shareholders of the merging companies to be informed adequately and as objectively as possible and to have their rights protected appropriately;

Whereas it is also indispensable that the staff of the merging companies should be informed and consulted about the repercussions of the merger on them;

Whereas the creditors, whether debenture-holders or not, and the holders of other securities of the company acquired must be protected with a view to ensuring that they do not suffer from the implementation of the merger;

Whereas the publication requirements of Directive No. 68/151/ EEC of 9 March 1968 must be extended to the transactions involved in a merger so that third parties are adequately informed of them;

[1] J.O. 1968, L65; see p. 51, *ante.*
[2] J.O. 1970, C48; see p. 62, *ante.*

74

Whereas it is necessary to extend the safeguards afforded under the merger procedure to members and other parties to certain legal transactions which in major points are akin to mergers so as to ensure that this protection cannot be evaded;

Whereas it is necessary, with a view to ensuring certainty in the legal relations between the companies involved, between these companies and third parties, and between members, to limit the number of grounds on which a merger may be annulled, while establishing the principle that defects attaching to a merger may be remedied wherever this is possible, and to fix a short period of time within which annulment may be claimed,

Has adopted the present Directive:

SCOPE OF APPLICATION

Article 1

1. The co-ordination measures laid down in this directive shall apply to Member States' statutory and administrative provisions relating to the following types of company:
— Germany: *die Aktiengesellschaft*
— Belgium: *la société anonyme*
      de naamloze vennootschap
— France: *la société anonyme*
— Italy: *la società per azioni*
— Luxembourg: *la société anonyme*
— Netherlands: *de naamloze vennootschap*
— Denmark: *Aktieselskab*
— Ireland: *companies incorporated with limited liability*
— the United Kingdom: *companies incorporated with limited liability.*

2. The Member States shall be free to refrain from applying the provisions of this directive to cooperative societies established in one of the forms of companies listed in the preceding paragraph.

CHAPTER I: REGULATION OF MERGER BY THE TAKEOVER OF ONE COMPANY BY ANOTHER AND MERGER BY FORMATION OF A NEW COMPANY

Article 2

1. The Member States shall as regards companies existing under their national laws, make provision for rules governing merger by takeover of one company by another and merger by formation of a new company.

2. For the purposes of this directive " merger by takeover "

means the operation whereby one company transfers to another, following a resolution for winding up without but not involving implementation of the liquidation procedure, the whole of its assets and liabilities, in exchange for the issue to the shareholders of the company taken over of shares in the acquiring company and, if appropriate, an equalization payment in cash not exceeding ten per cent of the nominal value of the shares so issued or, where they have no nominal value, of their proportional value.

3. For the purposes of this directive " merger by formation of a new company" means the operation whereby several companies transfer to a company which they form, following resolutions for their own winding up but not involving implementation of the liquidation procedure, the whole of their assets and liabilities in exchange for the issue to their shareholders of shares in the new company and, if appropriate, an equalization payment in cash not exceeding ten per cent of the nominal value of the shares so issued or, where they have no nominal value, of their proportional value.

4. Merger by takeover may also be effected if the company taken over is in liquidation, provided the latter has not yet begun to distribute its assets amongst its shareholders.

5. Merger by formation of a new company may also be effected where the companies which cease to exist are in liquidation, provided they have not yet begun to distribute their assets amongst their shareholders.

CHAPTER II: MERGER BY TAKEOVER

Article 3

1. The management organs of the merging companies shall draw up in writing a draft of the terms of merger.

2. The draft terms of merger shall specify at least:

(a) The name, legal form and registered office of each of the companies merging;

(b) The share exchange ratio and, where appropriate, the amount of the equalization payment;

(c) The terms relating to issue of shares in the acquiring company and the date from which such shares entitle the holders to participate in the profits;

(d) The date from which the business of the company taken over is to be regarded as being carried on on behalf of the acquiring company;

(e) The protection afforded by the acquiring company to the shareholders with special rights and the holders of securities other than shares, or the measures proposed concerning them.

3. The proposed terms of merger must be published in manner provided in Directive No. 68/151/EEC of 9 March, 1968, for each of the companies merging, at least one month before the date of meeting of the General Meeting which is to decide thereon.

Article 4

1. Merger shall require the approval of each of the merging companies in General Meeting. The laws of the Member States shall apply as regards the convening, composition and holding of the General Meetings and as regards the requirements as to quorum and majorities. In no case may the majority be less than two thirds either of the votes attached to the securities represented at the meeting or of the share capital represented thereat. Moreover, in appropriate cases, the rules relating to alteration of the statutes shall apply.

2. The general meetings shall discuss the approval of the merger plan and any amendment of the articles of association that its implementation may require.

Article 5

1. The management organs of each of the merging companies shall draw up a detailed report explaining the draft terms of merger, and in particular the share exchange ratio, and setting out the legal and economic grounds therefor.

2. In addition, for each of the merging companies one or more independent experts designated or approved by a legal or administrative authority shall examine the draft terms of merger and draw up a report for the shareholders. These experts may be the persons responsible for auditing the company's accounts.

Each expert shall be entitled to obtain from merging companies all relevant information and documents and to carry out all necessary investigations.

In their report the experts must state whether in their opinion the share exchange ratio is justified or not. In support of their statement they shall give at least the following particulars:

(a) The relationship between the companies' net assets on the basis of actual values;

(b) The relationship between the earnings yields of the companies, taking future prospects into account;

(c) The criteria used in evaluating the net assets and earnings yields.

In addition, the report shall indicate what special difficulties of evaluation have arisen, if any.

3. Every shareholder shall be entitled to have access to the following documents at the registered office at least two months before the date of meeting of the General Meeting which is to decide on the proposed merger:

(a) The draft terms of merger;

(b) The balance-sheets, profit and loss accounts and annual reports of the merging companies for the last three financial years;

(c) A financial statement drawn up as at the first day of the second month preceding the date of the draft terms of merger, if the last balance-sheet relates to a financial year which ended more than six months before that date;

(d) The reports of the management organs of the merging companies provided for in paragraph 1 of this Article and in Article 6 (1);

(e) The experts' reports provided for in paragraph 2 of this Article.

4. The financial statement provided for in paragraph 3 (c) shall be drawn up in accordance with the same methods and in the same form as the last annual balance-sheet.

However:

(a) No fresh physical inventory shall be taken;

(b) The figures in the last balance-sheet shall be altered only to reflect changes in the accounts; the following shall nevertheless be taken into account:
— interim depreciation and provisions;
— material changes in actual value not shown in the accounts.

5. Every shareholder shall be entitled to obtain free of charge on request copies, in full or in part, of the documents referred to in paragraph 3.

Article 6

1. The management organs of each of the merging companies shall draw up a detailed report explaining the legal, economic and social effects of the merger on the employees over a period of at least two years and indicating the measures to be taken regarding them.

2. Every employee or employees' representative shall be entitled to have access to the report provided for in paragraph 1 and the

other documents referred to in Article 5 (3) at the company's registered office at least two months before the meeting of the General
Meeting which is to decide on the merger.

3. Before the General Meeting discusses the merger the management organs of the merging companies shall discuss the reports provided for in paragraph 1 with the employees' representatives. The
latter may deliver a written opinion. The General Meeting which
is to decide on the merger shall be informed of that opinion.

4. If the merger is prejudicial to the employees' interests the
management organs shall initiate negotiations with the employees'
representatives, before the General Meeting discusses the merger,
with a view to reaching agreement on the measures to be taken
regarding the employees. If no agreement is reached in these negotiations, each of the parties may ask the public authority to act as
intermediary.

5. Every employee or employees' representative shall be entitled
to obtain free of charge on request copies, in full or in part, of the
documents referred to in paragraphs 2 to 4.

6. This Article is without prejudice to the laws of those Member
States which are more favourable to employees in cases of merger.

Article 7

1. If, as a result of the merger, the acquiring company increases
its capital, this transaction shall be governed by the rules of Directive
No. .... of ....[3]

2. The Member States shall, however, be free to refrain from
applying the provisions of this directive concerning valuation of
contributions in kind (Article 8), increases in capital through money
brought in for shares issued previously and to be paid up in full
(Article 21, paragraphs 1 and 2), and the right to preferential
subscription (Article 25).

Article 8

Where the laws of the Member States do not provide for judicial or
administrative preventive control over the legality of mergers, or
where such control does not extend to all acts in the law required
for merger, the minutes of the General Meetings which decide on the
merger and, where appropriate, the merger contract subsequent to
such General Meetings shall be authenticated by notarial act. In
such case, the notary must check and certify the existence and legality
of the acts in the law and formalities required of the company in
respect of which he is acting and of the draft terms of merger within
the meaning of Article 3.

[3] J.O. 1970, C48.

Article 9

Merger shall take effect on one of the following dates:

 (a) Where the laws of Member States provide for administrative or judicial preventive control over the legality of mergers, on the date on which the control formalities are completed as regards the company taken over;

 (b) Where the laws of Member States do not provide for the control referred to in (a), on the date of the notarial act recording the resolution of the General Meeting of either the company taken over or the acquiring company, whichever was last to approve the merger;

 (c) Where the laws of Member States provide for the merger contract to be concluded after the merger has been approved, by the companies involved, on the date on which the contract is concluded.

Article 10

1. Particulars of the merger shall be disclosed in accordance with the procedure laid down in Directive No. 68/151/EEC of 9 March, 1968 in respect of each of the merging companies.

2. The acquiring company may itself carry out the disclosure formalities in respect of the company taken over.

Article 11

1. The laws of the Member States shall fix the rules governing the rights of creditors other than debenture-holders to obtain security for their debts.

Such laws may make it possible for the company to be discharged of this obligation if the creditors already have adequate security or if the solvency of the acquiring company is such that they incur no damage. They may also provide that the company be authorized to repay the debts ahead of schedule instead of providing security.

2. The protection provided for in this Article must be granted at least to all creditors of the company acquired whose claims arose prior to the publication of the merger plan. It may, however, be dispensed with for creditors whose claims are secured on property which is subject to administrative control laid down by a special law.

Article 12

Without prejudice to the rules relating to collective exercise of their rights, Article 11 shall apply to the debenture holders of the company taken over, except where the merger has been approved by a General Meeting of debenture holders or, where the laws of Member States do not provide for such Meeting or do not confer the power upon it to approve mergers, by the debenture holders individually.

Article 13

Without prejudice to Article 12, shareholders with special rights and holders of (rights or) securities other than shares must in the acquiring company have rights equivalent to those they possessed in the company taken over, unless the variation of their rights has been approved by a General Meeting of the holders or, in Member States in which no provision exists for such meeting or in which power is not conferred on such General Meeting to approve changes in their rights, by the holders of those (rights or) securities individually.

Article 14

[*Article 14 is deleted in the amended version.*]

Article 15

1. Merger shall have the following consequences automatically:
   (a) The transfer, both as between the company taken over and the acquiring company and as regards third parties, of the whole of the assets and liabilities of the company taken over to the acquiring company;
   (b) The shareholders of the company taken over shall become shareholders of the acquiring company;
   (c) The company taken over shall cease to exist.

2. However, no shares in the acquiring company shall be issued in exchange for shares held by it in the company taken over, and such shares shall be cancelled.

3. This Article is without prejudice to the laws of those Member States which, in the event of merger, require certain formalities to be complied with in order for the transfer of certain assets of the company taken over to be effective as against third parties of good faith.

4. The acquiring company may itself carry out those formalities.

Article 16

1. The laws of the Member States shall lay down rules governing the tortious liability of the members of the administrative and supervisory organs of the company acquired in order to ensure that compensation be made for any loss suffered by the shareholders of this company as a result of wilful or negligent acts committed by these organs in preparing and implementing the merger.

2. The arrangements for liability laid down in the preceding paragraph must comply with the following principles:
   (a) The liability is towards the individual shareholders of the company acquired. The laws of the Member States may,

however, lay down rules on arrangements by these shareholders to have themselves represented collectively for this
purpose and on the distribution of damages recovered.
(b) The members of each of the appropriate organs of the company acquired are jointly and severally liable. Members
may, however, free themselves of this liability if they prove
that no blame for any wilful or negligent act attaches to
them personally.

Article 17

1. The laws of the Member States shall lay down rules on the
tortious liability of the experts responsible for drawing up, on behalf
of the company acquired, the report referred to in Article 5, second
paragraph, with a view to ensuring that the shareholders of this
company receive compensation for loss suffered through wilful or
negligent acts committed by these experts in the performance of
their duties.

2. Article 16, paragraph 2 shall apply to the liability laid down
in the preceding paragraph.

Article 18

1. The laws of the Member States shall as regards nullity of
merger make provision only as follows:
(a) A merger may be annulled only by a court decision;
(b) Mergers already carried through may be annulled only if
there has been no judicial or administrative control or no
document drawn up by a notary, and if *restitutio in integrum*
is still possible and the rights acquired in good faith by third
parties are safeguarded;
(c) Nullity proceedings may not be commenced where six months
have expired following the date on which the merger is effective as against the person alleging the nullity;
(d) Where it is possible to remedy a defect liable to entail annulment of a merger, the appropriate court shall grant the
companies involved a time-limit within which to remedy
such defect;
(e) The question whether a decision of nullity pronounced by a
court of law may be relied on as against third parties shall
be governed by Article 3 of Directive No. 68/151/EEC of
March 9, 1968;
(f) Where the laws of the Member States entitle a third party to
challenge the decision, he may do so only within six months
of public notice of the decision of the court being given as
provided for in the Directive referred to under (e);

(g) A decision of nullity of merger shall not of itself affect the validity of commitments entered into by or with the acquiring company prior to publication of the decision and subsequent to the time referred to in Article 9;

(h) The companies which were parties to the merger shall be jointly and severally liable in respect of the acquiring company's commitments referred to in (g).

2. The laws of the Member States shall provide for appropriate penalties in cases where mergers are defective as to substance or form but where nullity cannot be ordered.

CHAPTER III: MERGER BY FORMATION OF A NEW COMPANY

Article 19

1. Articles 3 to 6 and Articles 8 to 17 shall apply to merger by formation of a new company. For this purpose the expressions " merging companies " and " company taken over " refer to the companies which will cease to exist and " acquiring company " refers to the new company.

2. Article 3 (2) (a) shall also apply to the new company.

3. The draft terms of merger, the instrument of constitution and, if they are contained in a separate instrument, the statutes of the new company, shall be approved in General Meeting by each of the companies which will cease to exist.

4. It shall be permissible for the Member States not to apply to the formation of a new company the rules relating to verification of capital subscribed in kind which are laid down in Article 8 of Directive No. .... of .... [4]

5. Merger shall take effect on the date on which the new company acquires legal personality.

6. The new company may itself carry out the disclosure formalities relating to the companies which cease to exist.

7. Nullity of the merger may be ordered only in case of nullity of the new company.

CHAPTER IV: TAKEOVER OF A COMPANY BY ANOTHER COMPANY WHICH IS ITS SOLE SHAREHOLDER

Article 20

1. The Member States shall make provision, in respect of that company which is governed by their national law, for the operation whereby a company is wound up, but without implementation of the liquidation procedure, and transfers the whole of its assets and

[4] J.O. 1970, C48.

liabilities to another company which is the holder of all its shares and other securities carrying the right to vote at General Meetings of the shareholders. This operation shall be regulated by the provisions of Chapter II, with the exception of Articles 3 (2) (b) and (c), 5 (1) and (2), 7, 15 (1) (b), 16 and 17.

2. The reports provided for in Article 5 (1) and (2) shall be drawn up only in respect of the acquiring company.

[Paragraph 3 is deleted in the amended version.]

4. Completion of the transaction shall entail the cancellation of the shares of the company acquired and of the other securities mentioned in paragraph 1.

CHAPTER V: OTHER OPERATIONS

Article 21

1. Chapters II and III of this directive, with the exception of Article 15 (1), shall apply where Member States make provision, in respect of companies governed by their national law, for operations other than those defined in Articles 2 and 20 of this directive and whereby a company transfers to one or more companies which already exist or are to be formed the whole or part of its assets and liabilities in consideration, in full or in part, of the issue to its shareholders of shares in the transferee companies.

2. For the purpose of the preceding paragraph, the company transferring its assets shall be considered to be the company acquired, the existing companies to which the assets are transferred to be the acquiring companies, and the companies to be formed and to which the assets are transferred to be new companies, in accordance with the following distinctions:

(a) Articles 3, 4, 5, 6, 8, 16, 17 and 18 shall apply to the acquiring and the acquired companies. Where the transaction is for the benefit of one or more new companies, the memorandum of association and—if they are the subject of a separate document—the articles of association of these companies shall be appended to the merger plan and approved by the general meetings of the companies acquired.

Article 5 need not be applied, however, if the shareholders of the company acquired have the right to obtain consideration covering the value of their shares and if, in case of dispute, this consideration is determined by the court;

(b) Articles 9 and 10 shall apply to the acquiring companies, the companies taken over and the new companies;

(c) Articles 11, 12 and 15 (3) and (4) shall apply where the operation entails automatically the transfer, both as between the companies concerned and as regards third parties, of all or part of the liabilities of the company taken over to the acquiring company or the new company;

(d) Article 13 shall apply where the company taken over has issued shares conferring special rights or securities other than shares and the rights attached to those securities are transferred to the acquiring companies or the new companies;

(e) Article 15 (3) and (4) shall apply where the operation entails automatically the transfer, both as between the companies concerned and as regards third parties, of all or part of the assets of the company taken over to the acquiring company or the new company.

CHAPTER VI: GENERAL AND FINAL PROVISIONS

Article 22

[Article 22 is deleted in the amended version.]

Article 23

The Member States shall within 18 months of the date of promulgation of this directive make all changes in their statutory and administrative provisions that are necessary to give effect to its provisions and shall immediately inform the Commission accordingly.

The Governments of the Member States shall communicate to the Commission, for its information, the texts of draft laws and regulations, together with a statement explaining their purpose, in the field covered by this directive. This communication must be made no later than six months before the date envisaged for the entry into force of the draft.

Article 24

The present directive is addressed to the Member States.

Text 4

Fourth Draft Directive submitted by the Commission to the Council on November 10, 1971, concerning the annual accounts of limited liability companies

The Council of the European Communities

Having regard to the Treaty establishing the European Economic Community, and in particular Article 54 (3) (g) thereof;

Having regard to the proposal from the Commission;

Having regard to the Opinion of the European Parliament;

Having regard to the Opinion of the Economic and Social Committee;

Whereas coordination of the national provisions concerning the presentation and contents of the annual accounts and report, methods of valuation and publication of those documents in respect of the Société anonyme, the Aktiengesellschaft, the Società per azioni and the naamloze vennootschap and in respect of the Société à responsabilité limitée, the Gesellschaft mit beschränkter Haftung, the Società a responsabilità limitata and the Vennootschap met beperkte aansprakelijkheid is of special importance for the protection of members and third parties;

Whereas simultaneous coordination is requisite in these fields for those forms of company because, on the one hand, the activities of those companies frequently extend beyond the frontiers of their national territory and, on the other hand, they offer no safeguards to third parties beyond the amount of their net assets; whereas moreover the necessity and urgency of such coordination have been recognised and confirmed in Article 2 (1) (f) of Directive No. 68/151/EEC of 9 March 1968;

Whereas it is also necessary to establish in the Community equivalent legal requirements as regards the extent of the financial information that should be made available to the public by companies that are in competition with one another and have the same legal form;

Whereas the annual accounts must reflect as accurately as possible the company's assets and liabilities, financial position and results; whereas to this end a lay-out comprising items that in principle are obligatory must be prescribed for drawing up the balance sheet and profit and loss account; and whereas on the other hand the different

86

methods permitted in the Member States for valuation of assets and liabilities must be coordinated to ensure that annual accounts present equivalent information;

Whereas the annual accounts of sociétés anonymes, Aktiengesellschaften, società per azioni and naamloze vennootschappen must be available in the fullest possible measure to shareholders and third parties; and whereas to that end it is essential that they be published in full in a national gazette;

Whereas so far as regards sociétés à responsabilité limitée, Gesellschaften mit beschränkter Haftung, società a responsabilità limitata and vennootschappen met beperkte aansprakelijkheid a distinction may be made between the information to be given to the members and that to be given to third parties; whereas the members thereof should be given the same information as the shareholders in a société anonyme, Aktiengesellschaft, società per azioni and naamloze vennootschap; whereas for the information of third parties the same particulars should as a general rule be disclosed as in the case of these latter types of company by reason of the fact that the liability of the members is limited, but some relief can nevertheless be allowed in the case of the smaller companies;

Has adopted this Directive :

Article 1

1. (*a*) The coordination measures prescribed by Articles 2 to 47 of this Directive apply to the laws, regulations and administrative provisions of the Member States relating to the following types of company :
— in Germany :
die Aktiengesellschaft, die Kommanditgesellschaft auf Aktien;
— in Belgium :
la société anonyme, de naamloze vennootschap; la société en commandite par actions, de commanditaire vennootschap op aandelen;
— in France :
la société anonyme, la société en commandite par actions;
— in Italy :
la società per azioni, la società in accomandita per azioni;
— in Luxembourg :
la société anonyme, la société en commandite par actions;
— in the Netherlands :
de naamloze vennootschap, de commanditaire vennootschap op aandelen.

(*b*) The coordination measures prescribed by Articles 48 to 50 of this Directive apply to the laws, regulations and administrative provisions of the Member States relating to the following types of company:

— in Germany:
die Gesellschaft mit beschränkter Haftung;

— in Belgium:
la société de personnes à responsabilité limitée, de personen-vennootschap met beperkte aansprakelijkheid;

— in France:
la société à responsabilité limitée;

— in Italy:
la società a responsabilità limitata;

— in Luxembourg:
la société à responsabilité limitée;

— in the Netherlands:
de besloten vennootschap met beperkte aansprakelijkheid.

2. Until the safeguards required of credit institutions and insurance companies are in due course coordinated, it shall be permissible for the Member States not to apply the provisions of this Directive to those undertakings.

SECTION 1: GENERAL REQUIREMENTS

Article 2

1. The annual accounts shall comprise the balance sheet, the profit and loss account and the notes on the accounts. These documents shall constitute a composite whole.

2. The annual accounts shall conform to the principles of regular and proper accounting.

3. They shall be drawn up clearly and, in the context of the provisions regarding the valuation of assets and liabilities and the lay-out of accounts, shall reflect as accurately as possible the company's assets, liabilities, financial position and results.

SECTION 2: LAY-OUT OF THE ANNUAL ACCOUNTS

Article 3

The lay-out of the balance sheet and of the profit and loss account, particularly as regards the form adopted for their presentation, may not be changed from one year to the next. Departures from this principle shall be permitted in exceptional cases. Where it is departed from, an indication thereof shall be given in the notes on the accounts together with an explanation of the reasons therefor.

Article 4

1. In the balance sheet, and also in the profit and loss account, the items referred to in Articles 8, 9, and 20 to 23 of this Directive shall be shown separately. A more detailed sub-division of the items that are preceded by Arabic numerals is authorized.

2. In exceptional cases a different lay-out shall, where the special nature of the undertaking so requires, be permitted for the balance sheet and profit and loss account items that are preceded by Arabic numerals. Any such different lay-out shall, however, present an equivalent view and be explained in the notes on the accounts.

3. The Member States may authorize a regrouping of the balance sheet and profit and loss account items that are preceded by Arabic numerals where they are of secondary interest only in relation to the object of Article 2 (3) of this Directive.

4. In respect of each balance sheet and profit and loss account item the figures for the preceding financial year shall be shown.

Article 5

The Member States may authorize adaptation of the lay-out of the balance sheet and profit and loss account in order to bring out the allocation of the results.

Article 6

Any set-off between assets and liabilities, or between expenditure and income, is prohibited.

SECTION 3: BALANCE SHEET LAY-OUT

Article 7

For the presentation of the balance sheet, the Member States shall introduce into their legislation the lay-outs prescribed by Articles 8 and 9 of this Directive, and shall leave the companies to choose between them.

Article 8

ASSETS

A. *Subscribed capital unpaid*
 — *of which there has been called.*
B. *Formation expenses in so far as the national law permits them to be recorded as assets.*
C. *Fixed assets:*
   I. Intangible assets:

1. Cost of research and development, in so far as the national law permits them to be recorded as assets,
2. Concessions, patents, licences, trade marks, and similar rights and values, if they were:
    (*a*) acquired for valuable consideration and are not to be shown under CI3,
    (*b*) created by the undertaking itself, in so far as the national law permits them to be recorded as assets,
3. Goodwill, to the extent that it was acquired for valuable consideration,
4. Payments on account.

II. Tangible assets:
1. Land and buildings,
2. Plant and machinery,
3. Other fixtures, tools and equipment,
4. Payments on account and tangible assets in process of construction.

III. Participating Interests and other financial assets:
1. Holdings in associated undertakings,
2. Claims on associated undertakings,
3. Participating interests,
4. Claims on undertakings with which the company is associated by virtue of a participating interest,
5. Securities ranking as fixed assets,
6. Other claims,
7. Own shares (indicating their nominal value or proportionate value) to the extent that the national law permits them to be included in the balance sheet.

D. *Current assets :*
I. Stocks:
1. Raw and auxiliary materials,
2. Goods in course of production and waste products,
3. Finished products and stock in hand,
4. Payments on account.

II. Debtors:
(Amounts becoming due and payable within one year shall be shown separately for each item)
1. Claims in respect of sales and services rendered,
2. Claims on associated undertakings,
3. Claims on undertakings in which the company has a participating interest,
4. Other claims.

III. Securities forming part of the current assets, and liquid assets:
1. Holdings in associated undertakings,
2. Bills of exchange,
3. Bank balances, postal cheque account balances, cheques and cash in hand,
4. Own shares (indicating their nominal value or proportionate value) to the extent that the national law permits them to be included in the balance sheet,
5. Other securities.

E. *Pre-payments.*
F. *Loss:*
  I. For the year,
  II. Brought forward.

LIABILITIES

A. *Subscribed capital :*
(The shares must be shown by classes, indicating their nominal value or proportionate value).

B. *Reserves :*
1. Legal reserve,
2. Share premium account,
3. Revaluation reserve,
4. Reserve for own shares,
5. Statutory reserves,
6. Optional reserves.

C. *Value adjustments to the extent that these do not appear among the assets or in the notes on the accounts :*
1. On formation expenses,
2. On intangible fixed assets,
3. On tangible fixed assets,
4. On participating interests and other financial assets,
5. On stocks,
6. On claims forming part of the current assets,
7. On securities forming part of the current assets and liquid assets.

(As regards the figures mentioned in items 2 to 7, a corresponding breakdown to that used on the assets side should be included).

D. *Provisions for contingencies and charges :*
1. Provisions for pensions and similar obligations,
2. Provisions for taxation including future taxation,
3. Other provisions.

E. *Creditors :*

(Amounts becoming due and payable within one year, amounts becoming due and payable after more than five years, and amounts covered by valuable security furnished by the company, must be shown separately for each item)

1. Debenture loans, showing convertible loans separately,
2. Debts to credit institutions,
3. Payments received on account of orders,
4. Debts in respect of purchases and services received,
5. Debts represented by bills of exchange,
6. Debts to associated undertakings,
7. Debts to undertakings with which the company is associated by virtue of a participating interest,
8. Other creditors.

F. *Accruals :*

G. *Profit :*
   I. For the year,
   II. Brought forward.

Article 9

A. *Subscribed capital unpaid*
   — of which there has been called.
B. *Formation expenses in so far as the national law permits them to be recorded as assets.*
C. *Fixed assets :*
   I. Intangible assets:
      1. Cost of research and development, in so far as the national law permits them to be recorded as assets.
      2. Concessions, patents, licences, trade marks, and similar rights and values, if they were:
         (*a*) acquired for valuable consideration and are not to be shown under CI3,
         (*b*) created by the undertaking itself, in so far as the national law permits them to be recorded as assets,
      3. Goodwill, to the extent that it was acquired for valuable consideration,
      4. Payments on account.
   II. Tangible assets:
      1. Land and buildings,
      2. Plant and machinery,
      3. Other fixtures, tools and equipment,
      4. Payments on account and tangible assets in process of construction.

III. Participating interests and other financial assets:
    1. Holdings in associated undertakings,
    2. Claims on associated undertakings,
    3. Participating interests,
    4. Claims on undertakings with which the company is associated by virtue of a participating interest,
    5. Securities ranking as fixed assets,
    6. Other claims,
    7. Own shares (indicating their nominal value or proportionate value) to the extent that the national law permits them to be included in the balance sheet.

D. *Current assets :*
  I. Stocks:
    1. Raw and auxiliary materials,
    2. Goods in course of production and waste products,
    3. Finished products and stock in hand,
    4. Payments on account.
  II. Debtors:
  (Amounts becoming due and payable within one year must be shown separately in each case)
    1. Claims in respect of sales and services rendered,
    2. Claims on associated undertakings,
    3. Claims on undertakings with which the company is associated by virtue of a participating interest,
    4. Other claims.
  III. Securities forming part of the current assets, and liquid assets:
    1. Holdings in associated undertakings,
    2. Bills of exchange,
    3. Bank balances, postal cheque account balances, cheques and cash in hand,
    4. Own shares (indicating their nominal value or proportionate value) to the extent that the national law permits them to be included in the balance sheet,
    5. Other securities.

E. *Pre-payments.*

F. *Debts becoming due and payable within one year :*
(Amounts covered by valuable security furnished by the company must be shown separately for each item)
1. Debenture loans, showing convertible loans separately,
2. Debts to credit institutions,
3. Payments received on account of orders,
4. Debts in respect of purchases and services received,
5. Debts represented by bills of exchange,

    6. Debts to associated undertakings,

    7. Debts to undertakings with which the company is associated by virtue of a participating interest,

    8. Other debts.

G. *Current assets in excess of the debts becoming due and payable within one year.*

H. *Total amount of asset items after deduction of the debts becoming due and payable within one year.*

I. *Creditors for amounts becoming due and payable after more than one year :*

(Amounts becoming due and payable after more than five years and amounts covered by valuable security furnished by the company must be shown separately for each item)

    1. Debenture loans, showing convertible loans separately,

    2. Debts to credit institutions,

    3. Payments received on account of orders,

    4. Debts in respect of purchases and services received,

    5. Debts represented by bills of exchange,

    6. Debts to associated undertakings,

    7. Debts to undertakings with which the company is associated by virtue of a participating interest,

    8. Other creditors.

J. *Value adjustments to the extent that these do not appear in the notes on the accounts :*

    1. On formation expenses,

    2. On intangible fixed assets,

    3. On tangible fixed assets,

    4. On participating interests and other financial assets,

    5. On stocks,

    6. On claims in respect of current assets,

    7. On securities forming part of the current assets and liquid assets.

(As regards the figures mentioned in items 2 to 7, a corresponding breakdown to that used under C and D should be included)

K. *Provisions for contingencies and charges :*

    1. Provisions for pensions and similar obligations,

    2. Provisions for taxation, including future taxation,

    3. Other provisions.

L. *Accruals.*

M. *Subscribed capital.*

(The shares must be shown by classes, indicating their nominal value or proportionate value)

N. *Reserves :*
   1. Legal reserve,
   2. Share premium account,
   3. Revaluation reserve,
   4. Reserve for own shares,
   5. Statutory reserves,
   6. Optional reserves.
O. *Result for the year.*
P. *Results brought forward.*

Article 10

1. Where a component of the assets or liabilities pertains to several items in the balance sheet, its relationship to other items shall be indicated either under the item where it appears or in the notes on the accounts, unless such indication is not essential to the comprehension of the annual accounts.

2. Own shares and holdings in associated undertakings shall be shown only under the item respectively that relates thereto.

Article 11

All commitments by way of guarantee of any kind entered into for account of third parties shall, if there is no obligation to show them under liabilities, be clearly set out below the balance sheet or in the notes on the accounts, distinguishing between the various types of guarantee which the national law recognizes, and specifying what valuable security, if any, has been provided. Commitments of this kind existing in respect of associated undertakings shall be shown separately.

SECTION 4: SPECIAL PROVISIONS RELATING TO CERTAIN ITEMS IN THE BALANCE SHEET

Article 12

1. Whether particular assets are to be classified as fixed assets or current assets shall depend upon the purpose for which they are intended.

2. Fixed assets shall comprise those elements which are intended to be used on a continuing basis to enable the undertaking to operate.

3. (*a*) Movements in the various items of fixed assets shall be shown in the balance sheet or in the notes on the accounts. To this end there shall be shown, starting with the initial purchase price or production cost, separately for each of the items of fixed assets, on the one hand the additions, disposals, transfers and upward corrections during the year, and on the other hand the cumulative value adjustments as at the date of the balance sheet. If the value adjust-

ments are indicated in the balance sheet they may be shown under either assets or liabilities.

(*b*) Where at the time the first annual accounts are drawn up in accordance with this Directive, the purchase price or production cost of an element of fixed assets cannot be determined without untoward expense or delay, the residual value at the beginning of the year may be treated as the purchase price or production cost. Any use made of this provision must be mentioned in the notes on the accounts.

(*c*) In the case of application of Articles 30 and 31 of this Directive, the presentation of the movements in the various items of fixed assets referred to under (*a*) shall be supplemented by separate mention, for each of the various items, of the cumulative amounts at the date of the balance sheet, on the one hand of the differences referred to in Article 30 (2) and in Article 31 (2), and on the other hand of the additional value adjustments.

4. (*a*) Movements in the various items of current assets shall be presented in the balance sheet or the notes on the accounts. To this end there shall be shown, separately for each of the items of current assets, on the one hand the purchase price or production cost of the elements shown in the balance sheet, and on the other hand the value adjustments. If the value adjustments are indicated in the balance sheet they may be shown under either assets or liabilities.

(*b*) The provisions of paragraph 3 (*c*) shall apply to the presentation of the item relating to stocks.

5. The provisions of paragraph 3 (*a*) and (*b*) shall apply to the presentation of the item " formation expenses ".

Article 13

Under the item " land and buildings " shall be shown land not built on as well as the land built on and the buildings thereon, together with fixtures and fittings.

Where national law authorizes the inclusion under assets of rights in real estate which are of like nature to rights of ownership, they shall be included under the item " land and buildings ".

Article 14

The term " participating interests " is used in this Directive to mean rights in the capital of other undertakings, whether or not represented by certificates which by creating a durable link with them, are intended to contribute to the activities of the company. A holding of 10% of the subscribed capital of another undertaking shall be presumed to constitute a participating interest.

Article 15

Under " Pre-payments " on the assets side shall be shown expenditure incurred during the year but relating to a subsequent year, together with the earnings relating to the year to the extent that they will not be received until after the close of the year. The latter, however, may also be shown under debtors.

Article 16

The value adjustments are adjustment items relating to elements of assets and are intended to take account of depreciation established in respect of those elements at the date of the balance sheet, whether that depreciation is definitive or not.

Article 17

The provisions for contingencies and charges are intended to cover either the certain cost of major maintenance work or of major repairs which will be incurred in the course of subsequent years, or losses or charges the nature of which is clearly defined but which at the date of the balance sheet are either likely to be incurred, or are certain to be incurred but are indeterminate as to amount or as to the date on which they will arise.

The provisions for contingencies and charges shall not be used to adjust the value of elements of assets.

Article 18

Under " Accruals " on the liabilities side shall be shown income received before the date of the balance sheet but attributable to a subsequent year, together with charges which, though relating to the year in question, will only be paid in the course of a subsequent year. The latter, however, may also be shown under creditors.

SECTION 5: LAY-OUT OF THE PROFIT AND LOSS ACCOUNT

Article 19

For the presentation of the profit and loss account, the Member States shall adopt into their laws the lay-outs appearing in Articles 20 to 23 of this Directive, and shall leave the companies to choose between them.

Article 20

    I. Operating result (excluding any earnings and changes shown under II):

       1. Net turnover,

    2. Changes in stocks of finished and semi-finished products,

    3. Work effected by the undertaking for its own account and shown under assets,

    4. Other operating receipts,

    5. Cost of raw and auxiliary materials,

    6. Staff costs,

    7. (*a*) Value adjustments in respect of formation expenses and of tangible and intangible fixed assets,

        (*b*) Value adjustments in respect of elements of current assets,

    8. Other operating expenses,

    9. Operating result.

  II. Financial result:

    10. Earnings from participating interests, showing separately those derived from associated undertakings,

    11. Earnings from other securities and from claims forming part of the fixed assets, showing separately those derived from associated undertakings,

    12. Other interest and similar earnings, showing separately those derived from associated undertakings,

    13. Value adjustments in respect of participating interests and other financial assets and of securities forming part of the current assets,

    14. Interest and similar charges, showing separately those concerning associated undertakings,

    15. Financial result.

  III. Exceptional result:

    16. Exceptional earnings,

    17. Exceptional charges,

    18. Exceptional result,

    19. Sub-total.

  IV. Taxes:

    20. Taxes on the result:

        — actual,

        — future,

    21. Other taxes not shown under I, II or III above.

  V. Result for the year.

Article 21

A. *Charges*

  I. Operating expenses (excluding any shown under II):

    1. Reduction in the stock of finished and semi-finished products,

   2. Cost of raw and auxiliary materials,
   3. Staff costs,
   4. (*a*) Value adjustments in respect of formation expenses
      and of tangible and intangible fixed assets,
      (*b*) Value adjustments in respect of elements of current
      assets,
   5. Other operating expenses.
II. Financial charges:
   1. Value adjustments in respect of participating interests and
      other financial assets and of securities forming part of
      the current assets,
   2. Interest and similar charges, showing separately those
      concerning associated undertakings.
III. Exceptional charges.
IV. Taxes:
   1. Taxes on the result:
      — actual,
      — future,
   2. Other taxes not shown under I, II and III above.
V. Result for the year.

B. *Receipts*
   I. Operating receipts (excluding any shown under II):
      1. Net turnover,
      2. Increase in stocks of finished and semi-finished products,
      3. Work effected by the undertaking for its own account and
         shown under assets,
      4. Other operating receipts.
   II. Financial earnings:
      1. Earnings from participating interests, showing separately
         those derived from associated undertakings,
      2. Earnings from other securities and from claims forming
         part of the fixed assets, showing separately those derived
         from associated undertakings,
      3. Other interest and similar earnings, showing separately
         those derived from associated undertakings.
   III. Exceptional earnings.
   IV. Result for the year.

Article 22
   I. Operating result (excluding any earnings and charges shown
      under II):
      1. Net turnover,

    2. Production costs of output supplied and making-up the turnover (including value adjustments),

    3. Gross result achieved from turnover,

    4. Distribution expenses (including value adjustments),

    5. Administrative expenses (including value adjustments),

    6. Other operating receipts,

    7. Operating result.

  II. Financial result:

    8. Earnings from participating interests, showing separately those derived from associated undertakings,

    9. Earnings from other securities and from claims forming part of the fixed assets, showing separately those derived from associated undertakings,

    10. Other interest and similar earnings, showing separately those derived from associated undertakings,

    11. Value adjustments in respect of participating interests and other financial fixed assets and of securities forming part of the current assets,

    12. Interest and similar charges, showing separately those concerning associated undertakings,

    13. Financial result.

  III. Exceptional result:

    14. Exceptional earnings,

    15. Exceptional charges,

    16. Exceptional result,

    17. Sub-total.

  IV. Taxes:

    18. Taxes on the result:

      — actual,

      — future,

    19. Other taxes not shown under I, II or III above.

  V. Result for the year.

Article 23

A. *Charges*

  I. Operating expenses (excluding any shown under II):

    1. Production costs of output supplied and making-up the turnover (including value adjustments),

    2. Distribution expenses (including value adjustments),

    3. Administrative expenses (including value adjustments).

  II. Financial charges:

    1. Value adjustments in respect of participating interests and

other financial fixed assets and of securities forming part of the current assets,

2. Interest and similar charges, showing separately those concerning associated undertakings.

III. Exceptional charges.

IV. Taxes:
1. Taxes on the result:
   — actual,
   — future,
2. Other taxes not shown under I, II or III above.

V. Result for the year.

B. *Receipts*

I. Operating receipts (excluding any shown under II):
1. Net turnover,
2. Other operating receipts.

II. Financial earnings:
1. Earnings from participating interests, showing separately those derived from associated undertakings,
2. Earnings from other securities and from claims forming part of the fixed assets, showing separately those derived from associated undertakings,
3. Other interest and similar earnings, showing separately those derived from associated undertakings.

III. Exceptional earnings.

IV. Result for the year.

Article 24

The Member States may authorize companies for which at the date of the balance sheet:

— the balance sheet total reduced by the value adjustments, if these are entered under liabilities, does not exceed one million units of account,

— the net turnover does not exceed two million units of account,

— the average number of employees during the year did not exceed one hundred,

to adopt lay-outs different from those appearing in Articles 20 to 23 of this Directive within the following limits:

(a) in Article 20, under I, items 1 to 5 inclusive may be grouped together under one item called Gross result;

(b) in Article 21, items AI, 1 and 2, and BI, 1 to 4 inclusive may be grouped together under one item called Gross earnings or Gross charges as the case may be;

(c) in Article 22, under I items, 1, 2, 3 and 6 may be grouped together under one item called Gross result;

(d) in article 23, items AI, 1 and BI, 1 and 2, may be grouped together under one item called Gross earnings or Gross charges as the case may be.

If subsequently any one of the numerical limits set out above is exceeded, the exemptions provided for in this provision may again be applied only if all the conditions specified above are satisfied for two consecutive years.

The amounts in units of account specified in this provision may vary by not more than 10 per cent. up or down for purposes of conversion into national currencies.

SECTION 6: SPECIAL PROVISIONS RELATING TO CERTAIN ITEMS IN THE PROFIT AND LOSS ACCOUNT

Article 25

The net amount of turnover includes receipts from sales of products, goods and services falling within the usual operations of the company, after allowing for any price-reduction in respect of those sales, and for value-added tax and other taxes directly tied to the turnover.

Article 26

1. Under the items Exceptional earnings and Exceptional charges, shall be shown earnings and charges that are attributable to another year, together with any earnings and charges that do not arise out of the usual operations of the undertaking.

2. Unless such earnings and charges are of no importance in the assessment of the results, explanations of their amount and nature shall be given in the notes on the accounts.

Article 27

Under the item Taxes on the Result shall be shown the actual amount of taxes payable for the year, and separately, the amount of the future liability to tax.

SECTION 7: VALUATION RULES

Article 28

1. The Member States shall ensure that the valuation of the items shown in the annual accounts is made in accordance with the following general principles:

(a) The methods of valuation may not be changed from one year to another.

(*b*) Only the profits earned at the date of the balance sheet may be included in it; account shall nevertheless be taken of all contingencies foreseeable at that date.

(*c*) Account shall be taken of any deficiencies that do not become apparent until after the date of the balance sheet, but before it is drawn up, if they arose in the course of the year to which the annual accounts relate.

(*d*) Account shall be taken of any depreciation, whether the year closes with a loss or with a profit.

(*e*) The components of the asset and liability items shall be valued separately.

(*f*) The balance sheet at the close of one year shall correspond to the opening balance sheet for the following year.

2. Departures from these general principles shall be permitted in exceptional cases. Where they are departed from, an indication thereof shall be given in the notes on the accounts together with an explanation of the reasons and an assessment of the effect on the assets, liabilities, financial position and result.

Article 29

The valuation of the items shown in the annual accounts shall be made in accordance with Articles 32 to 39 of this Directive, based on purchase price or production cost.

Article 30

1. Notwithstanding the provisions of Article 29 of this Directive, the Member States may authorize valuation on the basis of replacement value for tangible fixed assets with a limited useful life, and for stocks.

They shall make provision that in cases where this method is employed an indication thereof shall be given in the notes on the accounts, specifying the items concerned, and that the use of that method is justified as regards the value shown.

2. Where paragraph 1 is applied the amount of the difference in valuation on the basis of replacement value and valuation in accordance with the general rule contained in Article 29 shall be shown under liabilities in the item Revaluation Reserve. This item shall be sub-divided into:

— Reserve for tangible fixed assets,
— Reserve for stocks.

3. The Revaluation reserve may be capitalized at any time.

4. The Revaluation reserve shall be reduced to the extent that the amounts transferred thereto are no longer required for the purpose

of replacement of the asset items concerned. The amounts in question shall be added to the result for the year. They shall be shown separately in the profit and loss account.

5. Save as provided in paragraphs 3 and 4 the Revaluation reserve shall not be reduced.

6. The value adjustments shall be calculated each year on the basis of the replacement value adopted for the year in question.

Article 31

1. Notwithstanding Article 29 of this Directive the Member States may authorize revaluation of the tangible fixed assets and of the participating interests and other financial assets.

They shall make provision that in cases where revaluation takes place an indication thereof shall be given in the notes on the accounts, specifying the items concerned and that the making of the revaluation is justified as regards the value shown.

2. In the event of paragraph 1 being applied, the amount of the difference in valuation made in accordance with paragraph 1 above and the valuation made in accordance with the general rule contained in Article 29 shall be shown under liabilities in the Revaluation Reserve. This item shall be sub-divided into:
— Reserve for tangible fixed assets,
— Reserve for participating interests and other financial assets.

3. The Revaluation reserve may be capitalized at any time.

4. The Revaluation reserve shall be reduced to the extent that the increases in value concerned have been actually realised. The amounts in question shall be added to the result for the year. They shall be shown separately in the profit and loss account.

5. Save as provided in paragraphs 3 and 4 the Revaluation reserve shall not be reduced.

Article 32

1. (*a*) Where the national law authorizes the inclusion of formation expenses under assets, they shall be written off over a maximum period of five years.

(*b*) In so far as the formation expenses have not been completely written off, no distribution of profits shall take place unless the amount of the optional reserves is at least equal to the amount of the expenses not written off.

2. The amounts entered under this item shall be explained in the notes on the accounts.

Article 33

1. (*a*) The items of fixed assets shall, without prejudice to the

provisions of (*b*) and (*c*) below, be valued at purchase price or production cost.

(*b*) The purchase price or production cost of the items of fixed assets which have a limited useful life shall be reduced by value adjustments calculated according to a method that satisfies the requirements of good management.

(*c*) (aa) Value adjustments may be made in respect of the items of fixed assets, whether or not their useful life is limited, so that they are valued at the lowest figure attributable to them at the date of the balance sheet.

(bb) Value adjustments shall be made if the depreciation in value is expected to be permanent.

(cc) The value adjustments referred to in (aa) and (bb) shall be shown separately in the profit and loss account or in the notes on the accounts.

(dd) Valuation at the lowest value provided for in (aa) and (bb) shall be discontinued if the reasons for which the value adjustments were made have ceased to apply.

(*d*) If the items of fixed assets are the subject of exceptional value adjustments under fiscal law, the amount of the adjustments shall be indicated in the notes on the accounts.

2. The purchase price shall be calculated by adding to the price paid the expenses incidental thereto.

3. (*a*) The production cost shall be calculated by adding to the purchase price of the raw and auxiliary materials the manufacturing costs directly attributable to the product in question.

(*b*) A reasonable proportion of the manufacturing costs which are only indirectly attributable to the product in question may be added to the production cost to the extent that they relate to the period of manufacture.

(*c*) Costs of distribution shall not be included in production cost.

4. (*a*) The Member States may authorize the inclusion in production cost of interest on capital borrowed to finance the manufacture of fixed assets to the extent that it relates to the period of such manufacture. In that event they shall make provision for an indication to be given in the notes on the accounts that such interest is included under assets.

(*b*) They may also authorize the inclusion in the production cost of interest on own capital utilized for the purpose of financing the manufacture of fixed assets to the extent that it relates to the period of such manufacture. In that event they shall make provision for the amount thereof to be shown in the notes on the accounts.

Article 34

1. Article 32 of this Directive shall apply to the item "Cost of research and development".

2. Articles 32 (1) (*a*) shall apply to item CI3 under Articles 8 and 9.

Article 35

Tangible fixed assets, raw and auxiliary materials, which are constantly being replaced and of which the overall value is of secondary importance to the undertaking may be shown under assets at a fixed quantity and value, if the quantity, value and composition thereof do not vary appreciably.

Article 36

1. (*a*) The items of current assets shall be valued at purchase price or production cost, without prejudice to the provisions of (*b*) and (*c*) below.

(*b*) Value adjustments shall be made in respect of the items of current assets so that they are valued at the lowest figure attributable to them at the date of the balance sheet.

(*c*) The Member States may authorize exceptional value adjustments if, on the basis of a reasonable commercial assessment, these are necessary so that the valuation of these items does not have to be modified in the near future because of fluctuations in value. The amount of these value adjustments shall be shown separately in the profit and loss account or in the notes on the accounts.

(*d*) Valuation at the lowest value provided for in (*b*) and (*c*) shall be discontinued if the reasons for which the value adjustments were made have ceased to apply.

(*e*) If the items of current assets are the subject of exceptional value adjustments under fiscal law, the amount of the adjustments shall be indicated in the notes on the accounts.

2. The definitions of purchase price and of production cost contained in Article 33 (2) to (4) shall apply.

Article 37

The purchase price or production cost of stocks of goods in the same category may also be calculated either on the basis of weighted average prices or by the "First in—first out" (Fifo) method or "Last in—first out" (Lifo) method, or some similar method.

Article 38

1. Where the amount of any debt repayable is greater than the

amount received, the difference may be shown as an asset. It shall be shown separately in the balance sheet or in the notes on the accounts.

2. The amount of such difference shall be written off not later than the time when repayment of the debt is made.

Article 39

Provisions for contingencies and charges shall not exceed in amount the sums which a reasonable businessman would consider necessary.

The provisions shown in the balance sheet under the item " Other provisions " shall be specified in the notes on the accounts if they are at all substantial.

SECTION 8: CONTENTS OF THE NOTES ON THE ACCOUNTS

Article 40

The notes on the accounts shall contain commentary on the balance sheet and profit and loss account in such manner as to give as true and fair a view as possible of the company's assets, liabilities, financial position and results.

Article 41

In addition to the information required under other provisions of this Directive, the notes on the accounts shall set out information in respect of the following matters in any event:

1. The valuation methods applied to the various items in the annual accounts, and the methods employed in calculating the value adjustments;

2. The name and head office address of each of the undertakings in which the company holds at least 10% of the capital, showing the proportion of the capital held and the amount of the subscribed capital, the amount of the reserves and the results for the latest business year of the undertaking concerned;

3. The way in which the authorized capital has been employed, if any such capital has been created;

4. Whether there are any entitlements carrying the right to a share of profits, and whether there are any convertible debentures or similar securities or rights, specifying the number thereof and what rights they confer;

5. The overall amount of the financial commitments that are not shown in the balance sheet, in so far as this information is of assistance in assessing the financial position. Commitments existing with regard to associated undertakings shall be shown separately;

6. The whole of the personnel costs relating to the accounting period unless they are shown separately in the profit and loss account;

7. The taxes included in the operating result, the financial result or exceptional result;

8. The amount of the changes in the result for the year due to the application of fiscal laws;

9. The amount of the emoluments granted during the year to the members of the administrative, managerial and supervisory bodies by reason of their responsibilities, showing the total for each category;

10. The amount of advances and credits granted to the members of administrative, managerial and supervisory bodies, and commitments entered into on their account by way of guarantees of any kind, showing the total for each category.

Article 42

The Member States may allow the particulars prescribed by Article 41 (2):

    (*a*) to take the form of a statement deposited in accordance with Article 3, paragraphs 1 and 2 of Directive 68/151/EEC of 9 March 1968. This shall be mentioned in the notes on the accounts.

    (*b*) to be omitted when their nature is such that, in the view of a reasonable business man, they would be seriously prejudicial to any of the undertakings to which this provision relates. The omission of the particulars shall be mentioned in the notes on the accounts.

SECTION 9: CONTENTS OF THE ANNUAL REPORT

Article 43

1. The annual report shall contain a detailed review of the development of the company's business and of its position.

2. The report shall also give particulars of:

    (*a*) any important events that have occurred since the close of the business year;

    (*b*) the company's likely future development.

SECTION 10: PUBLICATION

Article 44

1. The annual accounts duly approved and the annual report, together with the report submitted by the person responsible for auditing the accounts, shall be deposited without delay in accordance with Article 3 paras. (1) and (2) of Directive 68/151/EEC of 9 March 1968.

2. In derogation from Article 3 para. (4) of that Directive, the annual accounts shall be published in full in a national gazette designated by the Member State. The report submitted by the person responsible for auditing the accounts shall be published therein at the same time.

3. The annual report shall be published in accordance with the requirements of Article 3 para. (4) of the Directive referred to in paragraph 1.

Article 45

On any other occasion when publication is made in full, the annual accounts and report shall be reproduced in the form and text on the basis of which the person responsible for auditing the accounts drew up his report. They shall be accompanied by the full text of the certificate. If the person responsible for auditing the accounts made any qualification or refused to certify the accounts, the fact shall be stated and the reasons given.

Article 46

If the annual accounts are not published in full, it shall be pointed out that the version published is abridged, and reference shall be made to the national gazette in which they were published. The certificate of the person responsible for auditing the accounts shall not accompany this publication, but it shall be stated whether the certificate was made with or without qualification, or was refused.

Article 47

There shall be published along with the annual accounts, and in like manner:
— the proposed allocation of the results,
— the allocation of the results
in cases where these items do not appear in the annual accounts.

SECTION 11: SPECIAL PROVISIONS RELATING
TO THE SOCIÉTÉ À RESPONSABILITÉ LIMITÉE,
THE GESELLSCHAFT MIT BESCHRÄNKTER HAFTUNG,
THE SOCIETÀ A RESPONSABILITÀ LIMITATA AND THE
VENNOOTSCHAP MET BEPERKTE AANSRAKELIJKHEID

Article 48

The companies referred to in Article 1 (1) (*b*) shall draw up their annual accounts and report for the information of their members in accordance with the requirements of Articles 2 to 23 and 25 to 43 of this Directive, subject to the following qualifications:

(a) In Article 8 a separate item, " Claims on members ", shall be included under assets at CIII and DII and a further separate item, " Debts to members "; under liabilities at E;

(b) In Article 9 a separate item, " Claims on members ", shall be included at CIII and DII and a further separate item, " Debts to members "; at F and I.

Article 49

1. The companies referred to in Article 1 (1) (b) shall cause their annual accounts and report to be audited by one or more persons authorized by the law of the country to audit accounts.

2. The Member States may exempt from the obligation imposed under paragraph 1 companies of which at the date of their balance sheet:

— the balance sheet total reduced by the value adjustments, if these are entered under liabilities, does not exceed one hundred thousand units of account,

— the net turnover as defined in Article 25 of this Directive does not exceed two hundred thousand units of account,

— the average number of employees during the year did not exceed twenty.

In that case they shall introduce appropriate sanctions into their law for cases in which the annual accounts and reports of such companies are not drawn up in accordance with the requirements of this Directive.

If subsequently any one of the numerical limits set out above is exceeded, the exemption provided for in this provision may again be applied only if all the conditions specified above are satisfied for two consecutive years.

The amounts in units of account specified in this provision may vary by not more than 10 per cent. up or down for purposes of conversion into national currencies.

Article 50

1. (a) The companies referred to in Article 1 (1) (b) shall publish their annual accounts and report, and the report drawn up by the person responsible for auditing the accounts, in accordance with Article 44 of this Directive.

(b) Articles 45 to 47 of this Directive shall equally apply to the companies referred to in paragraph 1 (a).

2. Notwithstanding paragraph 1 (a) the Member States may permit

(a) companies other than those referred to in Article 49 (2),

in the case of which at the date of their balance sheet:

— the balance sheet total reduced by the value adjust-

ments, if these are entered under liabilities, does not exceed one million units of account;
— the net turnover as defined in Article 25 of this Directive does not exceed two million units of account;
— the average number of employees during the year did not exceed one hundred,

to publish their profit and loss account in the abridged form provided for in Article 24 of this Directive. If subsequently any one of the numerical limits set out above is exceeded, the exemption provided for in this provision may again be applied only if all the conditions specified above are satisfied for two consecutive years.

The amounts in units of account specified in this provision may vary by not more than 10 per cent. up or down for purposes of conversion into national currencies.

(b) the companies referred to in Article 49 (2) of this Directive to publish merely an abridged balance sheet showing only the items preceded by letters and Roman numerals set out in Articles 8 and 9 with separate particulars of the claims on and debts to members and notes on the accounts but not necessarily including the explanations required under Article 41 (4) to (10);

(c) the publication requirements laid down for the companies referred to in (a) and (b) to be effected in manner prescribed by Article 3 of Directive 68/151/EEC of 9 March 1968.

SECTION 12: FINAL PROVISIONS

Article 51

1. (a) The Member States shall, within eighteen months of notification of this Directive, make all the necessary amendments to their laws, regulations and administrative provisions so as to comply with the provisions of this Directive, and shall inform the Commission thereof immediately. They shall bring the amendment into force within thirty months of notification of this Directive.

(b) The Governments of the Member States shall communicate to the Commission for information the draft texts of the laws and regulations together with the statements of grounds, relating to the matters covered by this Directive. These shall be communicated at least six months before the date envisaged for final adoption of the texts.

2. The obligation to show in the annual accounts the items

prescribed by Articles 8, 9 and 20 to 23 which relate to associated undertakings, and the obligation to provide information concerning these undertakings in accordance with Articles 10 (2), 11 or 41 (5) of this Directive shall enter into force simultaneously with a Council Directive relating to consolidated accounts.

Article 52

This Directive is addressed to the Member States.

Text 5

Fifth Draft Directive, submitted by the Commission to the Council on October 9, 1972, concerning the structure of sociétés anonymes and the powers and obligations of their organs

The Council of the European Communities,

Having regard to the Treaty establishing the European Economic Community, and in particular Article 54 (3) (g) thereof;

Having regard to the proposal from the Commission;

Having regard to the Opinion of the European Parliament;

Having regard to the Opinion of the Economic and Social Committee;

Whereas the co-ordination provided for in Article 54 (3) (g) was begun by Directive No. 68/151/EEC of 9 March 1968 [1] governing the disclosure, validity of obligations entered into by the representative organs and the nullity of *sociétés anonymes, sociétés en commandite par actions* and *sociétés à responsabilite limitée* [2];

Whereas the co-ordination of national laws relating to such limited liability companies was continued by Directive No. . . . of . . . [3] on the annual accounts;

Whereas further the co-ordination of laws relating to *sociétés anonymes* [2] must be given priority because these companies much more than others carry on cross-frontier activities;

Whereas the laws of the Member States relating to the formation and capital of *sociétés anonymes* were co-ordinated by Directive No. . . . of . . . [4] and those relating to mergers of such companies were co-ordinated by Directive No. . . . of . . . [5];

Whereas so that the protection afforded to the interests of members and others is made equivalent, the laws of the Member States relating to the structure of *sociétés anonymes* and to the powers and obligations of their organs must be co-ordinated;

Whereas in the fields aforesaid equivalent legal conditions must be created in the Community for *sociétés anonymes*;

[1] The First Directive, see p. 51, *ante*.
[2] Where the French terms are used in the recitals of this Proposal they are to be taken to include a reference to the corresponding types of company existing in each of the six Member States.
[3] The Fourth Draft Directive, see p. 86, *ante*.
[4] The Second Draft Directive, see p. 62, *ante*.
[5] The Third Draft Directive, see p. 74, *ante*.

Whereas so far as concerns the organization of the administration of this type of company two different sets of arrangements at present obtain in the Community; whereas one of these provides for one administrative organ only while the other provides for two, namely a management organ responsible for managing the business of the company and an organ responsible for controlling the management body; whereas in practice, even under the arrangement which provides for only one administrative organ, a *de facto* distinction is made between active members who manage the business of the company and passive members who confine themselves to supervision; whereas in order to delimit clearly the responsibilities of the persons who are charged respectively with one or other of these duties it is preferable that there be separate organs whose responsibility it is to carry them out; whereas further the two-tier system will facilitate the formation of *sociétés anonymes* by members or groups of members from different Member States and, thereby, interpenetration of undertakings within the Community; whereas to this end the introduction of the two-tier system on an optional basis would not be sufficient and whereas that structure must be made compulsory for all *sociétés anonymes*;

Whereas the laws of certain Member States provide for worker participation within the supervisory body but no such provision exists in other Member States; whereas differences in the laws relating to this field must be eliminated not least because they constitute a barrier to the application of the Community rules which are necessary to facilitate transnational operations involving reconstruction and interpenetration of undertakings, in particular in so far as concerns the giving of effect to Article 220 of the Treaty which provides, *inter alia*, for international merger and transfer of the seat; whereas in order to make provision for worker participation in appointing and dismissing members of the supervisory organ the Directive does not make rules uniform for all the Member States but leaves them to choose between a number of equivalent arrangements;

Whereas the members of the management and supervisory organs must be made subject to special rules relating to civil liability which provide for joint and several liability, reverse the burden of proof in respect of liability for wrongful acts and ensure that the bringing of proceedings on behalf of the company for the purpose of making those persons liable is not improperly prevented;

Whereas as regards the preparation and holding of general meetings, the shareholders must be protected by equivalent provisions relating to the form, content and period of notice, the right to attend and to be represented at meetings, written or oral information, exercise of the right to vote, the majorities required for the passing of resolutions and, finally, the right to bring proceedings in respect of void or voidable resolutions;

Whereas certain rights of shareholders should be capable of being exercised by a minority of them;

Whereas in the interests of members and others the audit of the annual accounts should be carried out by experts whose independence is guaranteed by special provisions;

Has adopted this Directive:

SCOPE OF APPLICATION

Article 1

1. The co-ordination measures prescribed by this Directive apply to the laws, regulations and administrative provisions of the Member States relating to the following types of company:
— in Germany: *die Aktiengesellschaft*
— in Belgium: *de naamloze vennootschap, la société anonyme*
— in France: *la société anonyme*
— in Italy: *la società per azioni*
— in Luxembourg: *la société anonyme*
— in the Netherlands: *de naamloze vennootschap.*

2. It shall be permissible for the Member States not to apply the provisions of this Directive to co-operatives whose legal form is that of one of the types of company indicated in the foregoing paragraph.

CHAPTER I: STRUCTURE OF THE COMPANY

Article 2

1. The Member States shall make provision so that the structure of the company takes the form provided for in Chapters II and III of this Directive, the company thereby having not less than three separate organs:

(*a*) the management organ responsible for managing and representing the company;

(*b*) the supervisory organ responsible for controlling the management organ;

(*c*) the general meeting of shareholders.

2. They shall, further, make provision for the annual accounts to be drawn up and audited in manner provided in Chapter IV of this Directive.

CHAPTER II: THE MANAGEMENT ORGAN
AND THE SUPERVISORY ORGAN

Article 3

1. The members of the management organ shall be appointed by the supervisory organ.

2. Where the management organ has more than one member, the supervisory organ shall specify which member of the management organ is responsible for questions of personnel and worker relations.

3. The provisions of this Article shall be without prejudice to national laws under which the appointment or dismissal of any member of the management organ cannot be effected against the wishes of the majority of the members of the supervisory organ who were appointed by the workers or by their representatives.

Article 4

1. The laws of the Member States shall make provision that, at any rate for companies which employ five hundred staff or more, the appointment of members of the supervisory organ shall be made in manner provided in paragraphs 2 or 3.

2. Without prejudice to the provisions contained in the following subparagraphs, the members of the supervisory organ shall be appointed by the general meeting.

Not less than one third of the members of the supervisory organ shall be appointed by the workers or their representatives or upon proposal by the workers or their representatives.

The laws of the Member States may provide in relation to the appointment of members of the supervisory board that some of those who are not appointed in manner provided in the preceding subparagraphs may be appointed otherwise than by the general meeting.

3. The members of the supervisory organ shall be appointed by that organ. However, the general meeting or the representatives of the workers may object to the appointment of a proposed candidate on the ground either that he lacks the ability to carry out his duties or that if he were appointed there would, having regard to the interests of the company, the shareholders or the workers, be imbalance in the composition of the supervisory organ. In such cases the appointment shall not be made unless the objection is declared unfounded by an independent body existing under public law.

4. As regards companies which employ a lesser number of workers than that fixed in pursuance of paragraph 1 the members of the supervisory organ shall be appointed by the general meeting.

5. The members of the first management organ and of the first supervisory organ may be appointed in the statutes or in the instrument of constitution.

Article 5

1. Only natural persons may be appointed as members of the management organ.

2. Where the laws of the Member States provide that legal persons may be members of the supervisory organ, those legal persons shall designate a permanent representative who shall be subject to the same conditions and obligations as if he were personally a member of the supervisory organ, but without prejudice to the liability of the legal person which he represents.

Article 6

No person may be at the same time a member of the management organ and of the supervisory organ.

Article 7

The members of the management organ and of the supervisory organ shall be appointed for a specified period not exceeding six years. They shall be eligible for reappointment.

Article 8

The management organ and the supervisory organ shall not fix the remuneration of their own members.

Article 9

1. The members of the management organ shall not, without the authorization of the supervisory organ, carry on within another undertaking any activity, whether remunerated or not, for their own account or for account of any other person.

2. The general meeting shall be informed each year of the authorizations given.

3. A natural person shall not be a member of the supervisory organ of more than 10 companies.

Article 10

1. Every agreement to which the company is party and in which a member of the management organ or of the supervisory organ has an interest, even if only indirect, must be authorized by the supervisory organ at least.

2. Where a member of the management organ or supervisory organ becomes aware that such circumstances as are described in paragraph 1 obtain, he shall inform those two organs thereof. The interested member shall not take part either in the discussion or decision relating to the relevant agreement within the management organ or the discussion or decision relating to the giving of the

authorization required under paragraph 1 within the supervisory organ.

3. The general meeting shall be informed each year of the authorizations given under paragraph 1.

4. Want of authorization by the supervisory organ or irregularity in the decision giving authorization shall not be adduced as against third parties save where the company proves that the third party was aware of the want of authorization or of the irregularity in the decision, or that in view of the circumstances he could not have been unaware thereof.

Article 11

1. The management organ shall not less than every three months send to the supervisory organ a report on the progress of the company's affairs.

2. The management organ shall within three months following the end of each financial year present to the supervisory organ the draft annual accounts and draft annual report within the meaning of Articles 2 and 43 of Directive No. . . . of . . .[6]

3. The supervisory organ may at any time request from the management organ a special report on the affairs of the company or on certain aspects thereof.

4. The supervisory organ or one third of the members thereof shall be entitled to obtain from the management organ all information and relevant documents and to undertake all such investigations as may be necessary. The supervisory organ may authorize one or more of its members or one or more experts to exercise these powers.

5. Each member of the supervisory organ shall be entitled to examine all reports, documents and information supplied by the management organ to the supervisory organ.

Article 12

1. The authorization of the supervisory organ shall be obtained for decisions of the management organ relating to:

   (a) the closure or transfer of the undertaking or of substantial parts thereof;
   (b) substantial curtailment or extension of the activities of the undertaking;
   (c) substantial organizational changes within the undertaking;
   (d) establishment of long-term co-operation with other undertakings or the termination thereof.

2. The law or the statutes may provide that the authorization of

6 The Fourth Draft Directive, see p. 86, *ante*.

the supervisory organ must be obtained also for the effecting of other operations.

3. The provisions of Article 10 (4) shall apply as regards third parties.

Article 13

1. The members of the management organ may be dismissed by the supervisory organ.

2. The members of the supervisory organ may be dismissed at any time by the organs or persons who appointed them and under the same procedures. However, the members of the supervisory organ who were appointed by it under Article 4 (3) may be dismissed only where proper grounds for dismissal are found to exist by judgment of the court in proceedings brought in that behalf by the supervisory organ, the general meeting or the workers' representatives.

Article 14

1. The laws of the Member States shall make such provision relating to the civil liability of the members of the management organ and of the supervisory organ as to ensure that, at minimum, compensation is made for all damage sustained by the company as a result of breaches of law or of the statutes or of other wrongful acts committed by the members of those organs in carrying out their duties.

2. Each member of the organ in question shall be jointly and severally liable without limit. He may however exonerate himself from liability if he proves that no fault is attributable to him personally.

3. The provisions of the preceding paragraphs shall apply even where the powers vested in the organ have been allocated among its members.

4. The authorization given by the supervisory organ shall not have the effect of exempting the members of the management organ from civil liability.

5. Furthermore, any discharge, instruction or authorization given by the general meeting shall not have the effect of exempting the members of the management organ or of the supervisory organ from civil liability.

Article 15

1. Proceedings on behalf of the company to enforce the liability referred to in Article 14 shall be commenced if the general meeting so resolves.

2. Neither the law nor the statutes may require for the passing of

a resolution in that behalf a majority greater than an absolute majority of votes of the shareholders present or represented.

Article 16

It shall be provided that proceedings on behalf of the company to enforce the liability referred to in Article 14 shall also be commenced if so requested by one or more shareholders:

(a) who hold shares of a certain nominal value or proportional value which the Member States shall not require to be greater than 5 per cent. of the capital subscribed; or

(b) who hold shares of a certain nominal value or proportional value which the Member States shall not require to be greater than 100,000 units of account. This figure may vary up to not more than 10 per cent. for purposes of conversion into national currency.

Article 17

The bringing of proceedings on behalf of the company to enforce the liability referred to in Article 14 shall not be made subject, whether by law, the statutes or any agreement:

(a) to prior resolution of the general meeting or other organ of the company; or

(b) to prior decision of the Court in respect of wrongful acts of the members of the management organ or of the supervisory organ, or in respect of the dismissal or replacement of members thereof.

Article 18

1. Renunciation by the company of the right to bring proceedings on behalf of the company to enforce the liability referred to in Article 14 shall not be implied:

(a) from the sole fact that the general meeting has approved the accounts relating to the financial year during which the acts giving rise to damage occurred;

(b) from the sole fact that the general meeting has given its discharge to the members of the management organ or of the supervisory organ in respect of that financial year.

2. For renunciation to take place the following minimum conditions must be satisfied:

(a) an act giving rise to damage must actually have occurred;

(b) the general meeting must expressly resolve to renounce; the resolution shall in no way affect the right conferred by Article 16 on one or more shareholders who satisfy the requirements of that Article, provided they voted against the resolution or made objection thereto which was recorded in the minutes.

3. This Article shall apply to all compromises relating to the bringing of proceedings to enforce the liability aforesaid which have been agreed between the company and the member whose liability is in question.

Article 19

1. Proceedings on behalf of the company to enforce the liability referred to in Article 14 may also be brought by a creditor of the company who is unable to obtain payment from it.

2. Action by the creditor under the preceding paragraph shall in no way be affected by such renunciation or transactions as are referred to in Article 18.

Article 20

1. The Member States shall make such provision relating to the civil liability of the members of the management organ and of the supervisory organ as to ensure that compensation is made for all damage sustained personally by shareholders and third parties as a result of breaches of law or of the statutes or of other wrongful acts committed by the members of those organs in carrying out their duties.

2. The provisions of Article 14 (2) to (5) shall apply.

Article 21

The period in which action to enforce the liability referred to in Article 14, 19 or 20 may be brought shall not be less than three years from the date of the act giving rise to damage or, if the act has been dissembled, from the time when it has become known.

CHAPTER III: GENERAL MEETING

Article 22

1. The general meeting shall be convened at least once each year.

2. It may be convened at any time by the management organ.

Article 23

1. It shall be provided that one or more shareholders who satisfy the requirements of Article 16 may request the company to convene the general meeting and settle the agenda therefor.

2. If, following a request made under paragraph 1 no action has been taken by the company within one month, the competent court must have power to convene the general meeting or to authorize it to

be convened either by the shareholders who requested that it be convened or by their agents.

Article 24

1. The laws of the Member States may provide that the general meeting of a company all of whose shares are registered may be convened by notice sent by registered letter. In every other case the meeting shall be convened by notice published at least in the company's national gazette designated in that behalf pursuant to Article 3 (4) of Directive No. 68/151/EEC of 9 March 1968.

2. The notice shall contain the following particulars at least:

(a) the name of the company and the address of its registered office;

(b) the place and date of the meeting;

(c) the type of general meeting (ordinary, extraordinary or special);

(d) a statement of the formalities, if any, prescribed by the statutes for attendance at the general meeting and for the exercise of the right to vote;

(e) any provisions of the statutes which require the shareholder, where he appoints an agent, to appoint a person who falls within certain specified categories of persons;

(f) the agenda;

(g) the wording of proposed resolutions concerning each of the items on the agenda.

3. The length of the period between the date of dispatch by registered letter of the first notice of meeting and the date of the first meeting of the general meeting shall be not less than two weeks, and the length of the period between the date of first publication of the notice of meeting and the date of the first meeting of the general meeting shall be not less than one month.

Article 25

1. It shall be provided that one or more shareholders who satisfy the requirements of Article 16 may request that one or more new items be included in the agenda of a general meeting of which notice has already been given.

2. Requests for inclusion of new items in the agenda shall be sent to the company within five days following the date of dispatch by registered letter of the first notice of general meeting or within 10 days following the first publication of the notice of general meeting.

3. The items whose inclusion in the agenda has been requested under the last foregoing paragraph shall be communicated or pub-

lished in the same way as the notice of meeting, not less than five days or 10 days, respectively, before the meeting.

Article 26

Every shareholder who has completed the formalities prescribed by law or by the statutes shall be entitled to attend the general meeting.

Article 27

1. Every shareholder shall be entitled to appoint a person to represent him at the general meeting.

2. The statutes may restrict the choice of representative to one or more specified categories of persons. Every shareholder must, however, have the right to appoint another shareholder to represent him.

3. The appointment shall be made in writing which shall be sent to the company and be retained by it for not less than three years.

Article 28

1. If any person publicly invites shareholders to send their forms of proxy to him and offers to appoint agents for them, Article 27 and the following provisions shall apply:

(a) The appointment shall relate only to one meeting; it shall, however, be valid for a second meeting having the same agenda;

(b) the appointment shall be revocable;

(c) the invitation shall be sent in writing to every shareholder whose name and permanent address are known;

(d) the invitation shall contain the following particulars at least:

(aa) the agenda of the meeting;

(bb) the wording of proposed resolutions concerning each of the items on the agenda;

(cc) a statement to the effect that the documents referred to in Article 30 are available to any shareholder who requests them;

(dd) a request for instructions concerning the exercise of the right to vote in respect of each item on the agenda;

(ee) a statement of the way in which the agent will exercise the right to vote if the shareholder gives no instructions;

(e) the right to vote shall be exercised in accordance with the instructions of the shareholder or, if none are given by him, in accordance with the statement made to the shareholder;

(*f*) the agent may, however, depart from the instructions given by the shareholder or from the statement made to him if circumstances arise which were not known at the time the instructions or invitation were sent and the interests of the shareholder might be detrimentally affected;

(*g*) where the right to vote has been exercised in a manner contrary to the shareholder's instructions or to the statement made to him, the agent shall forthwith inform the shareholder and explain the reasons therefor.

2. The provisions of the foregoing paragraph shall apply where the company invites the shareholder to send his form of proxy to it and it appoints an agent for him.

Article 29

A list of persons present shall be drawn up in respect of each general meeting before any business is transacted. The list shall contain the following particulars at least:

(*a*) the name and permanent address of each shareholder present;

(*b*) the name and permanent address of each shareholder represented and of the person representing him;

(*c*) the number, class, nominal or proportional value and number of votes attaching to the shares of each shareholder present or represented.

Article 30

1. The documents relating to the annual accounts within the meaning of Article 2 (1) of Directive No. . . . . of . . .⁶ together with the report of the persons responsible for auditing the accounts (Article 60 of this Directive) shall be available to every shareholder at latest from the date of dispatch or of publication of the notice of general meeting convened to examine or adopt the annual accounts and the appropriation of the results of the financial year.

2. Paragraph 1 shall apply also to contracts in respect of which the approval of the general meeting is required.

Article 31

1. Every shareholder who so requests at a general meeting shall be entitled to obtain correct information concerning the affairs of the company if such information is necessary to enable an objective assessment to be made of the items on the agenda.

2. The management organ shall supply the information.

3. The communication of information may be refused only where:

(*a*) communication might cause material detriment to the company, or

(*b*) the company is under legal obligation not to divulge the information in question.

4. Disputes as to whether a refusal to supply information was justified shall be determined by the court.

Article 32

1. The general meeting shall not pass any resolution concerning items which do not appear on the agenda.

2. Paragraph 1 shall not apply provided all the shareholders are present or are represented at the general meeting and no shareholder requires his objection that the business in question should not be discussed to be recorded in the minutes.

3. It shall, however, be permissible for the Member States not to apply paragraph 1 to resolutions relating to the following matters:

(*a*) dismissal of members of the management organ or supervisory organ or of the persons responsible for auditing the accounts, provided that at the same meeting of the general meeting other persons are appointed to replace them;

(*b*) the bringing of proceedings on behalf of the company to enforce the liability of the members of the management organ or of the supervisory organ, provided that the annual accounts have been discussed or been the subject of a resolution at the same meeting;

(*c*) the calling of a new meeting.

Article 33

1. The shareholder's right to vote shall be proportionate to the fraction of capital subscribed which the share represents.

2. Notwithstanding paragraph 1, the laws of the Member States may authorize the statutes to allow:

(*a*) restriction or exclusion of the right to vote in respect of shares which carry special advantages;

(*b*) restriction of votes in respect of shares allotted to the same shareholder, provided the restriction applies at least to all shareholders of the same class.

3. In no case may the right to vote be exercised where payment up of calls made by the company has not been effected.

Article 34

Neither a shareholder nor his representative shall exercise the right to vote attached to his shares or to shares belonging to third persons where the subject matter of the resolution relates to:

(a) discharge of that shareholder;
(b) rights which the company may exercise against that share-
    holder;
(c) the release of that shareholder from his obligations to the
    company;
(d) approval of contracts made between the company and that
    shareholder.

Article 35

Agreements whereby a shareholder undertakes to vote in any of
the following ways shall be void:
(a) that he will always follow the instructions of the company or
    of one of its organs;
(b) that he will always approve proposals made by the company
    or by one of its organs;
(c) that he will vote in a specified manner, or abstain, in considera-
    tion of special advantages.

Article 36

1. Resolutions of the general meeting shall be passed by absolute
majority of votes cast by all the shareholders present or represented,
unless a greater majority or other requirements be prescribed by law
or by the statutes.

2. The foregoing paragraph shall not apply to the appointment of
members of the management organ or of the supervisory organ or
of the persons responsible for auditing the accounts of the company.

Article 37

1. A resolution of the general meeting shall be required for any
alteration of the statutes.

2. The laws of the Member States may, however, provide that the
general meeting may authorize another organ of the company to alter
the statutes, provided:
(a) the alteration is effected only for the purpose of giving effect
    to a resolution already passed by the general meeting; or
(b) the alteration is imposed by an administrative authority whose
    approval is necessary in order for alterations of the statutes
    to be valid;
(c) the alteration is effected solely in order that the statutes
    comply with compulsory provisions of law.

Article 38

The complete text of the alteration to the statutes which is to be
put before the general meeting shall be set out in the notice of
meeting.

Article 39

1. A majority of not less than two thirds either of votes carried by shares represented at the meeting or of the capital subscribed which is represented thereat shall be required for the passing by the general meeting of resolutions altering the statutes.

2. Where, however, the laws of the Member States provide that the general meeting may validly transact business only if at least one half of the capital subscribed is represented, resolutions for alteration of the statutes shall require a majority not less than that required under Article 36.

3. Resolutions of the general meeting which would have the effect of increasing the liabilities of the shareholders shall require in any event the approval of all shareholders involved.

Article 40

1. A resolution of the general meeting shall, where the share capital is divided into different classes and the resolution is detrimental to the holders of shares of those classes, be valid only if consented to by separate vote at least of each class.

2. Article 39 shall apply.

Article 41

1. Minutes shall be prepared of every meeting of the general meeting.

2. The minutes shall contain the following particulars at least:
   (a) the place and date of the meeting;
   (b) the resolutions passed;
   (c) the result of the voting;
   (d) objections made by shareholders to discussion of particular items of business.

3. There shall be annexed to the minutes:
   (a) the list of persons present;
   (b) the documents relating to the calling of the general meeting.

4. The minutes and the documents annexed thereto shall be held at the disposal at least of the shareholders and shall be kept for not less than three years.

Article 42

The Member States shall ensure that, without prejudice to rights acquired in good faith by third parties, all resolutions of the general meeting are void or voidable where:
   (a) the general meeting was not called in conformity with Article 24 (1), (2) (b) and (d) and (3);

(b) the subject matter of the resolution was not communicated and published in conformity with Article 24 (2) (f) or Article 25 (3), but without prejudice to the provisions of Article 32 (2) or (3);

(c) contrary to Article 26, a shareholder was not allowed to attend the general meeting;

(d) contrary to Article 30, a shareholder was unable to examine a document or, contrary to Article 31, information was refused to him;

(e) in the course of transacting business the provisions of Articles 33 and 34 relating to the exercise of the right of vote were not observed and as a result thereof the outcome of the vote was decisively affected;

(f) the majority required under Article 36 or 39 was not obtained.

Article 43

Proceedings under Article 42 for nullity or voidability may be brought at least:

(a) in the case of Article 42 (a)
by any shareholder who was not present or represented at the general meeting;

(b) in the case of Article 42 (b)
by any shareholder unless he was present or represented at the general meeting but did not cause to be recorded in the minutes his objection that the business in question should not be discussed;

(c) in the case of Article 42 (c)
by any shareholder who was not allowed to attend the general meeting;

(d) in the case of Article 42 (d)
by any shareholder who was unable to examine any document or to whom information was refused;

(e) in the case of Article 42 (e)
by any shareholder who was excluded from voting or who disputes the right to vote of some other shareholder who voted;

(f) in the case of Article 42 (f)
by any shareholder.

Article 44

Proceedings for nullity or voidability shall be brought within a period which the Member States shall fix at not less than three months nor more than one year from the time when the resolution of the general meeting could be adduced as against the person who claims that the resolution is void or voidable.

Article 45

A resolution of the general meeting shall not be declared void where it has been replaced by another resolution passed in conformity with the law or the statutes. The competent court must have power to allow the company time to do this.

Article 46

The question whether a decision of nullity pronounced by a court of law in respect of a resolution of the general meeting may be relied on as against third parties shall be governed by Article 12 (1) of Directive No. 68/151/EEC of 9 March 1968.

Article 47

Where the laws of the Member States provide for special meetings of holders of certain classes of shares, the provisions of Chapter 3 shall apply to such meetings and to the resolutions thereof.

CHAPTER IV:
THE ADOPTION AND AUDIT OF THE ANNUAL ACCOUNTS

Article 48

1. The annual accounts within the meaning of Article 2 of Directive No. . . . of . . .[6] shall be adopted by the general meeting.

2. The laws of the Member States may, however, provide that the annual accounts shall be adopted not by the general meeting but by the management organ and the supervisory organ, unless those two organs decide otherwise or fail to agree.

Article 49

1. Five per cent. of the result for each year, reduced where appropriate by losses brought forward from previous years, shall be appropriated to legal reserve until that reserve amounts to not less than 10 per cent. of the capital subscribed.

2. So long as the legal reserve does not exceed the amount specified in the foregoing paragraph it shall not be used except to set off losses and then only if other reserves are inadequate for that purpose.

Article 50

1. The general meeting shall decide how the results for each year, reduced where appropriate by the amount of the losses brought forward from previous years, are to be appropriated.

2. The statutes may, however, provide for the appropriation of a maximum of 50 per cent. of the result referred to in paragraph 1.

Article 51

1. One or more persons shall be made responsible for auditing the accounts of the company.

2. The audit shall in any event cover the annual accounts within the meaning of Article 2 of Council Directive No. . . . . of . . .[6] and the annual report within the meaning of Article 43 of that Directive.

Article 52

Only persons who are independent of the company and who are nominated or approved by a judicial or administrative authority may be charged with the responsibility of auditing the accounts of the company.

Article 53

1. The audit of the accounts shall in no case be undertaken by persons who are members, or who during the last three years have been members, of the management organ, supervisory organ or staff of the company whose accounts are to be audited.

2. Further, the audit of the accounts shall in no case be undertaken by companies or firms whose members or partners, members of the management organ or supervisory organ, or of which the persons who have power of representation are members, or during the last three years have been members, of the management organ, supervisory organ or staff of the company whose accounts are to be audited.

Article 54

1. The persons who have audited the accounts shall in no case be or, for a period of three years following cessation of their duties, become members of the management organ, supervisory organ or staff of the company whose accounts have been audited.

2. Further, the members or partners, members of the management organ or supervisory organ or the persons who have power of representation of the companies or firms who have audited the accounts shall in no case become members of the management organ, supervisory organ or staff of the company whose accounts have been audited, less than three years after cessation of their duties.

Article 55

1. The persons who are to audit the accounts shall be appointed by the general meeting. This Directive shall, however, be without

prejudice to the provisions of law of the Member States relating to the appointment of such persons at the time of formation of the company.

2. Where appointment by the general meeting has not been made in due time or where any of the persons appointed is unable to carry out his duties, the management organ, the supervisory organ or any shareholder must have the right to apply to the Court for appointment of one or more persons to audit the accounts.

3. Further, the court must have power to dismiss, where there are proper grounds, any person appointed by the general meeting to audit the accounts, and must also have power to appoint some other person for that purpose if application is made by the management organ, supervisory organ or by one or more shareholders who satisfy the requirements of Article 16.

Such application shall be made within two weeks following the date of the appointment by the general meeting.

Article 56

The persons who audit the accounts shall be appointed for a period certain of not less than three years nor more than six years. They shall be eligible for reappointment.

Article 57

1. The remuneration of the persons appointed by the general meeting to audit the accounts shall be fixed for the whole of their period of office before it commences.

2. Apart from the remuneration fixed pursuant to paragraph 1, no remuneration or benefit shall be accorded to the persons in question in respect of their auditing of the accounts.

3. The provisions of paragraph 2 shall apply to the persons appointed by the Court to audit the accounts.

Article 58

1. The persons appointed to audit the accounts shall in all cases examine whether the annual accounts within the meaning of Article 2 of Directive No. . . . of . . .[6] and the annual report within the meaning of Article 43 of that Directive are in conformity with the law and the statutes.

2. If they have no reservation to make, the persons responsible for the audit shall so certify on the annual accounts; otherwise they shall issue their certificate subject to reservations or shall refuse their certificate.

Article 59

The persons responsible for auditing the accounts shall be entitled to obtain from the company all information and relevant documents and to undertake all such investigations as may be necessary.

Article 60

The persons responsible for auditing the accounts shall prepare a detailed report relating to the results of their work. The report shall contain the following at least:

(*a*) an indication of whether the provisions of Article 51 (1) have been observed;

(*b*) observations concerning any infringements of law or of the statutes which have been found in the company's accounts, in its annual accounts or in the management report;

(*c*) observations concerning any facts noted which constitute a serious danger to the financial situation of the company;

(*d*) the complete text of the certificate given pursuant to Article 58 (2). Where reservations have been made, or where the certificate has been withheld, the reasons therefor shall be specified.

Article 61

Save where proper grounds exist, the persons responsible for auditing the accounts shall not be dismissed by the general meeting before the end of their period of office.

Article 62

Articles 14 to 21 of this Directive shall apply in respect of the civil liability of the persons responsible for auditing the accounts, so as to ensure that compensation is made for any damage sustained by the company, any shareholder or third party as a result of wrongful acts committed by those persons aforesaid in carrying out their duties.

Article 63

1. The Member States shall ensure that without prejudice to rights acquired in good faith by third parties, all resolutions of the organ whose responsibility it is to adopt the annual accounts are void or voidable where:

(*a*) the annual accounts have not been audited in conformity with Article 58 (1);

(*b*) the certificate relating to the annual accounts has been refused in accordance with Article 58 (2);

(*c*) the annual accounts have not been audited by a person nominated or approved in manner required by Article 52;

(*d*) the annual accounts have been audited by a person who, under Article 53, should not have been made responsible for the audit, or who has been dismissed by the Court in conformity with Article 55 (3) or by the general meeting in conformity with Article 61;

(*e*) the annual accounts have been audited by a person who, contrary to Article 55 (1), was not appointed by the general meeting or who, contrary to Article 55 (2) or (3), was not appointed by the Court.

2. Proceedings for nullity or voidability may be brought at least by any shareholder.

3. Articles 44 to 46 shall apply.

CHAPTER V: GENERAL PROVISIONS

Article 64

1. The Member States shall bring into force within eighteen months following the notification of this Directive all such amendments to their laws, regulations or administrative provisions as may be necessary to comply with the provisions of this Directive and shall inform the Commission thereof.

2. The Member States may provide that the amendments to their laws as referred to in paragraph 1 shall not apply to companies already in existence at the time of entry into force of those amendments until eighteen months after that time.

3. The Member States shall communicate to the Commission, for information, the texts of the draft laws and regulations, together with the grounds therefor, relating to the field governed by this Directive. The texts shall be communicated not later than six months before the proposed date of entry into force of the drafts.

Article 65

This Directive is addressed to the Member States.

Text 6

A. *(Unnumbered) Draft Directive, submitted by the Commission to the Council on September 26, 1972, concerning the content, checking and distribution of the prospectus to be published when securities issued by companies are admitted to official stock exchange quotation*

The Council of the European Communities

Having regard to the Treaty establishing the European Economic Community and, in particular, Article 54.3 g. thereof,

Having regard to the proposal from the Commission,

Having regard to the Opinion of the European Parliament,

Having regard to the Opinion of the Economic and Social Committee,

Whereas the enlargement of the size of the market in which enterprises operate to the dimensions of the Community involves a parallel widening of their financial requirements and of the capital markets on which they must call to satisfy these, and whereas admission to the stock exchanges of several Member States of transferable securities issued by companies and other legal persons in public and private law constitutes an important method of access to these capital markets, and whereas furthermore exchange restrictions on the purchase of transferable securities negotiated on the stock exchanges of another Member State have been eliminated as part of the liberalization of capital movements,

Whereas safeguards for the protection of the interests of company members and third parties investing whose savings are sought are required in most of the Member States of enterprises which make public call on savings, sometimes immediately the securities are issued and in any case at the time of their admission to official stock exchange quotation, and whereas these safeguards rest on the requirement that information which is adequate and as objective as possible must be furnished concerning in particular the financial situation of the issuing enterprise and the features of the securities for which quotation is requested and whereas the form under which this information is required usually consists of the publication of a prospectus,

Whereas at the same time the safeguards thus required diverge from one member country to another, both as regards the contents

134

and the layout of the prospectus and the efficacity, methods and timing of the check on the adequacy and sufficiency of the information given, and whereas the effect of these divergencies is not only to make it more difficult for enterprises to obtain admission to the stock exchanges of several Member States but also to hinder the acquisition by savers residing in a Member State of securities quoted on the stock exchanges of the other Member States and thus to inhibit the financing of the enterprises and investment by savers throughout the Community,

Whereas these divergencies should be eliminated by coordinating the rules and regulations without necessarily making them completely uniform, in order to achieve an adequate degree of equivalence in the safeguards offered in each Member State to ensure sufficient and objective information for company members and third parties who are present or potential security holders, and whereas at the same time, taking into account on the one hand the present degree of liberalization of capital movements in the Community and on the other the fact that a mechanism for checking at the time the securities are issued does not yet exist in all the Member States, it would appear sufficient at present to limit the necessary coordination to the conditions for admission of such securities to official stock exchange quotation,

Whereas the enterprises in the Member States which request the quotation of securities that they issue are all companies or other legal persons in public or private law within the meaning of Article 58 (2) of the Treaty so that the coordination of the safeguards which are made compulsory for them in the field of this Directive comes under Article 54.3 g.; and whereas these safeguards, because of their objective character and their nature as rules for the protection of savings and for the proper functioning of the stock exchanges, must necessarily also apply to applications for admission to quotation on a stock exchange in the Community of the securities issued by enterprises of third countries, and whereas the provisions of this Directive must consequently also concern the information required of these undertakings in the form of prospectuses and the checking of this information,

Has adopted this Directive :

SECTION I: GENERAL RULES AND FIELD OF APPLICATION

Article 1 : Requirement of issuing a prospectus

1. Member States shall ensure that, before securities are admitted to or introduced for official quotation on a stock exchange situated

within their territory, a prospectus checked by an authority appointed
for this purpose is published or made available to the public.

2. Notwithstanding the foregoing, securities issued by open-end
investment companies and unit trusts, i.e. organisations whose
securities are issued in a continuous fashion or in closely spaced
tranches and/or are bought back or redeemed directly or indirectly
at the request of the holder out of their assets, shall be excluded
from the field of application of this Directive.

3. The obligations of this Directive shall not apply either to
securities issued by the States or their local authorities.

Article 2 : Contents of the prospectus

The prospectus mentioned in Article 1 above must contain all
information which, according to the particular nature of the issuer
and the securities in question, is necessary to enable investors and
their investment advisers to form a well-founded opinion on the net
worth, financial situation, results and prospects of the issuer and also
on the rights pertaining to the securities for which application for
admission is being made.

Article 3 : Obligation to follow the schemes of presentation set out in the Schedules

1. In order to achieve the result envisaged in Article 2, Member
States shall ensure that the admission prospectus contains, in as easily
analysable and comprehensible a form as possible, at least those
items of information that are listed in Schedules A, B or C annexed
to the present Directive, depending on whether shares, debentures [1]
or certificates representing shares are involved.

The schemes of presentation in question are applicable in conjunction with the exception options provided for in Articles 4 and 5.

2. In the specific cases mentioned in Articles 6–12 the prospectus
shall be drawn up in accordance with the indications laid down
therein.

3. In cases where certain headings of the Schedules are inappro-
priate to the issuers' sphere of activity, a prospectus giving equivalent
information shall be drawn up by adapting the headings in question.

Article 4 : Right to waive publication of a prospectus or certain of its headings

1. Member States may, under conditions determined by them,
waive publication of a prospectus drawn up in accordance with the

---

[1] " Debenture " includes debenture stock, loan stock, bonds and any similar
securities of a company whether constituting a charge on the assets of the
company or not (Translator's note).

annexed schemes of presentation, or may even provide for complete exemption from the requirement of issuing a prospectus when the application for admission is in respect of the securities detailed below:

(*a*) securities for which, within a maximum of six months prior to the application for admission, an issue prospectus was published in the same member country in connection with a public issue, provided that the prospectus was drawn up in conformity with the provisions of the present Directive and can be held to be equivalent to the European admission prospectus; in such a case, the up-dating of that prospectus may if necessary be called for;

(*b*) securities already admitted to official quotation on another stock exchange in the same member country, provided that a prospectus has already been published which complies with the present Directive;

(*c*) shares (including shares having no capital value) allotted, consequent upon the capitalisation of reserves, issue premiums, revaluation surpluses or profits, to holders of shares of the same category already quoted on the same stock exchange;

(*d*) shares resulting from the conversion of convertible debentures when these convertible debentures and shares of the same category as those offered by way of conversion are already quoted on the same stock exchange;

(*e*) shares issued in connection with the exercise of warrants, when the debentures to which they were attached, as well as shares of the same category as those offered to holders of the warrants, are already quoted on the same stock exchange;

(*f*) supplementary certificates representing shares issued in exchange for original securities, where there is no increase of capital, when the certificates are already quoted on the same stock exchange;

(*g*) a number of securities amounting to less than 5 per cent. of the number of securities of the same category already admitted to quotation on the same stock exchange, provided that the aggregate market value of the additional securities does not exceed 500,000 units of account over a period of two years.

2. Where Member States intend to avail themselves of this exemption option, they must notify the Commission, at the latest by the expiry of the time-limit fixed in Article 20 (1), of the cases in which they intend to keep this option available and, where appropriate, of the particular provisions they are establishing for the scheme of

presentation. When, in these same cases, circumstances relating to the creation of extra securities call for special information the Member States must nevertheless prescribe the publication of the necessary information.

Article 5 : Dispensation from the provisions of certain headings in the annexed Schedules

The authorities of Member States may dispense the issuer from publishing certain information laid down in the Schedules when, in the particular circumstances of the issuer concerned :

1. this information has no more than minimal importance and is not likely to influence assessment of the net worth, financial position, results and prospects of the issuer;
2. the disclosure of this information would be contrary to the public interest or would be seriously detrimental to the issuer, provided that non-publication is not likely to mislead the public with regard to the facts and circumstances essential for assessment of the securities in question.

SECTION II: CONTENT OF THE PROSPECTUS IN SPECIAL CASES

Article 6 : Financial institutions

1. Upon admission to quotation for securities issued by financial institutions, the prospectus must contain at least the items of information specified in Chapters 1, 2, 3, 5 and 6 of Schedules A or B, according as shares or debentures are involved.

2. In addition, it must contain information adapted to the characteristics of the issuers in question and equivalent to that specified in Chapters 4 and 7 of Schedules A or B in accordance with the rules laid down for this purpose by the competent national authorities.

3. It shall be incumbent on Member States to define the financial institutions for which modified schemes for the presentation of prospectuses will be laid down.

The system provided for by this Article for financial institutions may be extended to investment companies and collective investment funds other than those covered in Article 1, to " pure " finance companies (i.e. those engaging in no other activities than assembling capital to make it available to a parent company or a company directly or indirectly affiliated with the parent company) and to " pure " holding companies (i.e. those that do not engage in any other activity than managing a portfolio of transferable securities, licences or patents).

Article 7 : Continuous or repeated loan issues by financial institutions

1. In the case of banks, savings banks, credit institutions and mortgage companies which publish their accounts regularly, which within the Community are corporations of public-law status or are subject to public supervision designed to protect savings, and which make continuous or repeated issues, not less than an average of twice a year, of debentures for which admission to quotation is sought, the complete prospectus drawn up in accordance with the method laid down for financial institutions in Article 6 need only be published every three years. This system may be extended to cover Dutch mortgage companies.

2. Nevertheless, on the occasion of each admission, the publication is required of information concerning, at the least, the signatories of the prospectus, the terms of the loan and conditions of the transaction (Chapters 1 and 2 of the annexed debentures Schedule), together with information concerning any events of importance for assessing the security which have occurred since the date of the latest annual statement of accounts. With regard to the latter, it may be made available to the public at the banks which are acting as paying agents.

In the case of debentures issued by the Italian banks' " special sections " with separate legal personality (*cartelle fondiarie* and other like securities), the annual accounts of the special sections must be published, and not those of the banks from which they stem.

Article 8 : Guaranteed loans

1. In the case of loans covered by a third company's guarantee other than in the form of material security, the prospectus must carry information as specified in the debentures Schedule concerning both companies when the issuing company and the guarantor company are specifically engaged in industry and commerce.

When one of the two companies is a financial institution, that part of the full prospectus which relates to that company shall be drawn up in accordance with the provisions of Article 6.

2. In the case of loans issued by a " pure " finance company having no other business than that of the issuing of loans and the placing of such funds at the disposal of the parent company or other companies affiliated to it, the prospectus must include, for the guarantor companies, the information specified in the debentures Schedule except for Chapter 2 and, for the issuing company, that is to say the " pure " finance company, the information specified in Chapters 1, 2 and 3 and under items 51 and 61 of the debentures Schedule.

When there is more than one guarantor, the information specified in the Schedule is required from each, but the prospectus may be abridged for the sake of making it easier to read, pursuant to instructions given by the authorities.

3. For group loans, information concerning all the guarantor companies is required in the prospectus. When these are too numerous, however, the authorities shall have discretionary power to allow abridgement of the information required of each.

4. In all cases of guaranteed loans, the guarantee contract must be annexed to the prospectus unless it is too voluminous or difficult for the public to understand. In such a case, a résumé of the contract must be published which will allow an assessment to be made of the nature and scope of the guarantee, whilst the contract itself must be made available to the public at the premises of the financial intermediaries through whom the request for admission is made.

Article 9 : Convertible loans or loans with warrants attached

1. When the request for admission relates to convertible debentures or to debentures carrying warrants, the prospectus must contain the information specified in the shares Schedule and in Chapter 2 of the debentures Schedule, i.e. information relating to the operation, as well as the subscription or conversion terms.

2. When the issuer of the debentures is a different Company from that which issues the shares, the prospectus must contain the information specified in the debentures Schedule for the first company and that specified in the shares Schedule for the second company.

However, in the event of the issuer of the debentures being a " pure " finance company, the prospectus need contain, in addition to the subscription or conversion terms, only the information specified in the debentures Schedule in the abridged form for the " pure " finance company, i.e. the information specified in Chapters 1, 2 and 3 and under items 51 and 61 of the debentures Schedule.

3. When the currency of the convertible debenture is different from that of the shares, the effects of any changes in currency parities upon the terms of conversion or upon the terms of subscription must be indicated.

Article 10 : Admission to stock exchange quotation of securities issued in connection with the merging or splitting of companies, the transfer of assets or a public exchange offer

1. When the application for admission relates to securities issued in connection with an operation involving the merging or splitting of companies, the transfer of assets or a public exchange offer, and when the operation took place within the last three years, the prospectus shall include, in addition to the information specified in

the shares Schedule or in the debentures Schedule as appropriate, the following material which may be inserted or simply annexed:
  (i) the documents presented to the general meeting, including the report of the merger, the valuation criteria and the justification for the exchange ratio;
  (ii) the opening balance sheet showing the effects of the operation in question;
  (iii) information relating to the financial background of each of the companies involved; this information may be brief for companies which are already quoted.

2. When less than six months before admission to stock exchange quotation equivalent and checked information has been published prior to an operation of the kind referred to in paragraph 1, the authorities of Member States may waive publication of a prospectus for admission to quotation, provided that this information is made available to the public.

Article 11 : Certificates representing shares

1. When the application for admission relates to certificates representing shares, the prospectus must contain the information specified in the shares Schedule as regards the shares represented, and the information specified in the certificates Schedule.

2. Nevertheless, the authorities may allow the issuer of the certificates to dispense with the publication of details of its financial position provided for in the annexed Schedule, when the issuer is:
  (i) a bank, savings bank, credit institution or mortgage company which is quoted on a stock exchange, which publishes its accounts regularly and which within the Community is a corporation of public-law status or subject to public supervision aimed at safeguarding savings;
  (ii) or an interprofessional organisation for the transfer of securities;
  (iii) or a trustee institution subject to special regulations for the safe custody of original shares.

Article 12 : Issuers in the public sector

1. In connection with the admission to stock exchange quotation of securities issued by corporate bodies under public law which are engaged in industrial, commercial or financial activities, the general rules laid down in this Directive shall apply with only such adaptations as the particularities of these enterprises may require.

2. When these issuers, or the debentures issued by them, are covered, both as to the redemption of the loan and interest payment, by the unconditional and irrevocable guarantee of a Member State,

the competent authorities may simplify that part of the prospectus which refers to the issuer and the issuer's financial position, while, at the same time, endeavouring to insist upon the publication of this information in accordance with sound practice as adopted on the international market.

SECTION III: ARRANGEMENTS FOR ENFORCING THE PROSPECTUS REQUIREMENTS AND FOR MAKING IT PUBLICLY AVAILABLE

Article 13 : Enforcement of the prospectus requirements

1. Member States shall instruct one or more national authorities, public or private, to supervise the enforcement of the rules in the present Directive and shall notify the Commission of these authorities, giving details of any division of responsibilities among them.

2. The prospectus may not be published, nor may it be made available to the public, before it has been passed by the competent authority as referred to in paragraph 1.

3. The competent authority shall give authorisation for the prospectus to be published or made available to the public only if it is of the opinion that the prospectus satisfies all the requirements of the present Directive, and if it has good reason to believe that it contains no particulars or omissions likely to mislead the public.

4. In order to carry out their task, the authorities appointed shall be endowed with all the necessary competence and powers of supervision. In particular, they must have the power to require the issuer of the securities for which admission to quotation is sought to furnish all the information and to produce all the documents necessary for them to judge whether or not the draft prospectuses submitted to them conform to the requirements laid down in the Directive, as well as powers to require the prospectus to be presented in the manner best suited to the characteristics of the issuer and of the securities.

They must also be provided with power to check whether an issuer complies with the conditions laid down in the Directive for a partial or total dispensation from some of its requirements.

Article 14 : Methods of publishing the prospectus

1. The prospectus for admission to quotation must be published:

    (i) either by insertion in an official gazette and in one or more other journals,

    (ii) or by making available to the public, free of charge, copies in pamphlet form at the headquarters of the stock exchange or stock exchanges on which the securities are being admitted to quotation and at the offices of the issuer as well as over the counters of the banks and other intermediaries involved in the application for admission or in the placing of the securities.

2. These two methods may be combined. In countries where publication of a prospectus in the press is prescribed not all the information specified in the Schedules annexed to the Directive need be published in the press, subject to the following conditions:

   (i) the information prescribed in the annexed Schedules but not published in the press must be made available to the public in pamphlet form;

  (ii) this pamphlet must always be accompanied by a reprint of the document published in the press;

 (iii) the document published in the press must mention the pamphlet and must state where members of the public may obtain the information document in full.

Finally, the apportionment of the information between the two methods must be carried out in accordance with the standards fixed by law or by the competent authorities and under their control.

3. It must be made compulsory for the prospectuses to be lodged in places and according to procedures laid down by the Member States.

Article 15 : Deadlines for publishing the prospectus

1. When shares are admitted to quotation the prospectus must be published or made available to the public as early as possible and at least eight days before the date on which the securities admitted to quotation can be the subject of dealings recorded in the official list. This same eight-day minimum requirement must be respected in the case of issues of convertible debentures or debentures with warrants attached carrying preferential subscription rights for current share-holders. Three days at least must be allowed in the case of issues of debentures, convertible debentures or debentures with warrants which do not carry preferential subscription rights for existing shareholders.

2. Moreover, where there is to be a market in subscription rights giving rise to dealings recorded in the official list, the prospectus must be published or made available to the public at least three days before this market opens.

3. In the event of the admission of debentures to quotation coinciding with the public issue, and when certain terms of the issue such as the issue price or the interest rate are only finalised at the last

moment, the authorities may confine themselves to insisting upon the publication, at least three days before admission, of a provisional prospectus omitting this information but indicating how it will be made known. This information must be made known to the public not later than the day before dealings commence, by putting out either a complete prospectus or an addendum sheet to the above-mentioned provisional prospectus, or alternatively by a notice in the press referring to the complete prospectus and indicating where it may be procured.

Article 16 : Publication of documents other than the prospectus

1. As soon as a checked prospectus is published for securities in connection with their admission to quotation, the bills, posters and documents confined to the announcement of these operations and to an indication of the essential characteristics of the securities must refer to the prospectus and must state where and how the public may procure it.

2. Documents containing more detailed information that are published by or on behalf of the issuer, and in particular the partial or abbreviated prospectus in countries where its issue is allowed by the authorities, must, in the same manner as the complete prospectus, be submitted for checking by the competent authorities, in order that they may verify that these informatory documents, though abbreviated or incomplete, would not be liable to distort the public's assessment of the securities and in order that they may call for amendments to be made, if necessary.

Furthermore, these documents must refer to the complete prospectus and must indicate where and how it may be obtained by the public.

3. It is recommended that Member States should encourage the publication of abbreviated prospectuses which are clearly presented and easy for the public to understand and which, whilst including only the essential elements of the annexed Schedules, convey an objective impression of the issuer and of the rights attaching to the securities.

4. The company or the financial intermediaries concerned in the placing of the securities or their admission to quotation may not, in this connection, give any information that might affect assessment of the securities if it does not appear in the prospectus or is not common knowledge.

Article 17 : New factors

Every important new factor arising between the time when the prospectus is finalised and when dealings commence in the stock market must be notified in a supplement to the prospectus, checked in the same way as the latter and made available by kindred procedures which will be decided by the competent authorities.

SECTION IV: PROCEDURES FOR COOPERATION BETWEEN MEMBER STATES IN THE APPLICATION OF THE DIRECTIVE

Article 18 : Operations affecting several Member States

1. In the case of simultaneous admission to quotation on the stock exchanges of several member countries of the Community, the authorities of the Member States concerned shall establish between themselves all the contacts necessary to coordinate to the maximum the requirements concerning prospectuses in order to avoid a multiplicity of formalities and to accept a single text for the greater part of the prospectus which would then only need a possible translation and supplement corresponding to the individual requirements of each Member State concerned.

2. In the event of admission to quotation being sought on a stock exchange in one or more Member States for securities which have been admitted to quotation in another Member State for less than six months, the authorities of the countries in which admission is being sought shall make contact with the authority which has already admitted the securities and shall, as far as is possible, exempt the issuer from drawing up a new prospectus subject to any need for updating, translation or the issue of a supplement in accordance with the individual requirements of each member country concerned.

3. In the case of a security which is quoted on the stock exchanges of several Member States, the authorities of the countries concerned must endeavour to get the issuer to arrange that information made available in one of these countries which might influence assessment of the merits of the security is also made available at the same time, or soon after, in the other countries in which the security is quoted.

Article 19 : Contact Group

1. A Contact Group shall be set up in the Commission. Its function shall be:

(*a*) to facilitate, without prejudice to the provisions of Articles 169 and 170 of the Treaty, harmonised application of the Directive through regular contacts designed to concert approaches to the practical problems connected with its application, and, in particular, with the annexed Schedules, about which exchanges of views might be deemed useful;

(*b*) to facilitate a concerted approach as regards supplements and improvements to the prospectus which it is permissible for the authorities of Member States to require or recommend at purely national level;

(*c*) to aid the Commission, if necessary, in drawing up new proposals to the Council with a view to supplementing or amending the Directive.

2. The Contact Group shall be composed of representatives of the Member States and of the Commission. The Commission's services shall provide the Secretariat.

SECTION V: FINAL PROVISIONS

Article 20

1. Member States shall put into effect, within twelve months of notification to them of the present Directive, all measures necessary for complying with its provisions and shall inform the Commission immediately of such measures.

2. The Member States shall communicate to the Commission the texts of the essential provisions of national law which they adopt in the areas covered by the present Directive.

Article 21

The present Directive is addressed to the Member States.

SCHEDULE A: SCHEME OF PRESENTATION FOR PROSPECTUSES FOR THE ADMISSION OF SHARES TO STOCK EXCHANGE QUOTATION

Chapter 1. Persons or bodies assuming responsibility for the prospectus

1.1. Name and function of the natural persons, name and registered office of the bodies corporate assuming responsibility for the prospectus or, as the case may be, for certain parts of it. Should they assume responsibility for certain parts of the prospectus only, mention these parts.

1.2. Declaration by the signatories of the prospectus that, to the best of their knowledge, the data appearing in that part of the prospectus for which they assume responsibility are in accordance with the facts and that there are no omissions likely to affect the bearing of the information.

1.3. Statement specifying whether or not the accounts have been checked by internal or outside auditing/accounting experts (e.g. accountants, sindaci, Wirtschaftsprüfer, etc.). The capacity (organ established under the " Statutes " [2] or external body) in which the verifications were carried out should be specified, as well as possible reservations. The same rule shall apply to the consolidated accounts contained in the prospectus.

Chapter 2. Information concerning admission to quotation and the securities for which application is being made

2.1. Nature of the operation (e.g., admission to quotation of securities already marketed; admission to quotation with a view to stock exchange marketing).

2.2. Information concerning the securities to be admitted to quotation.

2.2.1. Indication of the resolutions, authorizations and approvals by virtue of which the securities were created: type of operation and amount thereof. Number of securities created, if predetermined.

2.2.2. Concise description of the rights attaching to the securities, inter alia extent of the voting rights, entitlement to share in the profits and to the liquidation surplus, any privileges. Time-limit after which dividends lapse and indication of the party in whose favour this provision operates.

2.2.3. Arrangements for transfer of the securities and any restrictions on their free negotiability (e.g., clause establishing approval requirement).

2.2.4. Date from which dividends become payable.

2.2.5. The stock exchange or exchanges to which admission is or may be applied for.

2.2.6. The institutions which, at the time of admission, are the paying agents of the company in the country where the admission occurs.

2.3. Information concerning issue and placing of securities: should an issue prospectus not have been published and when the issue and the admission to quotation occur at the same time, or when the issue preceded admission to quotation by less than three months, the following items of information shall appear in the admission prospectus. The information provided for in point 2.3, so far as applicable, shall also be supplied for privately issued securities at the time of their admission to stock exchange quotation.

2.3.0. For the securities referred to in point 2.2, indication of any preferential rights or exclusion of preferential rights for existing shareholders. In the latter case, the reasons for the exclusion and, in the case of an issue for cash, for the choice of the issue price of the securities, with indication of the beneficiaries of the exclusion.

---

[2] In the case of a U.K. company this term corresponds to the memorandum and articles of association (Translator's note).

2.3.1. The total amount on offer to the public and the number of securities offered, where applicable by category.

2.3.2. If the public offer is being or has been made simultaneously on several markets and if a tranche is being or has been reserved for certain of these, indicate the tranches.

2.3.3. The issue or subscription price, distinguishing the par value or the amount placed to capital, the issue premium and the amount of any expenses explicitly charged to the purchaser or subscriber; the methods of payment of the price, *inter alia* as regards the paying-up of securities which are not fully paid-up.

2.3.4. The procedure for exercise of the preferential rights, the negotiability of subscription rights; what happens to unexercised rights.

2.3.5. Period during which the issue is or was open and indication of the financial institutions responsible for receiving the public's subscriptions.

2.3.6. Methods and time-limits for delivery of the securities, possible creation of scrip.

2.3.7. Indication of the persons underwriting or guaranteeing the issue for the issuing company. If the issue is being guaranteed privately by natural persons, this fact is to be indicated without mentioning them by name. Where not all of the issue is underwritten or guaranteed, the portion not covered is to be mentioned.

2.3.8. Estimate of the overall amount and/or amount per security of the charges relating to the issue operation, making a distinction at least between the legal and administrative expenses on the one hand, and the overall remuneration of the financial intermediaries on the other (including the underwriting commission or margin, guarantee commission, placing commission).

2.3.9. Net proceeds accruing to the company from the issue and planned appropriation of these proceeds (e.g., financing of the investment programme of reinforcement of the company's financial situation).

2.4. Information concerning admission to quotation.

2.4.1. Description of the securities the admission of which is applied for and, *inter alia*, number or overall par value, exact designation or category, serial numbers, coupons attached, etc.

2.4.2. If the securities are to be placed by introduction on the stock exchange, the number of securities made available to the market and/or the overall par value and, where applicable, the minimum sale price.

2.4.3. If known, the date on which the new securities will be listed.

2.4.4. If securities of the same category are already listed on one or more stock exchanges, mention is to be made of this or these stock exchanges and, in so far as the data mentioned below are available, for the last five financial years and for the current financial year as regards the principal stock exchange or stock exchanges:

2.4.4.1. The number of securities listed or their overall par value.

2.4.4.2. The volume of transactions by number of the securities and/or their market value.

2.4.4.3. The adjusted highest and lowest prices, i.e., rendered comparable so as to take account of operations that have occurred in respect of the capital (increase, decrease, splitting, rearrangement). The adjustment formulae utilised are to be indicated.

2.4.4.4. The adjusted profit per share and the adjusted dividend per share, i.e., rendered comparable so as to take account of operations that have occurred in respect of the capital (increase, decrease, splitting, rearrangement). The adjustment formulae utilised are to be indicated.

2.4.5. If securities of the same category are not yet admitted to quotation but are dealt in on markets other than that of official quotation, the most recent prices on those markets in so far as such publicity is permitted; the market on which these prices were recorded and the source from which they were taken. The data referred to above are given only if the market for the securities is sufficiently wide.

2.4.6. Public take-over bids or exchange offers involving the company's shares and public exchange offers which have been made by the company during the last financial year and the current financial year, mentioning the conditions of the offer and its result.

2.5. If, simultaneously or almost simultaneously with the creation of securities for which admission to quotation is being sought, securities of the same nature are subscribed or placed privately or if securities of other categories are created with a view to their public or private placing, details are to be given of the nature of these operations and of the number and characteristics of the securities to which they relate.

Chapter 3. Information of a general character about the company

3.1. Status of the company.

3.1.1. Name or style, registered office and, where appropriate, principal administrative establishment, if the latter is different from the registered office.

3.1.2. Date of incorporation and, if the life of the company is limited, the date of its expiration.

3.1.3. Legislation under which the company operates and legal form which it has adopted in the framework of this legislation.

3.1.4. Indication of the company's objects and reference to the Article of the " Statutes " in which they are described.

3.1.5. Indications of the places where it is possible to consult the coordinated " Statutes ", balance sheets and reports, decisions concerning the appointment and dismissal of members of the company's organs, as well as any other document quoted in the prospectus and accessible to the public, and of the place where the dispatch of the latest company report may be applied for. Places where the prospectuses relating to the operations in respect of issue or admission to quotation performed by the company in the course of the past five years may be consulted by the public.

3.1.6. Time-limits for and ways of calling general meetings. Date and place of the next General Meeting, if these are known.

3.2. Capital.

3.2.1. The amount of the capital subscribed and its composition; the part of the subscribed capital still to be paid up, with indication of the number (or the overall par value) and nature of the securities not yet fully paid-up, broken down, where applicable, according to the degree to which they have been paid up.

3.2.2. When there is an authorised capital or authority for a contingent capital increase, *inter alia* in connection with convertible bonds issued or subscription options granted, indicate:

    (i) the amount of this authorised or " contingent " capital and, where appropriate, the duration of the authorisation;

    (ii) the categories having a preferential right of subscription for these additional portions of capital;

    (iii) the terms and arrangements for the share issue corresponding to these portions.

3.2.3. If there exist several categories of securities, whether representing the capital or not, mention their principal characteristics and the number of shares or " parts " [3] issued.

3.2.4. Conditions governing changes in the capital and in the respective rights of the various categories of securities, in so far as they depart from the general law.

3.2.5. Outline table of changes in the capital covering, in principle, at least the last five years, as well as the most important events prior to that period. Date and concise description of the successive operations changing the capital or its composition (mentioning premiums on issues or assets brought in).

---

[3] " Parts " give profit-sharing rights but do not represent any capital value (Translator's note).

3.2.6. Indication of any person who directly or indirectly, alone or jointly with other shareholders, controls the company, mentioning the amount of his participation and in any case, in so far as it is known to the company, any holding of 25 per cent. or more of the subscribed capital.

Mention must also be made of the portions of 10 per cent. or more held directly or indirectly in the company by other natural persons or bodies corporate, whenever this holding is common knowledge.

By joint control must be understood the control exercised by several companies or several persons when they have concluded among themselves an agreement which may lead them to adopt a common policy vis-à-vis the company in question.

3.2.7. If the prospectus-publishing company belongs to a group of enterprises, a description of the group and of the place it occupies therein.

3.2.8. Book value and par value (or accounting par value) of its own securities repurchased or held by the company if these securities are not isolated in the balance sheet; origin and object of this repurchase.

Chapter 4. Information concerning the company's activity
4.1. Principal activities of the company.

In the sections where the description of the company's activity is required only for the current financial year and the last financial year and if it is considered that this period is too short to reflect meaningfully the company's development, it is advisable to add indications about the previous financial years. In so far as the company's development within the reference period has been influenced by exceptional events, e.g., an important merger, these events are to be indicated. If possible, the data should be presented in such a way as to enable a comparison to be made of the trend from one financial year to another.

4.1.1. Description of the company's principal activities, mentioning the main categories of products manufactured and sold and/or services performed. Indicate important new products and, as far as possible, the proportion of the turnover attributable to new products developed within the last five years.

4.1.2. The above description may contain indications concerning the development of the company's relative position in its principal branches of activities, if these indications can be based, as to their significance and comparability, on figures emanating from qualified institutions, and the source given.

4.1.3. Breakdown, by principal branches of activities, of the net amount of the turnover in the course of the past five financial years and, if these figures are significant, the production volumes of the principal products. Any relatively homogeneous activity which contributes more than 15 per cent. to the turnover is considered a branch of activity.

4.1.4. Information on the structure of markets and supplies for the last financial year and for the current financial year and their trend (with, if possible, breakdown of the net amount of the turnover by principal geographical or economic zones, in so far as this information may influence assessment of the net worth, financial position or results).

4.1.5. Location and importance of the company's principal establishments and, if necessary, their development in the course of recent financial years and the current financial year, and information about the real estate owned. Any establishment which accounts for more than 10% of turnover or production is considered to be a principal establishment.

4.1.6. For mining, extraction of hydrocarbons, quarrying, etc., description of the deposits, estimate of the economically exploitable reserves and expected period for which they will be exploited, indication of the period and principal conditions of the concessions and the economic conditions of their exploitation, indicating the state of progress of the actual exploitation.

4.2. Show clearly, if applicable, the company's dependence with respect to the grant, use or expiration of patents and licences, to the conclusion, maintenance or expiration of industrial, commercial and financial contracts, and to new manufacturing processes when these factors have great importance for the activity or profitability of the company.

If this is the case, all that will be required is to give indications about the degree of dependence, to describe concisely, and without divulging industrial secrets, the factors in question which have a particular importance, and to indicate, if they are significant in this respect, the dates of conclusion, obtaining or expiration of contracts, licences and patents.

4.3. Amount of the expenditure effected in the course of the past five financial years for research and development of new products.

4.4. Indications of lawsuits and factors interrupting activities (e.g.: strikes, accidents) which have had or might have a significant impact on the net worth, financial position or results of the company.

4.5. Average numbers employed and their trend in the course of the past five financial years (if this trend is significant) with, if possible, a breakdown of persons employed by principal branches.

4.6. Investments.

4.6.1. Description, with figures, of the principal investments, including trade investments acquired, in the course of the past five financial years.

4.6.2. General indications concerning the investment programme in course of implementation, including its overall cost, its methods of financing, the nature of the investments, in so far as these indications are necessary for assessing the use of the funds collected in relation to the programme as a whole. By investment programme in course of implementation is meant not only the projects whose execution has already started but, more widely, the whole body of investment projects which are inter-linked to an extent such that the commissioning or profitability of the investments already effected or in course of execution depends on the implementation of all the investment projects constituting the programme.

4.6.3. A table showing the sources and utilisation of funds must be supplied, relating to the past five financial years and the current financial year.

Chapter 5. Information concerning the net worth, financial situation and results of the company

5.1. General rules.

5.1.1. Comparative table summarising the annual accounts relating to the past five financial years so as to bring out the essential factors, ensuring however that the rearrangement of the published accounts does not affect their informative value.

5.1.2. The annual accounts relating to the last two completed financial years as approved by the general meeting of shareholders must be appended.

If more than nine months have elapsed since the date on which the last financial year was closed, a recent provisional financial statement (which may be submitted without having been checked by chartered accountants) must be inserted in the prospectus, or appended to it.

5.1.3. Should the annual accounts not be drawn up in conformity with the provisions of Council Directive No. ...... of ......,[4] and should they not give a sufficiently detailed and precise view of the net worth, financial situation and results of the company, they must be accompanied by explanatory notes and comments; more detailed disclosure in the prospectus may be called for and explicit mention must be made of corrections and amendments in relation to the published accounts.

[4] J.O. 1972, C7.

5.1.4. If the company draws up consolidated accounts, the information provided for in items 5.1.1, 5.1.2 and 5.1.3 shall, if possible, be given on the basis of the consolidated accounts as well.

5.2. Individual details relating to the enterprises in which the prospectus-publishing company holds at least 10 per cent. of the capital:

5.2.1. Name, registered office.

5.2.2. Proportion of capital held.

5.2.3. Capital subscribed.

5.2.4. Reserves.

5.2.5. Result of the last financial year.

These details shall be presented, if possible in the form of a synoptic table in the prospectus, unless they already appear in the annual accounts appended to it.

5.3. Individual details relating to the companies in which the prospectus-publishing company has a substantial holding likely to influence assessment of its net worth, financial situation or results.

These details must be given, *inter alia*, for the companies in which the prospectus-publishing company directly or indirectly holds at least 25 per cent. of the capital, or when the value of this holding represents at least 10 per cent. of the paid-up capital of the prospectus-publishing company, or when this holding accounts for at least 10 per cent. of the latter company's earnings.

However, for holdings in companies belonging to third countries, the details provided for in items 5.3.1. to 5.3.5. need not be given in an individual manner but may be amalgamated with the details provided for in item 5.4.

In addition to the details mentioned in items 5.2.1. to 5.2.5, the following indications must be given:

5.3.1. Field of activity.

5.3.2. Book value of the shares or " parts " held.

5.3.3. Amount still to be paid up on these shares or " parts " held.

5.3.4. Net turnover in the course of the last financial year.

5.3.5. Amount of dividends received in the course of the last financial year in respect of shares or " parts " held.

5.3.6. Amount of the prospectus-publishing company's claims on the company in which it has a substantial holding.

5.3.7. Amount of the prospectus-publishing company's debts to the company in which it has a substantial holding.

5.3.8. Amount for which the prospectus-publishing company guarantees, endorses or secures the commitments of the company in which it has a substantial holding.

5.4. Overall information relating to all the enterprises taken together in which the prospectus-publishing company holds at least 10% of the capital and which are not referred to in item 5.3:

Same details as those provided for in items 5.3.2 to 5.3.8 but presented in overall form and broken down as between companies of the country, companies of other member countries and companies of third countries.

5.5. When the prospectus comprises consolidated accounts, there shall be indicated in an annex:

5.5.1. The consolidation principles applied and, if applicable, any exceptions to and deviations from these principles.

The following details are to be indicated, *inter alia*:

(i) the selection criteria for the companies included in the consolidation;

(ii) the method(s) of consolidation utilised: overall or proportional integration, placing on an equivalent footing;

(iii) the rates of exchange used for the consolidation of the foreign companies;

(iv) the methods of eliminating profits resulting from transactions among the companies of the group;

(v) the way in which the stocks were integrated; in particular, explanations must be provided in the event of the non-elimination of the intra-group profit;

(vi) if appropriate, the details relating to the underlying fiscal situation of the group, taking account of timing differences in the payment of corporation tax;

(vii) the definition of the consolidated turnover;

(viii) the scope of the consolidation of the results (total, partial or simplified consolidation);

(ix) the changes which have occurred, in relation to the accounts published for the previous financial year, in the principles set forth above.

5.5.2. List of companies included in the consolidation, name and registered office. It may be sufficient to distinguish them by a sign in the list of companies for which details are provided for in item 5.2.

5.5.3. For each of the companies included in the consolidation, other than the prospectus-publishing company:

(i) the proportion of third-party interests, if the accounts of this company are consolidated globally;

(ii) the proportion of the consolidation calculated on the basis of the interests, if consolidation has been effected on a pro rata basis.

5.6. When the company performs a significant proportion of its activities through the intermediary of companies controlled by it and managed as a single unit, the details concerning the activity of the company (Chapter 4), its recent development and its prospects (Chapter 7) must be provided for the whole unit in addition to concise details for the prospectus-publishing company individually.

Chapter 6. Administration, Management, Supervision

6.1. Name, first name, place of residence and function in the company of the following persons, mentioning the principal activities performed by them outside the company when they are significant in relation to the prospectus-publishing company (*inter alia*, the most significant directorships and important functions in other companies). The activities of significance for the company performed by these same persons in the course of the past five years if they joined the company less than five years ago.

6.1.1. Members of the administrative, directing or supervisory organs, as well as the other persons who assume the management of the company at the highest level.

6.1.2. General partners in the case of a partnership limited by shares.

6.1.3. Founders, if the company has been established for less than five years.

6.2. Interests of the directors, etc., in the company.

6.2.1. Remuneration paid for the last completed financial year under any heading whatsoever, as a charge to overheads or the profit appropriation account, to the administrative, directing or supervisory organs. Overall amount for each category of organ. In addition, the total remuneration paid to the members of these organs of the prospectus-publishing company by all the companies controlled by it and managed as a single unit must be indicated.

6.2.2. Options granted to the members of the administrative, directing or supervisory organs and to the other persons referred to in point 6.1.1, with respect to securities of the company: terms and conditions of these options.

6.2.3. Information about the nature and extent of the direct or indirect interests of the directors and managers or of the persons they represent in transactions which are unusual by their character or their conditions, effected by the company (such as purchases outside the normal activity, acquisition or disposal or fixed asset items, lease contracts with subsidiaries or persons mentioned above) in the course of the last financial year and during the current financial year. When such unusual transactions were concluded in the course of previous financial years and their effects are still being felt, information on these transactions must also be given.

6.2.4. Overall indication of all the loans granted by the company to the persons referred to in point 6.1.1, as well as of the guarantees constituted by the company in their favour.

6.3. Staff benefits.

6.3.1. Brief description of the policy followed with regard to staff benefits and more particularly with regard to profit-sharing contracts or supplementary retirement pension contracts; as regards the latter point, steps taken to ensure provision for them.

Description of the special benefits of a contractual character when the probable trend of the charge they represent is likely to exert a marked influence on this category of expenditure.

6.3.2. Options granted to the staff on shares in the company.

6.3.3. Overall indication of all the loans granted by the company to the staff and of the guarantees constituted in their favour.

6.4. Name, address, capacity and occupation of the persons responsible for checking the accounts (e.g.: commissaires aux comptes, réviseurs d'entreprises, Wirtschaftsprüfer, sindaci, etc.).

Chapter 7.   Recent development and prospects of the company

7.1. General indications concerning the trend in the company's business since the end of the last financial year and comparison with the corresponding period of the previous financial year. When this information is already available in interim reports, it will suffice to append the said reports to the prospectus made available to the public. The following data are to be supplied, *inter alia*:

7.1.1. The net turnover since the beginning of the financial year.

7.1.2. A description of the most significant recent trends in production and stocks.

7.1.3. A description of recent trends in costs and selling prices.

7.1.4. The state of the order book.

7.2. Company prospects.

The prospectus must clearly bring out the fact that this part consists of estimates or intentions which might not materialise.

7.2.1. Brief indications on the projected investment programme in so far as the company has already made firm decisions on this or has prepared the ground by recent financial operations and where the programme is likely to exert an important influence on the company's future financial policy, particularly its self-financing policy.

7.2.2. An estimate concerning the company's commercial and financial prospects may be inserted in the prospectus, provided that it is backed by figures (concerning, for example, the trend of business conditions, of the markets and of the order book, the influence of capital spending by the company and its competitors) and by pointers that are highly likely to prove accurate.

7.2.3. If possible, general indications concerning the profit distribution and retention policies which the company contemplates following or proposing to the meeting of shareholders and particularly, if applicable, concerning the policy on the issue of securities in connection with capitalisation of all or part of the reserves or increases in value, and concerning the operation of any dividend equalisation reserve.

SCHEDULE B:

SCHEME OF PRESENTATION FOR PROSPECTUSES FOR THE ADMISSION TO STOCK EXCHANGE QUOTATION OF DEBENTURES ISSUED BY INDUSTRIAL OR COMMERCIAL UNDERTAKINGS

Chapter 1. Persons or bodies assuming responsibility for the prospectus

1.1. Name and function of the natural persons, name and registered office of the bodies corporate assuming responsibility for the prospectus or, as the case may be, for certain parts of it. Should they assume responsibility for certain parts of the prospectus only, mention these parts.

1.2. Declaration by the signatories of the prospectus that, to the best of their knowledge, the data appearing in that part of the prospectus for which they assume responsibility are in accordance with the facts and that there are no omissions likely to affect the bearing of the information.

1.3. Statement specifying whether or not the accounts have been checked by internal or outside auditing/accounting experts (e.g. accountants, sindaci, Wirtschaftsprüfer, etc.). The capacity (organ established under the " Statutes " [5] or external body) in which the verifications were carried out should be specified, as well as possible reservations. The same rule shall apply to the consolidated accounts contained in the prospectus.

Chapter 2. Information concerning the operation

2.1. Conditions of the loan.

2.1.1. The nominal amount of the loan; the nature and the amount of the denominations available and, where appropriate, their number and numbering.

---

[5] In the case of a U.K. company this term corresponds to the memorandum and articles of association (Translator's note).

2.1.2. The issue and redemption prices and the nominal interest rate; if several interest rates are provided for, an indication of the conditions for changes in the rate. In the event of the securities being issued continuously at a variable price following the trend of the markets, information is to be given concerning the limit issue prices applied.

2.1.3. The procedures for allocation of any other financial advantages of which account cannot be taken in the yield, for example prizes, share in profits, indexing, etc. and, where applicable, the basis of calculation of the variable factors and the publicity given to these; the probable incidence on yield of a variation of the parameter.

2.1.4. Tax withheld at source on the income from securities in the country of origin and/or the country of quotation. Indication as to whether the issuing company assumes responsibility for the withholding of tax at source.

2.1.5. Amortization.

2.1.5.1. The amortization plan for the loan with any possibilities of early redemption at the option of the issuer and/or subscriber and the way in which early redemptions or stock exchange or over-the-counter buying-in will affect the amortization plan; method of operation of any sinking fund.

2.1.5.2. Amortization procedure: technique of drawing by lot and publicity therefor, repurchase on the stock exchange, repurchase by mutual agreement.

2.1.6. The financial institutions which, at the time of admission, are the paying agents of the company in the country where the admission takes place.

2.1.7. Currency of the loan. If the loan is denominated in units of account, the contractual status of these; currency option.

2.1.8. Time limits.

2.1.8.1. Period of the loan and any interim due dates.

2.1.8.2. The date from which interest becomes payable and the due dates for interest.

2.1.8.3. The time limit on the validity of claims to interest and repayment of principal.

2.1.8.4. The procedures and time limits for the delivery of the securities and the creation of scrip, where applicable.

2.1.9. Any other factor necessary for the calculation of the yield or for the assessment of the value of the securities. The method of calculating the yield is to be specified.

2.2. Legal information.

2.2.1. Reference to the resolutions, authorizations and approvals by virtue of which the securities were created or which constitute a prior condition for issue or admission to quotation.

2.2.2. Nature and scope of the guarantees, sureties and commitments intended to ensure that the loan will be duly serviced as regards both interest and capital repayment. The texts of the contracts relating to such guarantees, sureties and commitments should be accessible to the public. When there are no such sureties, guarantees or commitments this fact must be mentioned.

2.2.3. Organization of representation for the body of debenture holders or trusteeships; name or denomination and head office of the representative of the debenture holders, the main conditions of such representation and particularly the conditions under which the representative may be replaced. The texts of the contracts relating to these forms of representation must be accessible to the public.

2.2.4. Mention of clauses subordinating the loan to other debts of the company already contracted or to be contracted in the future.

2.2.5. The legislation applicable to the securities and the courts competent in the event of litigation.

2.2.6. Arrangements for transfer of the securities, registered or bearer, and any restrictions on their negotiability.

2.3. Information concerning admission of the debentures to quotation.

2.3.1. The stock exchange or exchanges on which quotation is or will be applied for.

2.3.2. Indication of the persons underwriting or guaranteeing the issue for the issuing company and the extent of their commitments. If the issue is being guaranteed privately by natural persons this fact is to be indicated without mentioning who they are. Where not all of the issue is underwritten or guaranteed, the portion not covered is to be mentioned.

2.3.3. The number or global nominal value of the securities for which quotation is sought.

2.3.4. If the public offer, issue or admission to quotation takes place simultaneously on the markets of several countries and a tranche is reserved for certain of these markets, an indication of these tranches.

2.3.5. If, simultaneously or almost simultaneously with the creation of the securities which are the subject of the public issue or of the admission to quotation, securities of the same nature are subscribed or placed privately or securities of other categories are created with a view to their public or private placing, mention is to be made of the nature of these operations and of the number and characteristics of the securities concerned.

2.3.6. If the same debentures are already quoted on one or several stock exchanges, the following must be mentioned :

2.3.6.1. The stock exchange or exchanges on which they are quoted.

2.3.6.2. The latest price known.

2.3.7. If the securities are not yet admitted to quotation, but are dealt in on markets other than that of official quotation, the most recent prices on those markets insofar as these prices are meaningful; the market on which these prices were recorded and the source from which they have become known.

2.4. Information concerning the issue, in the case of a prospectus published at the time of issue, or if the issue is concomitant with admission to quotation or if it has taken place within the three months preceding such admission :

2.4.1. Any preferential rights and the procedure for exercising them : the negotiability of the rights and what happens to rights not taken up.

2.4.2. The amount of the subscription charges which are added to the purchase or subscription price and borne by the subscriber.

2.4.3. The procedure for payment of the purchase or subscription price.

2.4.4. The period during which the issue is or was open and an indication of any possibilities of early closure.

2.4.5. An indication of the financial establishments instructed to receive subscriptions from the public and of the persons responsible for allotment, where applicable, of the loan.

2.4.6. Indication of the net amount of the issue proceeds.

2.4.7. Purpose of the issue and allocation of its proceeds.

Chapter 3.   Information of a general character about the company

3.1. Status of the company.

3.1.1. Name or style, registered office and, where appropriate, principal administrative establishment, if the latter is different from the registered office.

3.1.2. Date of incorporation and, if the life of the company is limited, the date of its expiration.

3.1.3. Legislation under which the company operates and legal form which it has adopted in the framework of this legislation.

3.1.4. Indication of the company's objects and reference to the Article of the " Statutes " in which they are described.

3.1.5. Indications of the places where it is possible to consult the coordinated " Statutes ", balance sheets and reports, decisions concerning the appointment and dismissal of members of the company's organs, as well as any other document quoted in the prospectus and accessible to the public, and of the place where the dispatch of the latest company report may be applied for. Places where the prospectuses relating to the operations in respect of issue or admission to quotation performed by the company in the course of the past five years may be consulted by the public.

3.2. Capital.

3.2.1. The amount of the capital subscribed and its composition; the part of the subscribed capital still to be paid-up, with indication of the number (or the overall par value) and nature of the securities not yet fully paid-up, broken down, where applicable, according to the degree to which they have been paid-up.

3.2.2. In the case of a convertible loan or a loan with warrants attached and when there is an authorised capital or authority for a contingent capital increase, indicate :

(i) the amount of this authorised or " contingent " capital and, where appropriate, the duration of the authorisation;

(ii) the categories having a preferential right of subscription for these additional portions of capital;

(iii) the terms and arrangements for the share issue corresponding to these portions.

3.2.3. Indication of any person who directly or indirectly, alone or jointly with other shareholders, controls the company, mentioning the amount of his participation and in any case, in so far as it is known to the company, any holding of 25 per cent. or more of the subscribed capital. Mention must also be made of the portions of 10 per cent. or more held directly or indirectly in the company by other natural persons or bodies corporate, whenever this holding is common knowledge.

By joint control must be understood the control exercised by several companies or several persons when they have concluded among themselves an agreement which may lead them to adopt a common policy vis-à-vis the company in question.

3.2.4. If the prospectus-publishing company belongs to a group of enterprises, a description of the group and of the place it occupies therein.

3.2.5. Book value and par value (or accounting par value) of its own securities repurchased or held by the company if these securities are not isolated in the balance sheet; origin and object of this repurchase.

Chapter 4. Information concerning the company's activity

4.1. Principal activities of the company.

In the sections where the description of the company's activity is required only for the current financial year and the last financial year and if it is considered that this period is too short to reflect meaningfully the company's development, it is advisable to add indications about the previous financial years. In so far as the company's development within the reference period has been influenced by exceptional events, e.g., an important merger, these events are to be indicated. If possible, the data should be presented in such a way as to enable a comparison to be made of the trend from one financial year to another.

4.1.1. Description of the company's principal activities, mentioning the main categories of products manufactured and sold and/or services performed. Indicate important new products and, as far as possible, the proportion of the turnover attributable to new products developed within the last five years.

4.1.2. The above description may contain indications concerning the development of the company's relative position in its principal branches of activities, if these indications can be based, as to their significance and comparability, on figures emanating from qualified institutions, and the source given.

4.1.3. Breakdown, by principal branches of activities, of the net amount of the turnover in the course of the past five financial years and, if these figures are significant, the production volumes of the principal products. Any relatively homogeneous activity which contributes more than 15 per cent. to the turnover is considered a branch of activity.

4.1.4. Information on the structure of markets and supplies for the last financial year and for the current financial year and their trend (with, if possible, breakdown of the net amount of the turnover by principal geographical or economic zones, in so far as this information may influence assessment of the net worth, financial position or results).

4.1.5. Location and importance of the company's principal establishments and, if necessary, their development in the course of recent financial years and the current financial year, and information about the real estate owned. Any establishment which accounts for more than 10% of turnover or production is considered to be a principal establishment.

4.1.6. For mining, extraction of hydrocarbons, quarrying, etc., description of the deposits, estimate of the economically exploitable reserves and expected period for which they will be exploited, indication of the period and principal conditions of the concessions and the economic conditions of their exploitation, indicating the state of progress of the actual exploitation.

4.2. Show clearly, if applicable, the company's dependence with respect to the grant, use or expiration of patents and licences, to the conclusion, maintenance or expiration of industrial, commercial and financial contracts, and to new manufacturing processes when these factors have great importance for the activity or profitability of the company.

If this is the case, all that will be required is to give indications about the degree of dependence, to describe concisely, and without divulging industrial secrets, the factors in question which have a particular importance, and to indicate, if they are significant in this respect, the dates of conclusion, obtaining or expiration of contracts, licences and patents.

4.3. Amount of the expenditure effected in the course of the past five financial years for research and development of new products.

4.4. Indications of lawsuits and factors interrupting activities (e.g.: strikes, accidents) which have had or might have a significant impact on the net worth, financial position or results of the company.

4.5. Average numbers employed and their trend in the course of the past five financial years (if this trend is significant) with, if possible, a breakdown of persons employed by principal branches.

4.6. Investments.

4.6.1. Description, with figures, of the principal investments, including trade investments acquired, in the course of the past five financial years.

4.6.2. General indications concerning the investment programme in course of implementation, including its overall cost, its methods of financing, the nature of the investments, in so far as these indications are necessary for assessing the use of the funds collected in relation to the programme as a whole. By investment programme in course of implementation is meant not only the projects whose execution has already started but, more widely, the whole body of investment projects which are inter-linked to an extent such that the commissioning or profitability of the investments already effected or in course of execution depends on the implementation of all the investment projects constituting the programme.

4.6.3. A table showing the sources and utilisation of funds must be supplied, relating to the past five financial years and the current financial year.

Chapter 5. Information concerning the net worth, financial situation and results of the company

5.1. General rules.

5.1.1. Comparative table summarising the annual accounts relating to the past five financial years so as to bring out the essential factors, ensuring however that the rearrangement of the published accounts does not affect their informative value.

5.1.2. The annual accounts relating to the last completed financial year as approved by the general meeting of shareholders must be appended.

If more than nine months have elapsed since the date on which the last financial year was closed, a recent provisional financial statement (which may be submitted without having been checked by chartered accountants) must be inserted in the prospectus, or appended to it.

5.1.3. Should the annual accounts not be drawn up in conformity with the provisions of Council Directive No. .... of ... ,[6] and should they not give a sufficiently detailed and precise view of the net worth, financial situation and results of the company, they must be accompanied by explanatory notes and comments; more detailed disclosure in the prospectus may be called for and explicit mention must be made of corrections and amendments in relation to the published accounts.

5.1.4. If the company draws up consolidated accounts, the information provided for in items 5.1.1, 5.1.2 and 5.1.3 shall, if possible, be given on the basis of the consolidated accounts as well.

5.2. Individual details relating to the enterprises in which the prospectus-publishing company has a substantial holding likely to influence assessment of its net worth, financial situation or results.

These details must be given, *inter alia*, for enterprises in which the prospectus-publishing company directly or indirectly holds at least 25 per cent. of the capital, or when the value of this holding represents at least 10 per cent. of the paid-up capital of the prospectus-publishing company, or when this holding accounts for at least 10 per cent. of the latter company's earnings.

These details must be submitted if possible in the form of a synoptic table in the prospectus unless they already appear in the annual accounts annexed to it.

5.2.1. Name, registered office.

5.2.2. Portion of capital held.

5.2.3. Capital subscribed.

5.2.4. Reserves.

[6] J.O. 1972, C7.

5.2.5. Result of the last financial year.

5.3. Additional individual details regarding subsidiaries and indirect subsidiaries. By subsidiary is meant an enterprise in which the prospectus-publishing company holds shares or " parts " which represent over half that enterprise's subscribed capital or to which is attached a voting power of over 50 per cent. By indirect subsidiary is meant an enterprise in which the prospectus-publishing company holds directly or through one or more subsidiaries or indirect subsidiaries shares or " parts " which represent over half that enterprise's subscribed capital or to which is attached a voting power of over 50 per cent. However, for subsidiaries and indirect subsidiaries located in third countries the details provided for in items 5.3.1 to 5.3.8 need not be given in an individual manner but may be amalgamated with the details provided for in item 5.4.

In addition to the details mentioned in items 5.2.1 to 5.2.5, the following indications are to be given :

5.3.1. Field of activity.

5.3.2. Book value of the shares or " parts " held.

5.3.3. Amount still to be paid-up on these shares or " parts " held.

5.3.4. Net turnover in the course of the last financial year.

5.3.5. Amount of dividends received in the course of the last financial year in respect of shares or " parts " held.

5.3.6. Amount of the prospectus-publishing company's claims on the subsidiary or indirect subsidiary.

5.3.7. Amount of the prospectus-publishing company's debts to the subsidiary or indirect subsidiary.

5.3.8. Amount for which the prospectus-publishing company guarantees, endorses or secures the commitments of the subsidiary or indirect subsidiary.

5.4. Overall information relating to all enterprises referred to in item 5.2 and not referred to in item 5.3 :

Same details as those provided for in items 5.3.2 to 5.3.8 but presented in overall form and broken down as between companies of the country, companies of other member countries and companies of third countries.

5.5. When the prospectus comprises consolidated accounts, there shall be indicated in an annex :

5.5.1. The consolidation principles applied and, if applicable, any exceptions to and deviations from these principles.

The following details are to be indicated, *inter alia :*

    (i) the selection criteria for the companies included in the consolidation;

(ii) the method(s) of consolidation utilised: overall or proportional integration, placing on an equivalent footing;

(iii) the rates of exchange used for the consolidation of the foreign companies;

(iv) the methods of eliminating profits resulting from transactions among the companies of the group;

(v) the way in which the stocks were integrated; in particular, explanations must be provided in the event of the non-elimination of the intra-group profit;

(vi) if appropriate, the details relating to the underlying fiscal situation of the group, taking account of timing differences in the payment of corporation tax;

(vii) the definition of the consolidated turnover;

(viii) the scope of the consolidation of the results (total, partial or simplified consolidation);

(ix) the changes which have occurred, in relation to the accounts published for the previous financial year, in the principles set forth above.

5.5.2. List of companies included in the consolidation, name and registered office. It may be sufficient to distinguish them by a sign in the list of companies for which details are provided for in item 5.2.

5.5.3. For each of the companies included in the consolidation, other than the prospectus-publishing company:

(i) the proportion of third-party interests, if the accounts of this company are consolidated globally;

(ii) the proportion of the consolidation calculated on the basis of the interests, if consolidation has been effected on a pro rata basis.

5.6. When the company performs a significant proportion of its activities through the intermediary of companies controlled by it and managed as a single unit, the details concerning the activity of the company (Chapter 4), its recent development and its prospects (Chapter 7) must be provided for the whole unit in addition to concise details for the prospectus-publishing company individually.

Chapter 6. Administration, Management, Supervision

6.1. Name, first name, place of residence and function in the company of the following persons, mentioning the principal activities performed by them outside the company when they are significant in relation to the prospectus-publishing company (*inter alia*, the most significant directorships and important functions in other companies). The activities of significance for the company performed by these same persons in the course of the past five years if they joined the company less than five years ago.

6.1.1. Members of the administrative, directing or supervisory organs, as well as the other persons who assume the management of the company at the highest level.

6.1.2. General partners in the case of a partnership limited by shares.

6.1.3. Founders, if the company has been established for less than five years.

6.2. Interests of the directors, etc., in the company.

6.2.1. Remuneration paid for the last completed financial year under any heading whatsoever, as a charge to overheads or the profit appropriation account, to the administrative, directing or supervisory organs. Overall amount for each category of organ. In addition, the total remuneration paid to the members of these organs of the prospectus-publishing company by all the companies controlled by it and managed as a single unit must be indicated.

6.2.2. Information about the nature and extent of the direct or indirect interests of the directors and managers or of the persons they represent in transactions which are unusual by their character or their conditions, effected by the company (such as purchases outside the normal activity, acquisition or disposal of fixed asset items, lease contracts with subsidiaries or persons mentioned above) in the course of the last financial year and during the current financial year. When such unusual transactions were concluded in the course of previous financial years and their effects are still being felt, information on these transactions must also be given.

6.2.3. Overall indication of all the loans granted by the company to the persons referred to in point 6.1.1, as well as of the guarantees constituted by the company in their favour.

6.3. Staff benefits.

6.3.1. Brief description of the policy followed with regard to staff benefits and more particularly with regard to profit-sharing contracts or supplementary retirement pension contracts; as regards the latter point, steps taken to ensure provision for them.

Description of the special benefits of a contractual character when the probable trend of the charge they represent is likely to exert a marked influence on this category of expenditure.

6.3.2. Overall indication of all the loans granted by the company to the staff and of the guarantees constituted in their favour.

6.4. Name, address, capacity and occupation of the persons responsible for checking the accounts (e.g.: commissaires aux comptes, réviseurs d'entreprises, Wirtschaftsprüfer, sindaci, etc.).

Chapter 7. Recent development and propects of the company

7.1. General indications concerning the trend in the company's business since the end of the last financial year and comparison with the corresponding period of the previous financial year. When this information is already available in interim reports, it will suffice to append the said reports to the prospectus made available to the public. The following data are to be supplied, *inter alia:*

7.1.1. The net turnover since the beginning of the financial year.

7.1.2. A description of the most significant recent trends in production and stocks.

7.1.3. A description of recent trends in costs and selling prices.

7.1.4. The state of the order book.

7.2. Company prospects.

The prospectus must clearly bring out the fact that this part consists of estimates or intentions which might not materialise.

7.2.1. Brief indications on the projected investment programme in so far as the company has already made firm decisions on this or has prepared the ground by recent financial operations and where the programme is likely to exert an important influence on the company's future financial policy, particularly its self-financing policy.

7.2.2. An estimate concerning the company's commercial and financial prospects may be inserted in the prospectus, provided that it is backed by figures (concerning, for example, the trend of business conditions, of the markets and of the order book, the influence of capital spending by the company and its competitors) and by pointers that are highly likely to prove accurate.

7.2.3. If possible, general indications concerning the profit distribution and retention policies which the company contemplates following or proposing to the meeting of shareholders and particularly, if applicable, concerning the policy on the issue of securities in connection with capitalisation of all or part of the reserves or increases in value, and concerning the operation of any dividend equalisation reserve.

SCHEDULE C:

SCHEME OF PRESENTATION FOR PROSPECTUSES FOR THE ADMISSION TO STOCK EXCHANGE QUOTATION OF CERTIFICATES REPRESENTING SHARES

Chapter 1. Information on the issuer of the certificates

1.1. Name of style, registered office and, where appropriate, principal establishment if this is different from the registered office.

1.2. Date of incorporation and, if the life of the company is limited, date of its expiration.

1.3. Legislation under which the company operates and legal form which it has adopted in the framework of this legislation.

1.4. The amount of the authorized capital, if appropriate, and the amount of the capital subscribed and its composition; the part of the subscribed capital still to be paid-up with an indication of the number (or the overall par value) and nature of the securities not yet fully paid-up, broken down, where applicable, according to the degree to which they have been paid-up.

1.5. Indication of the chief holders of the capital.

1.6. Name, first name, place of residence and function in the company of the members of the administrative, directing or supervisory organs as well as of the other persons who assume the management of the company at the highest level and of the persons entrusted with checking the accounts.

1.7. Objects of the company. If the issue of certificates representing shares is not the only object of the company, the features of its other activities must be set out, those having a purely trustee character being dealt with separately.

1.8. Annual accounts for the last completed financial year. Commitment by the issuer to publish any information required by law, in particular any amendments to the " Statutes ", the annual accounts and publications for the information of security holders, and the places where such publication will be made.

Chapter 2. Information on the certificates themselves

2.1. Legal status. The issue terms must be inserted in the prospectus, with mention of the date and place of their publication.

2.1.1. Exercise and benefit of the rights attaching to the original securities, particularly as regards voting rights—conditions on which the company issuing the certificates may exercise these rights, and measures envisaged to obtain the instructions of the certificate holders—and the right to share in the profit and liquidation surplus.

2.1.2. Bank or other guarantees attached to the certificates and intended to underwrite the issuer's obligations, possibility of obtaining the conversion of the certificates into original securities and procedure for such conversion.

2.2. The amount of the commission and costs to be borne by the holder of the securities in connection with:

2.2.1. the issue of the certificates or " parts ",[7]

2.2.2. the payment of the coupons,

2.2.3. the creation of additional certificates,

2.2.4. the exchange of the certificates for original securities.

2.3. Negotiability of the securities:

---

[7] " Parts " give profit-sharing rights but do not represent any capital value (Translator's note).

2.3.1. Stock exchanges on which quotation is or will be applied for. If it is indicated that other markets will be organized, specify on whose initiative and responsibility.

2.3.2. Any restrictions on the free negotiability of the securities.

2.4. Supplementary information for admission to quotation:

2.4.1. If the securities are to be placed by introduction on a stock exchange: the number of securities made available to the market and/or the overall par value; the minimum sale price, if such a price is fixed.

2.4.2. Date on which the new securities will be quoted if this is known.

2.5. Indications of the tax arrangements with regard to any imposts and taxes to be borne by the holders and levied in the countries where the certificates are issued.

2.6. Competent courts in the event of litigation.

B. *Draft Council Recommendation, submitted by the Commission to the Council on September 26, 1972, concerning the contents of the propectus to be published when securities issued by the States or their local authorities are admitted to official stock exchange quotation*

The Council of the European Communities,

Whereas, in order to contribute to interpenetration of capital markets and at the same time ensure adequate protection for savings, it is appropriate to ensure that information which is sufficient and as objective as possible is provided for present and potential holders of the securities issued by the States or their local authorities when these securities are admitted for quotation on the Official List of a stock exchange; and whereas better information for the public concerning these securities is at the same time calculated to stimulate its interest in them, and thus to facilitate the financing of these public issuers;

Whereas, for this purpose, it would be desirable that the Member States should voluntarily introduce for securities issued by themselves, by another State, or by a local authority a prospectus similar to the one which is required of companies within the meaning of Article 58 (2) of the Treaty by Council Directive No. . . . . of . . . ;

Recommends the Member States to make it a condition of transferable securities issued by a State or by a local authority being admitted or introduced to the Official List of any stock exchange situated within their territory that a prospectus is published or made available to the public which comprises information concerning the prospectus signatories and the operation similar to that specified in Chapters 1 and 2 of the " debentures " Schedule B annexed to Council Directive No. . . . . of . . . and which contains information on the economic and financial situation of the issuer.

Text 7

Proposed Statute for the European Company, submitted by the Commission to the Council on June 30, 1970

The Council of the European Communities,

Having regard to the Treaty establishing the European Economic Community, and in particular Article 235,

Having regard to the proposal from the Commission,

Having regard to the Opinion of the Assembly,

Having regard to the Opinion of the Economic and Social Committee,

Whereas the harmonious development of economic activities within the Community as a whole calls for transition from the stage of customs union to that of economic union; whereas achievement of the latter presupposes, in addition to the elimination of obstacles to trade, a reorganization of the factors of production and distribution on a Community scale in order to ensure that the enlarged market will operate similarly to a domestic market; whereas to this end it is essential that undertakings whose activity is not confined to meeting purely local requirements should be able to plan and carry out the reorganization of their activities at Community level and improve their means of action and their competitiveness directly at this level; and whereas, if such improvement were to occur in the main at national level, it might tend to fragment markets and so constitute an impediment to economic integration;

Whereas structural reorganization at Community level presupposes the possibility of combining the potential of existing undertakings in a number of Member States by rationalization and merger, but these processes can only be conducted subject to the rules on competition; whereas the establishment of European undertakings is the obvious and normal means of achieving that result under the most satisfactory conditions; whereas this is a necessary instrument for attainment of one of the objectives of the Community;

Whereas, however, the establishment of such undertakings meets with legal, fiscal and psychological difficulties; and whereas the measures provided for in the Treaty by way of harmonization of legislation and the conclusion of conventions to enable the movement of companies to be effected by transfer of the registered office and by merger are calculated to alleviate some of these difficulties, they do not

173

dispense with the necessity of adopting a specific national legal system to invest an economically European undertaking with the legal status essential to a commercial company; still less do they eliminate the obstacle which a change of nationality constitutes for undertakings linked by name and tradition to a given country;

Whereas, therefore, the legal framework within which European undertakings must still operate, and which remains national in character, no longer corresponds to the economic framework within which they are to develop if the Community is to achieve its purpose; and whereas this situation, especially because of the psychological effects it produces, may seriously impede the regrouping of companies incorporated in different countries;

Whereas the only solution capable of effecting both economic and legal unity of the European undertaking is, accordingly, to permit the formation, side by side with companies governed by one or other national law, of companies wholly subject only to a specific legal system that is directly applicable in all the Member States, thereby freeing this form of company from any legal tie to this or that particular country;

Whereas the introduction of this uniform legal status effective throughout the Community thus appears necessary for the unimpeded formation and management of undertakings of European dimensions produced by regrouping the forces of national companies;

Whereas the requisite powers to formulate this legal status have not been provided for in the Treaty;

Whereas the purpose underlying the legal form of a European commercial company demands in any event, without prejudice to economic requirements which may arise in the future, that a European company may be formed to effect mergers between companies incorporated in different Member States, as well as to allow such companies to form holding companies and joint subsidiary companies; and whereas it is sufficient, in order to attain the desired economic objectives at the same time as the process of founding a European company through merger and the establishment of holding companies is simplified, to accept as founders—apart from other European companies— only companies incorporated under national law in the form of a *société anonyme, Aktiengesellschaft, società per azioni or naamloze vennootschap* *;

Whereas the form of a European company should itself be that of a company limited by shares, which is best suited, from both the finan-

---

* Translator's note: these are companies limited by shares. For the sake of convenience only, they are together hereinafter referred to by the expression " société anonyme " or, where the context requires the plural, by the expression " sociétés anonymes."

cial and management points of view, to the needs of companies operating at European level; and whereas, in order to ensure that such undertakings may operate on an acceptable scale, a minimum paid-up capital must be stipulated such that these companies have adequate resources at their disposal, but not such as thereby to restrict the formation of European companies by national undertakings of medium size; and whereas the amount of capital must none the less be smaller in the case of formation of subsidiaries;

Whereas to obtain maximum benefit from such uniformity of status, none of the regulations governing the founding, structure, operation and winding up of the European company must be subject to national laws; and whereas it is necessary for this purpose to formulate a statute for the European company containing a full set of standard provisions and to refer back to the general principles common to the laws of the Member States for solution of problems relating to matters governed by this Statute but which have not expressly been dealt with herein;

Whereas in order to ensure uniformity of status it is imperative that the founding of the European company be subject to a system of registration at a central registry, under legal control, to eliminate any possibility of invalidity of the company after incorporation; whereas one specific European legal body should be seised of this control in order to avoid discrepancies of judgment in the scrutiny of deeds and documents prepared by the founders; and whereas the requisite authority should naturally be vested in the judicial body of the Communities, the Court of Justice of the European Communities;

Whereas the Court of Justice must also have jurisdiction, to the exclusion of national courts, to decide whether a European company forms part of a group of companies within the meaning of this expression in Title VII of this Regulation; and whereas, indeed, the existence of a group, which has important legal implications for the management and shareholders of a company, being a member thereof, often cannot be established, in case of doubt, except by analysis of actual relationships between companies in different countries and hence of the *de facto* situations in these various countries, which require appraisal; and whereas an examination of this kind would be very difficult for a national tribunal whose powers of inquiry would not extend beyond the country concerned;

Whereas there are wide differences between the laws in force in the Member States as regards the representation of employees within undertakings and the extent to which their representatives participate in the decision-making machinery of *sociétés anonymes*, these questions should not be determined by national laws lest uniformity in the system of management of the European company be disrupted;

and whereas if national legislation concerning representation of workers at management level can continue to apply, it is nevertheless necessary, in the case of European companies with branches in several Member States, to provide for the formation of a European Works Council with appropriate power to deal with matters affecting a number of branches; and whereas it is equally necessary to allow representation of workers on the Supervisory Board, to enable them to express their point of view when important economic decisions are made upon matters of company management and on the appointment of members of the Board of Management;

Whereas the European company must remain subject to national fiscal requirements, since formulation of a fiscal system solely for the European company might be the source of discrimination, favourable or otherwise, in relation to *sociétés anonymes* subject to national law; whereas, however, allowance should be made in the calculation of the taxable profits of the European company for losses incurred by their permanent branches or subsidiaries in other countries, until taxation of the revenue of the companies can be brought under the exclusive control of their country of domicile for fiscal purposes; whereas it is necessary, moreover, to lay down a procedure for the settlement of possible disputes upon the determination of the domicile of the European company for fiscal purposes and to settle the terms and consequences of transfer of fiscal domicile from one country to another; and whereas, further, the European company is to benefit, on the same basis as companies incorporated under national law, from the provisions of the directive concerning the common fiscal system applicable to parent and subsidiary companies in different Member States and the directive on the common system applicable to mergers, scission and the contribution of assets effected between companies in different Member States, issued by the Council on . . .

Whereas, in order to ensure that breaches of duty on the part of the members of the administrative organs of the European company shall not remain without penalty, it is essential that Member States introduce into their criminal law appropriate uniform provisions for dealing with punishable offences; and whereas it is necessary that all Member States should prescribe penalties for the same offences and only for those offences, in order to avoid disparities prejudicial to uniformity of status,

Has adopted this Regulation

TITLE I: GENERAL PROVISIONS

Article 1

1. Commercial companies may be incorporated throughout the

European Economic Community as European companies (Societas Europaea " S.E.") on the conditions and terms set out in this Regulation.

2. The capital of the European company shall be divided into shares. The liability of the shareholders for the debts of the company shall be limited to the amount subscribed by them.

3. The S.E. is a commercial company whatever the object of its undertaking.

4. The S.E. has legal personality. In each Member State and subject to the express provisions of this Statute it shall be treated in all respects concerning its rights and powers as a *société anonyme* * incorporated under national law.

Article 2

Sociétés anonymes * incorporated under the law of a Member State and of which not less than two are subject to different national laws may establish an S.E. by merger or by formation of a holding company or joint subsidiary.

Article 3

1. An S.E. already in existence may itself establish an S.E. by merger or by formation of a holding company or of a joint subsidiary with other S.E.s or with *sociétés anonymes* * incorporated under the national law of a Member State.

2. An S.E. may establish a subsidiary in the form of an S.E.

Article 4

The capital of an S.E. shall amount to not less than:

500,000 units of account in the case of merger or formation of a holding company,

250,000 units of account in the case of formation of a joint subsidiary,

100,000 units of account in the case of formation of a subsidiary by an S.E.

Article 5

1. The registered office of an S.E. shall be situate at the place specified in its Statutes. Such place shall be within the European Community.

2. The Statutes may designate a number of registered offices.

Article 6

1. For the purposes of this Statute, a dependent undertaking is one which is legally autonomous and on which another undertaking

(hereinafter referred to as the " controlling company ") is able, directly or indirectly, to exercise a controlling influence, one of the two being an S.E.

2. An undertaking shall in any event be considered dependent on another when that other has the power, in relation to the first:

(*a*) to control more than half the votes attached to the whole of the issued share capital;

(*b*) to appoint more than half of its board of management or of its supervisory body;

(*c*) to exert, pursuant to contracts, a decisive influence on its management.

3. A controlling influence shall be presumed to exist where one undertaking has a majority shareholding in the capital of another.

4. In calculating the extent of the shareholding of a controlling company there shall be included the shares belonging to a dependent undertaking thereof. The same shall apply to the shareholding of an undertaking acting on behalf of the controlling company or of an undertaking dependent thereon.

Article 7

1. Save as otherwise provided, matters governed by this Statute, including those not expressly mentioned herein, shall not be subject to the national laws of the Member States. A matter not expressly dealt with herein shall be resolved:

(*a*) in accordance with the general principles upon which this Statute is based;

(*b*) if those general principles do not provide a solution to the problem, in accordance with the rules or general principles common to the laws of the Member States.

2. Matters which are not governed by this Statute shall be subject to the national law applicable in the circumstances.

Article 8

1. Every S.E. shall be registered in the European Commercial Register at the Court of Justice of the European Communities.

2. The formalities concerning the opening and maintaining of the European Commercial Register shall be laid down in rules prescribed by the Council on a proposal from the Commission.

3. Each Member State shall, in its own country, maintain a register supplementary to the European Commercial Register in which European companies, having their registered office in the territory of that State, shall also be registered. Entries appearing in the European Commercial Register and documents filed therein shall in case of con-

flict prevail over entries made in or copies issued out of the supplementary register.

4. The European Commercial Register, its supplementary registers and the documents filed therein shall be open to public inspection.

Article 9

1. All notices concerning the S.E. shall be published in the Official Gazette of the European Communities, in the official bulletins of company publications in the Member State in which the S.E. has its registered office, and in a daily newspaper circulating in that State.

2. The publications referred to in the preceding paragraph are hereinafter called " company journals ".

3. Where this Statute prescribes a time-limit computed from the date of publication in the company journals, such time-limit shall be computed from the date of publication of whichever of the relevant journals shall last be published.

Article 10

The S.E. shall state on its letters and order forms its registration number in the European Commercial Register, the address of its registered office, the amount of its capital and, if it is the fact, that the company is in liquidation.

TITLE II: FORMATION

Section One : General

Article 11

1. Application for registration of the S.E. shall be made to the Court of Justice of the European Communities for registration in the European Commercial Register.

2. There shall be attached to the application:
   (*a*) the document of constitution approved by the founder companies, together with its annexes;
   (*b*) the Statutes of each of the founder companies.

3. In addition, the application shall comply with the provisions of one of the following Sections of this Title, according to the form of constitution adopted.

Article 12

1. The document of constitution shall contain a general statement to the effect that the formation of the company complies with the conditions prescribed in Title I and shall also state the economic reasons for its formation.

2. There shall be attached to the document of constitution:
- (*a*) the Statutes of the S.E.;
- (*b*) the opening balance sheet of the S.E. with explanatory notes;
- (*c*) the auditor's report;
- (*d*) the composition of the first Board of Management and of the first Supervisory Board, where this does not appear in the Statutes.

3. The document of constitution and annexes mentioned in paragraph 2 (*a*) and (*d*) shall be authenticated by notarial act.

Article 13

The Statutes of the S.E. shall state at least:
- (*a*) the name of the company, with the suffix " S.E.";
- (*b*) the address of the registered office;
- (*c*) the precise object of the undertaking;
- (*d*) the amount of the capital, the nominal value and number of the shares, specifying whether they are bearer or registered shares, and, where there are different classes of shares, a description of each class;
- (*e*) the accounting currency of the company;
- (*f*) the period for which the company is formed, where this is fixed.

Article 14

1. The opening balance sheet of the S.E. and the accompanying explanatory notes shall comply with the requirements of this Statute relating to the balance sheet and to the explanatory notes contained in the annex to the annual accounts.

2. The explanatory notes shall show the approximate total expenses borne by the S.E. in respect of its formation and of matters incidental thereto.

3. The explanatory notes shall in addition contain particulars of the capital subscribed in kind, state its value and the names of the persons who subscribed the same and specify the nominal value and class of shares issued in respect thereof.

4. The benefits and special rights granted to each person taking part in the formation of the company shall be fully disclosed in the explanatory notes.

Article 15

1. The auditors' report shall be prepared by one or more auditors appointed by the founder companies.

2. Only persons who are suitably qualified and experienced may be appointed as auditors. They shall have obtained their professional qualifications by satisfying the requirements for admission and by passing a legally organized examination and shall be persons authorized in a Member State to act as auditors of the annual accounts of *sociétés anonymes* * whose shares are quoted on a stock exchange. Auditors shall be in no way dependent on the founder companies.

3. The auditors' report shall consist of a review of the entire operation of formation and, in particular, of:

(a) the opening balance sheet of the S.E. and the relevant explanatory notes;

(b) the valuation of the capital subscribed in kind;

(c) the payment up in full of the whole of the capital.

Article 16

1. If, within two years of formation, the S.E. shall acquire property owned by a founder company, or by a shareholder of the founder company or of the S.E., and the price shall exceed one tenth of the capital of the S.E., the purchase shall in addition be the subject of an audit. The provisions of Article 15, paragraphs 1 and 2, shall apply. The purchase shall be subject to ratification by the members in General Meeting. The auditors' report shall be published in the company journals.

2. Paragraph 1 shall not apply if the purchase had already been agreed upon at the time of formation of the S.E. and the explanatory notes to the opening balance sheet dealt with it.

Article 17

1. The Court of Justice of the European Communities shall examine whether the formalities required for formation of the S.E. have been complied with. A procedural regulation shall prescribe the conditions of this examination.

2. For purposes of this examination, the Court of Justice may, without stating its reasons, obtain the assistance of a qualified accountant, at the expense of the founder companies.

3. The Court of Justice shall refuse registration in the European Commercial Register in the following cases:

(a) the company has not been formed in accordance with this Statute;

(b) the document of constitution or its annexes are incomplete;

(c) the Statutes do not comply with the provisions of this Statute;

(d) the auditors' report does not establish that subscription of the whole of the capital is certain and, in particular, that the value of the capital subscribed in kind is at least equal to the nominal value of the shares issued in consideration thereof.

4. The Court of Justice is authorized to obtain from the founder companies all the information it may require. It may give them an opportunity to supplement or correct their applications.

5. If the Court of Justice finds no reason to refuse or to defer registration it shall order registration of the S.E. in the European Commercial Register and shall forward to the Registry the application made by the S.E., accompanied by its document of constitution and the annexes thereto.

Article 18

1. There shall be registered in the European Commercial Register:

  (a) the name of the company;
  (b) the address of the registered office;
  (c) the object of the undertaking;
  (d) the amount of the capital;
  (e) the names of the members of the Board of Management;
  (f) a statement of the type of constitution as defined in Articles 2 and 3;
  (g) particulars of the founder companies;
  (h) the titles of the company journals.

2. The registration and the particulars prescribed in paragraph 1, together with the conclusions contained in the auditors' report, shall be published in the company journals.

Article 19

1. The S.E. shall have legal personality from the date of publication of its registration in the Official Gazette of the European Communities. As from that date, it shall be treated as having been properly formed in all respects.

2. Any person acting in the name of the S.E., prior to the date of publication, shall be personally liable in respect of his acts; where several persons have acted together, they shall be jointly and severally liable.

Article 20

1. For a period of three years from the date of registration of the S.E. in the European Commercial Register, the founder companies and the persons responsible therefor shall be jointly and severally liable to the S.E. and to third parties for any omission or inaccuracy in the particulars included in the application.

2. The founder companies and the persons responsible therefor shall not be liable under paragraph 1 if they had no knowledge of such omissions or inaccuracies and could not have acquired knowledge thereof by exercising the standard of care incumbent on a prudent businessman. In this context, matters which are within the knowledge of persons responsible for a founder company shall be deemed to be within the knowledge of the company.

3. For a period of three years from the date of registration in the European Commercial Register, the auditors shall be jointly and severally liable to the S.E. and to third parties for any omission or inaccuracy in their report, unless they show that they have exercised the standard of care required in the practice of their profession.

Section Two : Formation by Merger

Article 21

Where an S.E. is formed by merger of *sociétés anonymes*, the entire undertaking of the founder companies, including their assets and liabilities, shall be transferred, in exchange for the issue to the shareholders of the merging companies of shares in the S.E. and, if appropriate, an equalization payment in cash not exceeding 10% of the nominal value of the shares so issued.

Article 22

1. The founder companies shall prepare a draft of the terms of merger, containing:

   (a) the draft document of constitution provided for in Article 12 and its annexes;
   (b) the terms covering the exchange ratio of shares in the founder companies for shares in the S.E.;
   (c) the basis of ascertainment of such share exchange ratio, duly approved by the auditors;
   (d) particulars of issue of the S.E. shares;
   (e) proposals as to the manner in which the rights of creditors are safeguarded;
   (f) proposals as to the preservation of the rights of third parties (not being shareholders) to profits.

2. The following shall be annexed to the draft terms of merger:

   (a) the Statutes of the founder companies brought up to date;
   (b) the balance sheets and profit and loss accounts for the last three financial years of each of the founder companies; the last balance sheet shall have been drawn up as at a date not more than six months earlier than the date for which the first General Meeting provided for in Article

24 is convened; if drawn up as at an earlier date, it shall be redrawn as at the date of the first day for which the General Meeting is convened. It shall not be necessary to draw up a fresh inventory. The values shown in the last balance sheet shall merely be altered to agree with the amendments in the books. However, depreciation and reserves for the intervening period shall be taken into account, together with any material change in the true value not shown in the books.

Article 23

The auditors are authorized to obtain from merging companies all information and documents which they consider useful, and to carry out all necessary investigations.

Article 24

1. The draft terms of merger shall be approved in General Meeting by each founder company. The resolution of approval shall satisfy the same conditions as are prescribed in the case of a resolution for winding up of the founder company. However, at a first General Meeting the quorum required shall not exceed one half of the shares carrying the right to vote; and at a second General Meeting the quorum shall not exceed one quarter of such shares. The majority required for the passing of a resolution of approval shall not exceed three quarters of the votes cast at the General Meeting. If the national law does not provide for a quorum, it shall not be permissible to require for the passing of the resolution of approval a majority exceeding three quarters of the votes cast and four fifths of the share capital represented.

2. From the date of convening of the General Meeting, the founder companies shall forthwith supply at the request of any interested person, upon payment of the cost price, a copy of the draft terms of merger and of its annexes. A note to this effect shall appear in the notice of General Meetings. The notice of meeting shall state, further, that only those shareholders who vote against the resolution in General Meeting and cause their dissent to be recorded in the Minutes may propose that it be withdrawn.

3. At least one month's notice of General Meetings shall be given.

4. Provided that the national law does not require more extensive information to be given to shareholders, each of them shall receive such information as he may request at the General Meeting upon essential points to enable him to make an assessment of the merger, including information relating to the other companies with which the merger is to be effected.

5. Minutes of General Meetings of the founder companies shall be drawn up by notarial act.

6. Minutes of General Meetings shall be filed without delay and at the latest within the two weeks following the General Meeting at which a decision has been taken, for inspection, free of charge, by any interested person. They shall be filed at the place designated by the national law of each of the founder companies for filing of their Statutes. Any shareholder or third party shall, as provided in Article 22, paragraph 1, be entitled to obtain, on request, a complete copy of the Minutes at cost price.

Article 25

1. Resolutions of General Meetings may be challenged only by shareholders who voted against the resolution at the General Meeting and caused their dissent to be recorded in the Minutes. Legal proceedings, whatever the cause of action, shall be commenced in the competent national court within one month of the passing of the resolution.

2. The Court of Justice of the European Communities may, on the application (which shall specify the reasons therefor) of a shareholder who was unable to take the action referred to in paragraph 1, after hearing the founder companies and before registration of the S.E. in the European Commercial Register, grant him an extension of time in which to commence proceedings in the competent national court for cancellation or declaration of nullity of the resolution provided that *prima facie* evidence be produced to the Court of Justice that a breach of the fundamental provisions of the Statutes or of the relevant national law has occurred.

3. The Court of Justice of the European Communities shall not forward the application of the S.E. to the European Commercial Register for registration until final judgment has been given in proceedings for cancellation or for a declaration of nullity.

4. Resolutions of General Meetings shall not be challenged after the date on which registration of the S.E. in the European Commercial Register was published in the Official Gazette of the European Communities.

Article 26

Minutes of General Meetings together with certificates of filing thereof shall be annexed to the application of the S.E. to the Court of Justice of the European Communities.

Article 27

1. The creditors and third parties mentioned in Article 22, paragraph 1, subparagraphs (*e*) and (*f*) may, if they consider that their

rights are curtailed by the merger, oppose the same in the Court of Justice of the European Communities within the two months following the filing of the Minutes, as provided for in Article 24, paragraph 6, stating the reasons on which they base their opposition. Until this period has expired, the Court of Justice shall not direct registration of the S.E. in the European Commercial Register.

2. If the Court of Justice of the European Communities, after hearing the founder companies, considers the opposition justified, it may require the founder company concerned to provide suitable sureties.

Article 28

1. Registration of the S.E. in the European Commercial Register shall be published in the company journals. The merger shall in addition be registered and published in manner required by the provisions of the national law governing the dissolution of the founder companies.

2. The founder companies shall cease to exist, without liquidation, on the date on which publication as aforesaid shall have been made in the Official Gazette of the European Communities. As from that date, the liability of the S.E. shall be substituted for that of the founder companies.

3. By virtue of publication, the shareholders of the founder companies shall become shareholders of the S.E.

4. After publication of the dissolution of the founder companies as provided for in paragraph 1, the commercial registers or the courts within whose jurisdiction the registered offices of the founder companies are situated shall automatically forward the documents of constitution and other documents in their possession to the supplementary registers of the European Commercial Register in the country in which the founder company concerned had its registered office.

Section Three : Formation of an S.E. as Holding Company

Article 29

1. Where an S.E. is formed as a holding company, all the shares in the capital of the founder companies shall pass to the S.E. holding company in exchange for shares in the S.E. holding company.

2. The founder companies shall continue to exist.

Article 30

1. The founder companies shall draw up a draft document of constitution which shall comply with the requirements of Article 12, paragraph 1. This draft shall contain:

(a) a proposal as to the ratio of exchange of shares in the founder companies for shares in the S.E.;

(b) proposals as to the terms upon which the shares of the S.E. shall be issued;

(c) the basis of ascertainment, duly approved by the auditors, of the ratio of exchange of shares in the founder companies for shares in the S.E.

This draft shall be authenticated.

2. In addition to the annexes provided for in Article 12, paragraph 2, there shall be attached to the draft document of constitution the balance sheets and profit and loss accounts for the last three financial years of each of the founder companies; the last balance sheet shall have been drawn up as at a date not more than six months earlier than the date for which the first General Meeting provided for in Article 32 of the relevant company is convened; if drawn up as at an earlier date, it shall be redrawn as at the date of the first day of the second month preceding the date for which the General Meeting is convened. It shall not be necessary to draw up a fresh inventory. The values shown in the last balance sheet shall merely be altered to agree with the amendments in the books. However, depreciation and reserves for the intervening period shall be taken into account, together with any material change in the true value not shown in the books.

Article 31

The auditors are authorized to obtain from the S.E. holding company all information and documents which they consider useful, and to carry out all necessary investigations.

Article 32

1. The draft document of constitution and its annexes shall be approved in General Meeting of each of the founder companies. The resolution of approval shall satisfy the same conditions as are prescribed in the case of a resolution for winding up of the founder company. However, at a first General Meeting the quorum required shall not exceed one half of the shares carrying the right to vote; and at a second General Meeting the quorum shall not exceed one quarter of such shares. If the national law does not provide for a quorum, it shall not be permissible to require for the passing of the resolution of approval a majority exceeding three quarters of the votes cast and four fifths of the share capital represented.

2. From the date of convening of the General Meeting, the founder companies shall forthwith supply at the request of any interested person, upon payment of the cost price, a copy of the draft document

of constitution together with all its annexes. A note to this effect shall appear in the notice of General Meeting. The notice shall state, moreover, that only those shareholders who vote against the resolution in General Meeting and who cause their dissent to be recorded in the Minutes may propose that it be withdrawn.

3. At least one month's notice of General Meetings shall be given.

4. Provided that the national law does not require more extensive information to be given to shareholders, each of them shall receive such information as he may request at the General Meeting upon essential points to enable him to make an assessment of the formation of the S.E. holding company.

5. Minutes of General Meetings of the founder companies shall be drawn up by notarial act.

6. Minutes of General Meetings shall be filed without delay and at the latest within the two weeks following the General Meeting at which the decision was taken, for inspection, free of charge, by any shareholder. They shall be filed at the place designated by the national law of each of the founder companies for filing of their Statutes. Any shareholder shall be entitled to obtain, on request, a complete copy of the Minutes at cost price.

Article 33

1. Resolutions of General Meetings may be challenged only by shareholders who voted against the draft document of constitution and caused their dissent to be recorded in the Minutes. Legal proceedings, whatever the cause of action, shall be commenced in the competent national court within one month of the passing of the resolution.

2. The Court of Justice of the European Communities may, on the application (which shall specify the reasons therefor) of a shareholder who was unable to take the action referred to in paragraph 1, after hearing the founder companies and before registration of the S.E. in the European Commercial Register, grant him an extension of time in which to commence proceedings for cancellation or declaration of nullity in the competent national court, provided that *prima facie* evidence be produced to the Court of Justice that a breach of the fundamental provisions of the Statutes or of the relevant national law has occurred.

3. The Court of Justice shall not forward the application of the S.E. to the European Commercial Register for registration until final judgment has been given in proceedings for cancellation or for a declaration of nullity.

4. Resolutions of General Meetings shall not be challenged by way of proceedings for cancellation or declaration of nullity after the

date on which registration of the S.E. in the European Commercial Register was published in the Official Gazette of the European Communities.

5. By virtue of publication, the shareholders of the founder companies shall become shareholders of the S.E.

Article 34

Minutes of the General Meetings together with certificates of filing thereof shall be annexed to the application of the S.E. to the Court of Justice of the European Communities by the founder companies.

Section Four : Formation of a Joint Subsidiary

Article 35

The document of constitution and the Statutes of the S.E. shall state the names of the founder companies and the amount of the participation of each of them in the joint subsidiary.

Article 36

If one of the founder companies is an S.E., the decision of the Board of Management to participate in the formation of a joint subsidiary shall be approved by the Supervisory Board.

Article 37

The terms of the resolutions of approval shall be communicated with the application of the joint subsidiary to the Court of Justice of the European Communities.

Section Five : Formation of a Subsidiary by an S.E.

Article 38

1. The document of constitution and the Statutes of the S.E. shall state the name of the founder company.

2. Article 11, paragraph 2 (*b*), shall not apply.

Article 39

The document of constitution and its annexes shall be approved by the Supervisory Board of the founder company.

TITLE III: CAPITAL; SHARES AND THE RIGHTS OF SHAREHOLDERS; DEBENTURES

Section One : Capital

Article 40

1. The capital of the S.E. shall be expressed in European Community units of account or in the currency of one of the Member States.

2. The capital of the S.E. shall be divided into shares. It shall be fully paid up, either in cash or in kind. Return of capital is prohibited, save in the event of a reduction of capital.

3. Capital subscribed otherwise than in cash shall be treated as subscribed in kind. Intangible assets shall be treated as capital subscribed in kind provided that they are transferable.

Article 41

1. Any increase of capital shall require a resolution of the General Meeting passed in like manner to a resolution for alteration of the Statutes.

2. The capital shall be increased either by capitalization of available reserves or by subscription of new capital which shall be paid up in full.

3. An increase of capital by subscription of new capital may also be effected by creation of approved capital. This shall not exceed one half the amount of capital specified in the Statutes. Approval may be given for a maximum period of five years, unless the creation of approved capital is contemporaneous with an issue of convertible debentures.

Article 42

1. Where the capital is increased by subscription of new capital, the shareholders shall be entitled to subscribe for new shares in proportion to their existing shareholdings. The Board of Management shall give notice in the company journals of the amount of the issue and of the period within which the right to subscribe shall be exercised. This period shall be not less than one month from the date of publication.

2. In the resolution for increase of capital by subscription of new capital, the General Meeting may exclude, in whole or in part, the right of members to subscribe. This may be agreed upon only where the Meeting has first received a report from the Board of Management giving reasons for exclusion, in whole or in part, of the right to subscribe and for the proposed price of issue. As from the date of notice of the General Meeting, the shareholders shall be entitled forthwith to obtain free copies of this report. A note to this effect shall appear in the notice of Meeting.

3. Where new capital is subscribed wholly or partly in kind, a report as to the value thereof, signed by at least two independent and qualified accountants appointed by the court within whose jurisdiction the registered office of the S.E. is situate, shall be submitted to the General Meeting. As from the date of notice of the General Meeting, the shareholders shall be entitled forthwith to obtain free copies of

this report. A note to this effect shall appear in the notice of General Meeting. The provisions of Article 15, paragraph 2, and of Article 203 shall apply to such accountants.

4. Where the capital is increased by capitalization of available reserves, the new shares shall be distributed amongst the shareholders in proportion to their existing shareholdings.

Article 43

1. Where approved capital is created, the Board of Management shall each year, in the annex to the annual accounts, give particulars of the manner in which it has been employed.

2. Paragraphs 1 to 3 of the preceding Article shall apply. Shareholders shall be entitled to obtain, with the annex to the annual accounts, free copies of the report mentioned in paragraph 3 of the preceding Article.

3. Where the approved capital has been fully applied or has been used only in part but the period aforesaid has expired, the Board of Management shall, pursuant to the resolution of the General Meeting for creation of approved capital, amend the Statutes, as necessary, to show the increase of capital which has been effected.

Article 44

1. Any reduction of capital shall require a resolution of the General Meeting passed in like manner to a resolution for alteration of the Statutes. The reasons for the reduction in capital shall be specified in the notice of General Meeting.

2. The reduction of capital shall be effected by decreasing the nominal value of the shares. The amount of nominal capital shall not, however, be reduced below the amount of minimum capital. Only when losses have been incurred may the General Meeting resolve to reduce the capital to an amount below that of the minimum capital; the General Meeting shall, at the same time, resolve to increase the capital so that it be raised to an amount equal to or exceeding the minimum capital. This provision shall not be treated as inconsistent with Article 249.

3. When the capital is reduced for the purpose of reconciling the same with the capital of the company as diminished by losses and, in consequence of the reduction, the assets are in excess of the liabilities, the balance shall be entered in a reserve account. For a period of three years, this reserve shall not be used for the purpose of distribution of dividends.

Article 45

1. Creditors who consider that their rights are prejudiced by the reduction of capital may, within two months of filing of the Minutes

of the General Meeting, apply to the court within whose jurisdiction the registered office of the company is situate.

2. The court within whose jurisdiction the registered office of the company is situate may, if satisfied as to the merits of the application, order that some or all of the creditors be paid off, or that appropriate security be given in their favour. The alteration of the Statutes shall not be forwarded for entry in the European Commercial Register before the expiration of two months from filing of the Minutes of the General Meeting.

Article 46

1. The acquisition of shares in the S.E. by the S.E. itself, by third parties on behalf of the S.E. or by undertakings controlled by the S.E. is prohibited. This prohibition extends to the taking of any pledge of shares of the S.E.

2. When an undertaking passes into the control of an S.E. in which it holds shares, it shall dispose of them within one year from the date upon which it passes into such control. In the meantime, the shares shall confer no rights on the controlled undertaking. The same rule shall apply in the case of merger.

Article 47

1. Reciprocal shareholding is prohibited when one of the undertakings is an S.E.

2. Reciprocal shareholding shall be deemed to exist where each company holds, either solely or jointly with others, whether directly or through a company controlled by it or through third parties acting on its behalf, more than 10% of the capital of the other.

3. Where there is reciprocal shareholding, the company whose holding of shares is the smaller shall reduce its holding to 10 per cent. within one year from the date on which such companies become aware of the reciprocal shareholding, unless, within the like period, they agree some other method of terminating the reciprocal shareholding. If the shareholdings are equal, both companies shall satisfy this obligation. However, where a company acquires a shareholding of 10 per cent. or more, or increases its holding to that percentage after having been informed by the other company that it has a 10 per cent. holding, the duty of disposal shall fall on the former.

4. After expiration of the period specified in the preceding paragraph, no rights accruing to the holder of the shares shall be exercised if the holdings are in excess of 10 per cent.

5. An S.E. which holds, either solely or jointly with others, whether directly or through a company controlled by it or through

third parties acting on its behalf, more than 10 per cent. of the capital of a company shall forthwith give notice in writing to such company of this shareholding and of any change therein, stating the exact amount. Every company whose shareholding in an S.E. reaches this level shall be under the like obligation. Until such notice be given, no rights accruing to the holder of such shares shall be exercised, if the holding exceeds 10 per cent.

Section Two : Shares and the Rights of Shareholders

Article 48

1. The nominal value of the shares shall be expressed in the same currency as the capital.

2. Shares of different nominal value may be issued.

3. Shares are indivisible. Where more than one person holds a share, the rights deriving therefrom may be exercised only by one common representative.

Article 49

1. Shares may carry different rights in respect of distribution of profits and assets of the company. Promises to pay, or payment of, fixed interest are prohibited.

2. Non-voting shares may be issued, subject to the following conditions:

(a) their total nominal value shall not exceed one half of the capital;

(b) they shall confer all the rights of a shareholder, save only the right to vote; they shall carry the right to subscribe only for non-voting shares;

(c) they shall not be included in computing a quorum or a majority required by this Statute or by the Statutes.

The foregoing provisions of this Article are without prejudice to paragraph 5 of this Article or to paragraph 2 of Article 235.

3. Shares carrying multiple voting rights are prohibited.

4. Shares carrying the same rights shall constitute one class of shares.

5. A resolution of the General Meeting varying the relationship between different classes of shares to the detriment of one class shall be valid only if approved by the holders of the shares of that class. In such a case, holders of non-voting shares shall be entitled to vote. The provisions of Title VIII shall apply in regard to convening, quorum and majority.

Article 50

1. Shares may be issued either in bearer or in registered form. The Statutes may entitle the shareholders to request conversion of their bearer shares into registered shares or vice versa.

2. Registered shares shall be recorded in the company's share register together with the name and address of the holder. Access to the information contained in the share register shall be given to any shareholder at his request.

Article 51

1. Every shareholder shall be entitled to receive a certificate for each of his shares, free of cost.

2. Pending the preparation of the certificates, the company shall, if so requested by the shareholder, issue provisional certificates. Such certificates shall be in registered form.

3. Where, in consequence of any change in the legal position, certificates issued have become inaccurate, the Board of Management may, following a request to the holders to this effect, declare void any such certificates that are not submitted for rectification or exchange. Certificates declared void shall be replaced by new certificates.

4. If a certificate has so deteriorated that it is no longer suitable for circulation, the shareholder shall be entitled, provided that the material content of the certificate remains legible, to request the issue to him by the company of a new certificate in exchange for the old. The shareholder shall pay the costs in advance.

5. When a certificate is lost or destroyed, the shareholder may apply to the court within whose jurisdiction the registered office of the company is situate for cancellation of the certificate and for delivery of a new certificate in its place. The applicant shall cause to be published, in the company journals, a public notice requesting any interested person to notify within three months his actual or potential rights in respect of the certificate. As to any other matter arising in connection therewith, the provisions of the national law of the country in which the registered office is situate shall apply.

6. The provisions of this Article shall apply to provisional certificates.

Article 52

Bearer shares shall be transferred by simple delivery.

Article 53

1. Transfer of registered shares shall be effected by registration in the share register of the company.

2. Registration shall be effected upon production of a declaration of transfer dated and signed by the transferor and by the transferee.

3. The Statutes may restrict the right of transfer. The restrictions shall be clearly stated in the Statutes. They shall not be such as to amount to a complete discretion, on the part of the company, in the matter of approval of a transfer, or such as to render the shares non-transferable in practice.

4. Declarations of transfer made during the four weeks preceding a General Meeting shall not be entered in the share register until after such meeting has been held.

Section Three : Debentures

Article 54

The Board of Management may issue debentures, subject to the approval of the Supervisory Board. The provisions of Article 60 shall apply to the issue of convertible debentures.

Article 55

Not less than fourteen days' notice of any public issue of debentures shall be given in the company journals. The notice shall specify the number, nominal amount, issue price and rate of interest of the debentures to be issued, and the date and conditions of redemption.

Article 56

1. Holders of debentures of the same public issue shall automatically constitute a body whose resolutions, subject to their being passed in accordance with the provisions of this Section, shall be binding on each of them.

2. A meeting of such body shall be competent to decide on any proposal of the company relating to the issue and, in particular, on any proposal which might vary the conditions of issue or vary or cancel any securities.

Article 57

1. Upon a public issue of debentures, the company shall appoint a person who is independent of the company to be the representative of the body of debenture holders. A meeting of the said body may at any time dismiss the representative and appoint another person in his place. In an emergency, any debenture holder may apply to the court in whose jurisdiction the registered office of the S.E. is situate for appointment of a representative.

2. The representative of the body of debenture holders shall represent the latter vis-à-vis the S.E. in any judicial or other proceed-

ings. He is entitled to attend General Meetings of the company and to exercise at such meetings all the rights, excepting the right to vote, of a shareholder, and in particular the right to request and receive information. The company shall make available to the representative all documents which shareholders are entitled to see, or of which they are entitled to obtain a copy.

Article 58

1. A meeting of the body of debenture holders shall be convened by the representative or by the Board of Management of the S.E. One or more debenture holders holding 5 per cent. of the debentures in circulation or a nominal value of 250,000 units of account may, in writing, request the representative or the Board of Management to convene such a meeting.

2. A meeting shall be validly held if three quarters of the debenture holders are present or are represented. Failing this quorum the meeting shall be reconvened. The second meeting shall be validly held whatever the number of debenture holders present or represented.

3. A majority of three quarters of the votes validly cast shall be required for the passing of resolutions.

4. Voting rights shall be proportional to the nominal amount of debentures held. The minimum nominal amount shall carry the right to one vote.

5. The representative or, in his absence, a member of the Board of Management of the company shall take the chair.

6. The provisions governing the convening and holding of meetings shall apply.

Article 59

1. The expenses incurred in convening and holding meetings of debenture holders, in remunerating the representative and in implementing the steps to be taken in the interests of the body of debenture holders and in the preservation of their rights shall be borne by the company.

2. Any disputes between the company and the body of debenture holders shall be decided by the court within whose jurisdiction the S.E. has its registered office.

Article 60

1. A decision to issue convertible debentures to persons who shall thereby have a vested right to exchange or subscribe for shares may be taken only by a General Meeting held in like manner as for passing a resolution altering the Statutes. The meeting shall simultaneously create approved capital, in respect of which the shareholders shall

waive their right of subscription. The amount of approved capital shall be equal to the amount which would be attained if the right to exchange or subscribe for shares were exercised in full.

2. Shareholders shall be entitled to apply for convertible debentures issued unless otherwise resolved in General Meeting.

3. So long as convertible debentures are in circulation, the company shall not alter its Statutes so as to reduce the rights of the holders of convertible debentures unless, not less than three months before the alteration, they be given the opportunity, by notice published in the company journals, of exercising their right of subscription or exchange, or unless approval be given by the body of debenture holders for alteration of the Statutes.

Section Four : Other Securities

Article 61

The company shall not issue to persons who are not shareholders of the company other securities conferring a right to participate in the profits or assets of the company.

TITLE IV: ADMINISTRATIVE ORGANS

Section One : Board of Management

Article 62

The company shall be administered by a Board of Management exercising its functions under the control of a Supervisory Board.

Article 63

1. Members of the Board of Management shall be appointed by the Supervisory Board. The Supervisory Board, on behalf of the company, shall conclude a contract with each member of the Board of Management containing the terms relating to, and the amount of, his remuneration.

2. Only natural persons shall be appointed members of the Board of Management.

3. Where the Board of Management comprises one or two members it shall be composed only of nationals of Member States. In all other cases, this requirement shall apply to the majority of the Board of Management.

4. The Board of Management shall not include persons not having legal capacity or persons who, by virtue of the laws of a Member State, are prohibited from assuming such office by reason of criminal conviction or bankruptcy.

5. The maximum number of members of the Board of Management shall be specified in the Statutes.

6. Where the Board of Management comprises more than one member, the Supervisory Board may appoint one such member as chairman. In the like case, the Supervisory Board shall also appoint one such member to be responsible for personnel and industrial relations.

7. The Supervisory Board may dismiss members of the Board of Management, including the chairman, where serious grounds justify such action. Dismissal shall entail immediate and final termination of office. The other effects of dismissal shall be determined in accordance with the contract and the law applicable thereto.

Article 64

1. The Board of Management shall have full power to act in the interests of the company, save as expressly reserved to other bodies by this Statute.

2. Where the Board of Management comprises more than one member, the members act collectively. Subject to the provisions of Article 63, paragraph 6, members of the Board of Management may divide their powers among themselves; division so made shall be for internal purposes only. The Supervisory Board may at any time make regulations for the internal operation of the Board of Management.

Article 65

1. Where the Board of Management comprises more than one member, each of them shall have authority to represent the company in its dealings with third parties, unless otherwise provided by the Statutes. Provisions of the Statutes to this latter effect may not be relied on to defeat claims by third parties.

2. The Board of Management may appoint agents with power of procuration and authorize them to exercise specified powers of representation, subject to approval of their appointment and of the extent of their powers by the Supervisory Board.

3. Notice of change in membership of the Board of Management, appointment or dismissal of an agent having power of procuration, the extent of the powers which they are authorized to exercise and any change therein shall be given to the European Commercial Register by the Board of Management.

4. Until publication in the company journals of the fact of registration of the contents of such notice, the same may not be relied on to defeat claims by third parties unless the company proves that they

had knowledge thereof. Third parties shall, however, be entitled to plead the same.

5. After registration of the names of the members of the Board of Management and of authorized agents, any irregularity in their appointment may not be relied on to defeat claims by third parties unless the company proves that they had knowledge thereof.

Article 66

1. The following acts of the Board of Management shall be subject to prior authorization by the Supervisory Board:

(a) closure or transfer of the undertaking or of substantial parts thereof;

(b) substantial curtailment or extension of the activities of the undertaking;

(c) substantial organizational changes within the undertaking;

(d) establishment of long-term cooperation with other undertakings or the termination thereof.

2. Apart from the cases mentioned in paragraph 1, the Statutes may specify that certain acts of the Board of Management shall be subject to prior authorization by the Supervisory Board. In the case of paragraph 1 and of this present paragraph, absence of prior authorization may not be relied on to defeat claims by third parties.

Article 67

In its dealings with third parties, the company shall be bound by the acts of members of the Board of Management, notwithstanding that such acts are outside the object of the company, unless the same are *ultra vires* the Board of Management as provided by this Statute. Limitations placed on the Board's powers by the Statutes may not be relied on to defeat claims by third parties.

Article 68

1. Within three months of the closing of each financial year the Board of Management shall submit to the Supervisory Board draft accounts and a draft management report relating thereto.

2. At least once each quarter, the Board of Management shall submit to the Supervisory Board a report on the progress of the company and of the companies controlled by it. Quarterly accounts shall be attached to the report.

3. Further, the Board of Management shall immediately inform the chairman of the Supervisory Board of any matter of importance. Any matter arising within a dependent company which may appreciably affect the S.E. shall be considered a matter of importance.

Matters so referred to the chairman of the Supervisory Board shall be incorporated in the subsequent quarterly report.

Article 69

1. A member of the Board of Management may not also be a member of the Supervisory Board.

2. Members of the Board of Management may not engage in other professional activities, nor accept appointment to the Supervisory Board of another company, unless specifically authorized so to do by the Supervisory Board.

3. Members of the Board of Management may not borrow, in any form whatever, from the company or from its dependent companies, nor obtain from them any overdraft, whether on current or other account, nor procure them to guarantee or endorse their commitments to third parties. This prohibition shall extend to the spouse, ascendants and descendants of each member of the Board of Management, and to any intermediary.

4. Prior authorization of the Supervisory Board shall be required for the making of any agreement to which the company is a party and in which a member of the Board of Management has an interest, direct or indirect. To this end, the member concerned shall advise the Supervisory Board, in writing, of the proposed agreement. Failure to obtain such authorization may not be relied on to defeat claims by third parties, unless the company proves that the third party knew that such authorization had not been obtained.

Article 70

1. In carrying out their duties of management, members of the Board of Management shall exercise the standard of care befitting a conscientious manager and promote the interests of the company and of its personnel.

2. They shall exercise proper discretion in respect of information of a confidential nature concerning the company or its dependent undertakings. They shall exercise the like discretion even after they have ceased to hold office.

Article 71

1. The members of the Board of Management are jointly and severally liable to the company for any failure to observe the provisions both of this Statute and of the Statutes of the company and for wrongful acts committed in the course of their administration.

2. They shall not be held liable if they prove that no fault is attributable to them and if they brought the relevant acts or omissions

to the attention of the Supervisory Board, in writing and without delay, after the same had come to their knowledge.

3. Authorization granted by the Supervisory Board shall not exonerate the members of the Board of Management from their responsibility.

4. The right of action in respect of liability of the members of the Board of Management shall be barred at the end of three years from the date of the act complained of or, if such act was concealed, from the date of its discovery.

5. Where the company becomes insolvent, an action in respect of liability against the members of the Board of Management shall lie also at the instance of the syndic.

Article 72

1. The Supervisory Board and the General Meeting may resolve that proceedings be instituted on behalf of the company in respect of liability of the members of the Board of Management or of any member thereof. The action shall be brought by the Supervisory Board. The Meeting may, however, appoint a special representative to bring the action.

2. An action may also be brought, on behalf and for account of the company, by one or more shareholders holding 5 per cent. of the capital or shares of a nominal value of 100,000 units of account. For this purpose, the shareholders, if there are more than one, shall appoint a special representative who shall be responsible for bringing the action.

3. The plaintiffs may sue for damages in full compensation for the loss sustained by the company, to which the damages and interest shall be paid. If the claim succeeds, the costs of the proceedings shall be borne entirely by the company.

4. If the claim envisaged under paragraph 2 of this Article shall fail, the plaintiffs may be ordered personally to pay the costs both of the company and of the defendants, and, if the action was malicious, to pay damages and interest to the defendants or to the company.

Section Two : The Supervisory Board

Article 73

1. The Supervisory Board shall exercise permanent control over the management of the company by the Board of Management.

At least every quarter, the Board of Management shall submit to the Supervisory Board a report on the administration of the company and of its subsidiaries or divisions. This report shall be concerned particularly with the company's dealings with undertakings within the group.

The Supervisory Board may at any time require the Board of Management to submit a special report on the administration of the company and on specific points concerning its business affairs. It may likewise request information on events occurring within affiliated undertakings in the group, where such events may have a substantial influence upon the position of the company.

It shall be part of the duty of the Board of Management to inform the Supervisory Board, on its own initiative and without delay, if it has knowledge of such events.

2. The Supervisory Board shall advise the Board of Management, either upon request thereof or on its own initiative, on any matter of importance to the company.

3. Save in the cases specifically provided for in this Statute, the Supervisory Board shall not intervene directly in the management of the company nor represent it in dealings with third parties. Vis-à-vis the Board of Management or any member thereof the Supervisory Board shall represent the company at law or in agreements made between the company and a member of the Board of Management.

4. In the event of a vacancy on the Board of Management or if one or more members thereof be unable to attend, the Supervisory Board may, for a period to be specified in advance but not exceeding one year, appoint one or more of its members as alternates. Whilst performing the duties of an alternate, such members shall not carry out those of a member of the Supervisory Board. The provisions of Section One of this Title shall apply to alternates.

Article 74

1. The number of members of the Supervisory Board shall be divisible by three. Where an S.E. has permanent establishments in several Member States, the Supervisory Board shall comprise not less than twelve members.

2. Only natural persons may be members of the Supervisory Board. Their maximum number shall be laid down by the Statutes. Article 63, paragraph 4, shall apply to them.

3. Subject to the provisions of Article 137, the members of the Supervisory Board shall be appointed by the General Meeting for a period, prescribed by the Statutes, of not more than five years.

Article 75

1. Members of the Supervisory Board shall be eligible for re-election.

2. Members appointed by the General Meeting may be dismissed by that body at any time.

3. Where an age limit is specified in the Statutes, members of the Supervisory Board who attain that age shall remain in office until the close of the following General Meeting.

4. If the number of members of the Supervisory Board shall fall below the legal minimum, the Board of Management shall forthwith convene a General Meeting for the purpose of bringing the Supervisory Board up to full strength.

5. Notice of any change in composition of the Supervisory Board shall forthwith be given by the Board of Management to the European Commercial Register.

Article 76

1. The Supervisory Board shall elect from its members a chairman and a vice-chairman.

2. The chairman of the Supervisory Board shall convene the same either on his own initiative or at the request of a member thereof or of a member of the Board of Management. Such request shall set out the reasons therefor. If, within fourteen days, the request be not complied with, the member who made it may convene the Supervisory Board.

3. Members of the Board of Management shall attend meetings of the Supervisory Board unless the latter shall otherwise decide. They shall attend in an advisory capacity.

Article 77

1. The Board of Management shall supply information in writing on each item on the agenda, which shall be settled by the chairman of the Supervisory Board. The agenda and the information in writing aforesaid shall be sent by the Board of Management to each member of the Supervisory Board.

2. Meetings of the Supervisory Board shall not be validly held unless at least one half of its members is present.

3. Unless a greater majority is specified in the Statutes, decisions shall be made by majority vote of members present.

4. Members not present may take part in decisions either by authorizing a member present to represent them, or by sending a written vote through him.

5. In the conditions mentioned in the Statutes, decisions on any specific matter may be made in writing, in particular by exchange of telegrams or telex messages, provided that no objection is raised to such procedure by any member.

6. Minutes of Supervisory Board decisions shall be prepared under supervision of the Board of Management; they shall be examined and signed by the chairman of the Supervisory Board. If no member of the Board of Management is present at a meeting of the Supervisory Board, or if the latter makes a decision in writing, the chairman shall appoint a member of the Supervisory Board to prepare the Minutes.

Article 78

The Supervisory Board shall have unlimited rights of inspection of and control over all company activities; it shall have direct access to ledgers, correspondence, minutes and, in general, all company documents.

Article 79

1. The remuneration of members of the Supervisory Board may be determined by the Statutes or, in default, by the General Meeting.

2. Members of the Supervisory Board may not borrow, in any form whatever, from the company or from its dependent companies, nor obtain from them any overdraft, whether on current or other account, nor procure them to guarantee or endorse their commitments to third parties. This prohibition shall extend to the spouse, ascendants and descendants of each member of the Supervisory Board, and to any intermediary.

3. Prior authorization of the Supervisory Board shall be required for the making of any agreement to which the company is a party and in which a member of the Supervisory Board has an interest, direct or indirect. Failure to obtain such authorization may not be relied on to defeat claims by third parties, unless the company proves that the third party was acting in bad faith. The member concerned shall make his request for authorization in writing and shall not take part in the vote on the application for approval.

Article 80

1. In carrying out their duties, the members of the Supervisory Board shall have regard to the interests of the company and of its personnel.

2. They shall exercise proper discretion in respect of information of a confidential nature concerning the company or its dependent companies. They shall exercise the like discretion even after they have ceased to hold office.

Article 81

1. The members of the Supervisory Board are jointly and severally liable to the company for any failure to observe the provi-

sions both of this Statute and of the Statutes of the company and for wrongful acts committed in the course of their administration.

2. They shall not be held liable in respect of acts in which they took no part, if they prove that no fault is attributable to them and that they brought such acts to the attention of the chairman of the Supervisory Board in writing and without delay, after the same had come to their knowledge.

3. The right of action in respect of liability of the members of the Supervisory Board shall be barred at the end of three years from the date of the act complained of or, if such act was concealed, from the date of its discovery.

4. Where the company becomes insolvent, an action in respect of liability against the members of the Supervisory Board shall lie at the instance of the syndic.

5. The General Meeting and the shareholders may also bring an action in respect of liability against the members of the Supervisory Board under the conditions prescribed by Article 72.

Section Three: Special Obligations Applicable to Members of the Board of Management, the Supervisory Board, the Auditors and Principal Shareholders

Article 82

1. Where the company's shares are quoted on a Stock Exchange, members of the Management and Supervisory Boards and the persons responsible for auditing the accounts of the company shall, within twenty days of acquisition, either cause to be converted into registered shares or lodge with a bank, shares in the capital of the S.E. which are owned directly, or through an intermediary, by them, their spouse or their infant children.

Subject to Article 47, paragraph 5, the same obligation shall apply to any person who holds, directly or through an intermediary, solely or jointly with his spouse or infant children, more than 10% of the capital of the company.

2. Persons who acquire any of the capacities mentioned in paragraph 1 shall forthwith give notice to the European Commercial Register for the purpose of entry therein, of the number, nominal value and, where appropriate, the class, of the shares to which the said paragraph applies, together with the name and status of the owner thereof. An extract from the register of registered shares or a certificate issued by the bank with which they are lodged shall be attached in support of the notice.

3. The like persons shall, further, give notice to the European Commercial Register within fifteen days of the end of each quarter

of the financial year, for the purpose of registration, of any sale or purchase of shares, to which paragraph 1 applies, effected during that quarter, specifying the price paid or received.

4. In respect of each person mentioned in paragraph 1, the European Commercial Register shall keep an up-to-date record of the number, nominal value and, where appropriate, the class, of shares held by him, together with a record of transactions of which notice has been given pursuant to paragraph 3. Any person having an interest may inspect the entries in the register and, on payment of the expenses, obtain a copy thereof.

5. Any profit made by a person mentioned in paragraph 1 on purchase and resale of shares, or vice versa, within six months, for his own account or that of his spouse or infant children shall automatically be the property of the S.E. The amount thereof shall be paid to the company within eight days from completion of the transaction from which the profit arose.

Section Four : The General Meeting

Article 83

Subject to the limitations prescribed by this Statute, the General Meeting may pass resolutions concerning the following matters:

    (*a*) increase or reduction of capital;

    (*b*) issue of debentures convertible into shares;

    (*c*) appointment or removal of members of the Supervisory Board;

    (*d*) legal proceedings on behalf of the company;

    (*e*) appointment of auditors;

    (*f*) appropriation of annual profits;

    (*g*) alteration of the Statutes;

    (*h*) winding-up of the company and appointment of liquidators;

    (*i*) conversion of the company;

    (*j*) merger or transfer of all or of a substantial part of the company's assets;

    (*k*) approval of contracts committing the S.E. in the following respects:

        to pool the whole or a part of its profits or of the profits of one or more of its establishments with the profits of other undertakings or of one or more of the establishments thereof, or to share the profit pooled;

        to lease its undertaking to another undertaking or otherwise grant possession thereof to another undertaking;

        to carry on its business on behalf of another undertaking.

Article 84

1. The General Meeting shall be convened by the Board of Management. It shall be held at least once each year, not later than six months after the end of the financial year, principally to review the annual accounts and the management report. Upon the application of the Board of Management this period may, in exceptional circumstances, be extended by order of the court within whose jurisdiction the registered office of the company is situate, from which there shall be no right of appeal.

2. The Board of Management may convene a General Meeting at any time and shall do so if the Supervisory Board so requires.

3. If the Board of Management shall fail to convene a General Meeting prescribed by this Statute or by the Statutes or as required by the Supervisory Board, the latter may convene the same.

Article 85

1. One or more shareholders holding between them not less than 5% of the capital or a nominal value of at least 100,000 units of account may by requisition in writing setting out their reasons and the items on the agenda, require that a General Meeting be convened. The Statutes may specify a lesser percentage and number of units.

2. If within one month the requisition mentioned in paragraph 1 has not been complied with, the requisitionist or requisitionists may apply to the court for an order that the meeting be convened. The application shall be heard by the court within whose jurisdiction the registered office of the S.E. is situate and there shall be no right of appeal against its decision. If, after hearing the company, the court shall consider the application justified, it shall authorize the requisitionist or requisitionists to convene the General Meeting at the expense of the company, shall settle the agenda and appoint the chairman.

3. Before the dispatch of notice of the next General Meeting, the shareholder or shareholders referred to in paragraph 1 of this Article shall be entitled to require that certain items be placed on the agenda. If the Board of Management shall refuse to include such items within one month, the requisitionist or requisitionists may apply to the court for an order that they be included. The application shall be heard by the court within whose jurisdiction the registered office of the S.E. is situate and there shall be no right of appeal against its decision. If, after hearing the company, the court shall consider the application justified, it shall order the Board of Management to place on the agenda one or more of the items forming the subject of the application.

Article 86

1. A General Meeting shall be convened by notice published in the company journals not less than four weeks before the date of the meeting.

2. The notice shall set out the agenda and the proposals concerning each item thereon.

3. The shareholder or shareholders referred to in paragraph 1 of Article 85 shall be entitled, within one week of publication of the notice provided for in the preceding paragraph, to require counter-proposals confined strictly to items on the agenda, to be published in like manner to the agenda not later than ten days prior to the meeting, unless such counter-proposals would involve a resolution inconsistent with this Statute or the Statutes of the company, or an identical counter-proposal has been rejected by a General Meeting during the previous five years.

4. The General Meeting may pass resolutions upon items not included in the duly published agenda only by unanimous vote of all the shareholders of the company. The meeting may, however, remove one or more members of the Supervisory Board appointed by the General Meeting, and may replace them without the matter appearing on the agenda, provided that one half of the capital is present or represented.

Article 87

1. The members of the Board of Management and of the Supervisory Board shall attend General Meetings in a consultative capacity.

2. Every shareholder and every holder of a share certificate or of debentures convertible into shares is entitled to attend the General Meeting.

3. The Statutes may make attendance at a General Meeting conditional upon the lodging of the scrip certificates with a bank at least fifteen days prior to the meeting and until the conclusion thereof. In such case, the banks shall forthwith give notice of such deposit to the company, indicating the nature and nominal value of the certificates and the names and addresses of the persons lodging the same.

4. In lieu of the lodging of certificates provided for by paragraph 3, the Statutes may require that notice of intention to attend the meeting be given in writing or by telegram at least eight days prior to the holding thereof. If so, the information required under paragraph 3 shall be communicated to the company.

5. Where the Statutes contain such provisions as are mentioned in paragraphs 3 and 4, a note to this effect shall appear in the notice convening the meeting.

Article 88

1. Shareholders who are entitled to vote may be represented by a proxy at General Meetings. Members of the Board of Management, members of the Supervisory Board and employees of the company, or of its dependent companies, may not act as proxies.

2. The appointment of a proxy shall be made in writing and the person appointed shall act without payment. It shall specify the shares in respect of which the right to vote will be exercised. The form of proxy shall be lodged with the company prior to the meeting.

3. The appointment of a proxy shall be valid for not more than six months. It may be revoked at any time. The appointee shall not delegate his powers.

4. No person may vote in his own name in respect of shares belonging to another, unless a form of proxy has been duly lodged. This prohibition shall not apply to companies which manage investment funds.

Article 89

1. Unless otherwise provided by the Statutes, the chairman of the Supervisory Board shall preside at General Meetings, or, in his absence, the vice-chairman of that Board, and in the absence of the vice-chairman, the oldest member thereof. In the absence of any member of the Supervisory Board, the meeting shall elect its own chairman.

2. A list of persons present shall be prepared by a notary. Before opening the meeting, the said list shall be made available in the assembly hall for perusal by those attending the meeting. It shall record the name and place of residence of all certificate holders present and represented, and also the number, description and nominal value of their shares and, if there is more than one class of shares, the class to which the certificates relate. Where a proxy is also attending in his own right as a shareholder, separate entries shall be made.

3. Any person attending a General Meeting is entitled to speak upon matters appearing on the agenda and which the chairman has opened to debate. Any shareholder may make counter-proposals on any item on the agenda. The chairman shall regulate the discussion and may take any steps which he considers appropriate for the orderly conduct of business.

4. The chairman shall determine the order of voting if there is more than one proposition on the same item. The Statutes may provide for a secret vote in respect of the appointment or removal of members of the Supervisory Board; a General Meeting may at any time, by majority vote, decide to the contrary. Voting in respect of

appointments may be by acclamation provided that no objection be raised by any shareholder entitled to vote.

Article 90

1. During the course of a General Meeting, any shareholder shall be entitled to be given information, at his request, by the Board of Management concerning the affairs of the company, where such information is necessary for realistic discussion of items on the agenda. The obligation to impart information shall extend to legal and business matters between the S.E. and its dependent or controlling companies or affiliated undertakings within a group.

2. The information supplied shall be true and fair in all respects.

3. The Board of Management may refuse to give information where:

(a) in the opinion of a reasonable businessman, it would be such as to cause considerable prejudice to the S.E. or to any of its dependent or controlling companies; or

(b) by divulging the same it would commit a criminal offence.

4. Where information is refused to a shareholder, he shall be entitled to require that his question and the grounds relied on for refusing to answer it be entered in the Minutes of the General Meeting.

5. A shareholder to whom information is refused may challenge the validity of the refusal in the court within whose jurisdiction the registered office of the S.E. is situate whose decision shall be final and without right of appeal. Application to the court shall be made within two weeks from the date of closure of the General Meeting.

6. If the plaintiff's right to be given the information is upheld, the Board of Management shall publish the question and the relevant information in the company journals within the ensuing four weeks.

Article 91

1. Subject to Article 49, paragraph 2, each share shall carry a right of vote proportionate to the share of capital which it represents; each share shall carry at least one vote.

2. A simple majority of the votes validly cast shall be required for the passing of resolutions by the General Meeting, save where this Statute prescribes a larger majority.

3. The Statutes may prescribe a larger majority in cases where this Statute does not do so, provided that the majority required shall not exceed four fifths of the votes validly cast.

Article 92

1. The voting rights attached to a share shall be exercised by the person entitled in possession to a life interest therein. Upon a resolution altering the Statutes, however, the right to vote shall be exercised by the legal owner of the share.

2. Voting rights in respect of shares which are in pledge shall be exercised by the legal owner. For this purpose, for a period of fifteen days prior to the General Meeting and until the conclusion thereof, the pledgee shall at the request of the debtor lodge the shares which he holds in pledge with a bank appointed by the company at the debtor's request.

3. A shareholder shall not exercise his right of vote, nor procure it to be exercised by any other person, upon a resolution concerning his own discharge or upon any other resolution in respect of which his own interest is in conflict with that of the company.

Article 93

1. Shareholders may, gratuitously, agree to entrust to one of their number, or to a third party, the decision as to the manner in which their right of vote is to be exercised. All agreements pursuant to which shareholders bind themselves to vote in accordance with the directions of the Board of Management or of the Supervisory Board, or in support of proposals of those organs, shall be void.

2. Notice of agreement shall be given to the company. The agreement shall not take effect, vis-à-vis the company, until such notice has been given. Votes cast in pursuance of such agreement, prior to the notice, shall be void.

3. The names of the parties to the agreement and the total nominal value of their shares shall be set out in the management report. The date of expiry of the agreement shall also be specified in the said report.

Article 94

1. The Minutes of the General Meeting shall be drawn up by a notary. They shall include the items discussed, the comments which speakers have asked to be placed on record and the resolutions passed by the General Meeting.

2. The list of persons present and the documents relating to the convening of the meeting shall be annexed to the Minutes together with the reports to shareholders on items placed on the agenda.

3. Immediately after the General Meeting the Board of Management shall file two authenticated copies of the Minutes and of the annexes thereto in the European Commercial Register.

Article 95

1. Subject to the special procedures and provisions set out in this Statute, resolutions of the General Meeting may, in accordance with the conditions hereinafter contained, be cancelled on the grounds of violation of the provisions hereof, or of the Statutes of the company.

2. Proceedings for cancellation may be brought by any shareholder or by any other interested person who shows that the observance of the provisions is a matter in which he has a proper interest.

3. The proceedings for cancellation shall be brought before the court within whose jurisdiction the registered office of the S.E. is situate, within three months of filing of the Minutes of the Meeting in the European Commercial Register, and shall be against the company. If the proceedings are based on grounds which have been concealed, they may be pleaded within the three months following discovery thereof.

4. On the application of the plaintiff and after hearing the company, the judge may suspend implementation of the resolution in question. He may, likewise, on the application of the company, and after hearing the plaintiff, order that the plaintiff provide security to cover any damage caused by the proceedings or by suspension of implementation of the resolution in the event of dismissal of the proceedings as being unfounded.

5. A judgment ordering cancellation or suspension of a resolution shall have effect in respect of all parties, subject to the rights acquired vis-à-vis the company by third parties acting in good faith. The Board of Management shall forthwith file two authenticated copies of the judgment or order in the European Commercial Register.

6. The judge may not order cancellation of a resolution where the resolution has been replaced by another passed in accordance with this Statute and the Statutes of the company. The judge may, if he thinks fit, allow such time as may be necessary for the meeting to pass such resolution.

Article 96

1. Any resolution of the General Meeting which is contrary to public policy or morality shall be void.

2. Any person having an interest may plead the provisions of the preceding paragraph within three years of the passing of the resolution. Where the grounds of invalidity have been concealed, they may, for a period of three years following the discovery thereof, be relied on as grounds for legal proceedings.

Section Five : Special Supervision of the Administrative Organs

Article 97

Where there are firm grounds for believing that the Board of Management or the Supervisory Board has committed a serious breach of its obligations or a member of either of them has committed such breach of his obligations or that those Boards (or either of them) are no longer in a position to perform their functions and that there is a consequent risk that the company may thereby suffer substantial prejudice:

  (i) shareholders owning between them either 10 per cent. of the capital of the company or shares to the value of 200,000 units of account; or

  (ii) the representative of a body of debenture holders; or

  (iii) the European Works Council

may apply, setting out the grounds of the application, for one or more special commissioners to be appointed by the court within whose jurisdiction the registered office of the company is situate or by the court specially designated by the Member States for hearing such application.

Article 98

1. The court shall deal with the application in chambers and shall hear both parties.

2. If, in the opinion of the court, the application is valid, it shall, at the expense of the company, appoint one or more special commissioners and specify the matters which they are to investigate. Their duties may, on their own application, be enlarged by the court, subject to hearing the company.

3. There shall be no appeal against a decision to appoint special commissioners or, where applicable, to enlarge their duties. Such decisions shall be published in the company journals.

4. The court may require the company to deposit a sum of money or procure a banker's guarantee to be given in respect of payment of fees of the special commissioners. The amount of their remuneration shall be determined by the court on completion of their investigations and after they have been heard by the court. The court may, during the course of the investigation, increase the amount required to be deposited.

5. Special commissioners shall have the same powers as the auditors of the annual accounts.

6. On completion of their investigations the special commissioners shall submit their report to the court which appointed them.

Article 99

1. The registrar shall notify the parties immediately after the special commissioners' report has been filed. The parties shall be entitled to obtain a copy thereof. The court shall act upon the application of the first party to apply.

2. Having full regard to the contents of the report and after hearing the parties, the court may:

(i) suspend from office one or more members of the Board of Management or of the Supervisory Board;
(ii) dismiss them;
(iii) appoint new members to these bodies on a temporary basis.

3. The court shall have power of control over action initiated by it. On application by the company it may curtail or extend the period of suspension. It shall determine the fees to be paid by the company to persons appointed on a temporary basis.

4. The court may make orders for giving interim effect to decisions which it has made under paragraphs 2 and 3. These shall apply in relation to third parties from the date of their publication in the company journals. They shall, further, be registered in the European Commercial Register.

TITLE V: REPRESENTATION OF EMPLOYEES IN THE EUROPEAN COMPANY

Section One : The European Works Council

SUBSECTION ONE: GENERAL

Article 100

A European Works Council shall be formed in every European company having establishments in more than one of the Member States.

Article 101

Unless otherwise expressly provided for in this Statute, organs of employee representation formed in the establishments of a European company pursuant to national laws shall continue in existence with the same functions and powers as are conferred upon them under that law.

Article 102

For establishments situate in the countries hereinafter specified in this Article, the following shall constitute employees' representative bodies within the meaning of Section One of this Title:

(i) The Federal Republic of Germany: the "Betriebsräte" established under the decree of 11 October 1952;
(ii) Belgium: the "ondernemingsraden" or "conseils d'entreprise" established under the law of 20 September 1948;
(iii) France: the "comités d'entreprise" established by the decree of 22 February 1945;
(iv) Italy: the "commissioni interne d'azienda" established in pursuance of the collective agreement of 18 April 1966;
(v) Luxembourg: the "délégations ouvrières principales" established under the law of 20 November 1962 and the "délégations d'employés" established under the law of 20 April 1962;
(vi) The Netherlands: the "ondernemingsraden" established under the law of 4 May 1950.

SUBSECTION TWO: COMPOSITION AND ELECTION

Article 103
1. The members of the European Works Council shall be elected by the employees in each establishment of the European company.
2. Where all the assets and liabilities of a European company having establishments in more than one of the Member States are transferred to another European company, the members of the European Works Council of the European company by which the transfer is made shall become members of the European Works Council of the European company to which the transfer is made.
3. Where all the assets and liabilities of a company incorporated under a national law, or of a European company having establishments only in one of the Member States, are transferred to a European company, the European Works Council of the European company to which the transfer is made shall be enlarged in order to accommodate those members who are elected by the representative bodies of the company by which the transfer is made.

Article 104
The election of members to the European Works Council shall be subject to the rules which apply to the election of employee members of the representative bodies referred to in Article 102.

Article 105
Each establishment of the S.E. shall elect to the European Works Council:
from 200 to 999 employees: 2 representatives
from 1,000 to 2,999 employees: 3 representatives
from 3,000 to 4,999 employees: 4 representatives

where there are more than 5,000 employees, 1 representative for
each additional 5,000 employees.

The same number of alternates shall be elected.

Article 106

Voting shall take place within two months following the formation
of the S.E.

SUBSECTION THREE: TERM OF OFFICE

Article 107

1. The European Works Council shall be elected for a period of
three years.

2. The election of an employee to the European Works Council
shall in no way affect his position as a member of the representative
bodies referred to in Article 102.

Article 108

The term of office of the members of the European Works Council
shall cease upon expiration of the mandate of the European Works
Council, or by their resignation, or by termination of their contract
of employment or by their ceasing to be eligible for membership.

Article 109

1. Two months before the date of expiration of the mandate of the
European Works Council, elections shall be held to choose the
members of the European Works Council for the following term.

2. The first meeting of the new European Works Council shall be
convened by the chairman of the old Council not later than one
month before expiration of the mandate thereof.

3. The old Council shall continue to deal with current business
until the first meeting of the new European Works Council is held.

Article 110

Any member of the European Works Council whose mandate
expires before its normal term or who is temporarily unable to carry
out his mandate shall be replaced by an alternate member.

SUBSECTION FOUR: MANAGEMENT

Article 111

1. After the European company has been formed, the first meeting
of the European Works Council shall be convened by the Board of
Management within one month from the date of the election.

2. The members present at that meeting shall elect a chairman
and draw up its internal rules of procedure.

3. The mandate of the European Works Council within the meaning of Article 107 shall have effect as from the day of the first meeting.

Article 112

No employee who is an actual or alternative member of the European Works Council shall be dismissed from his employment during his term of office on the European Works Council nor during the three years following the period thereof, save upon grounds which, in accordance with the national law applicable, entitle the European company to terminate the contract of employment without notice.

Article 113

1. During their term of office the members of the European Works Council shall be exempt from the obligation to carry out the duties of their employment to the extent to which they consider it necessary for the performance of their duties on the Council.

2. The members of the European Works Council shall continue to receive the wages and salaries and all allowances and bonuses which were payable to them before their election to the European Works Council. They shall be entitled to all benefits and increases in wages, salaries, allowances and bonuses.

Article 114

Present and former members of the European Works Council shall be bound particularly to keep the secrets of the undertaking and its affairs which come to their knowledge by virtue of their membership of the European Works Council and which have been declared secret by the Board of Management. This provision shall apply also to alternate members.

Article 115

The operating expenses of the European Works Council shall be borne by the S.E.

Article 116

1. At the request of one sixth of its members, the European Works Council may decide, by majority vote, that the delegate of a trade union represented in an establishment of the European company shall be entitled to attend certain meetings of the Council in an advisory capacity.

2. The question whether a trade union is represented in an establishment of the S.E. shall be determined in accordance with the law of the country in which the establishment is situate.

Article 117

The European Works Council may, for clarification of certain questions, consult one or more experts if it considers this to be necessary for the proper discharge of its duties.

The Board of Management shall make available to the experts, free of charge, all documentation necessary for their work, save where this would be seriously inimical to the interests of the company. The costs incurred in consulting experts shall be borne by the S.E.

Article 118

1. The European Works Council shall keep the employees regularly informed of its work by such means as it shall deem most suitable for this purpose.

2. The information supplied shall have regard to the interests of the S.E. and shall not disclose secrets appertaining to operations or processes which are specially protected in one of the Member States.

SUBSECTION FIVE: FUNCTION AND POWERS

Article 119

1. The European Works Council shall be responsible for representing the interests of the employees of the S.E.

2. The European Works Council shall confine itself to dealing with those matters which concern the S.E. as a whole or several of its establishments. It shall not be competent in matters which are the subject of a collective agreement within the meaning of Section Four of this Title.

3. The European Works Council shall ensure that effect be given to provisions of law existing for the benefit of the employees of the S.E., collective agreements made in accordance with Section Four, and agreements concluded within the company as a result of its efforts.

Article 120

1. The Board of Management and the European Works Council shall meet at regular intervals for joint discussion.

2. The Board of Management of the S.E. shall keep the European Works Council regularly informed of the general economic position of the S.E. and of its future development. To this end it shall send to it every quarter a report on the preceding quarter. This report shall contain at least:

    (a) a general survey of developments in the sectors of the economy in which the S.E. operates;

    (b) a survey of the development of the business of the S.E.;

(*c*) an exposé of likely developments and of their repercussions on the employment situation;

(*d*) a survey of investment resolved to be made.

3. The Board of Management shall inform the European Works Council of every event of importance.

Article 121

1. The European Works Council shall receive the same communications and documents as the shareholders.

2. The annual accounts shall after adoption be sent to the European Works Council together with the management report.

Article 122

1. The European Works Council may request written information from the Board of Management on any matter which it considers of importance and may give its opinion thereon.

2. The European Works Council may invite any member of the Board of Management to its meetings and request him to provide information on or explanations of certain business operations.

Article 123

1. Decisions concerning the following matters may be made by the Board of Management only with the agreement of the European Works Council:

(*a*) rules relating to recruitment, promotion and dismissal of employees;

(*b*) implementation of vocational training;

(*c*) fixing of terms of remuneration and introduction of new methods of computing remuneration;

(*d*) measures relating to industrial safety, health and hygiene;

(*e*) introduction and management of social facilities;

(*f*) daily time of commencement and termination of work;

(*g*) preparation of the holiday schedule.

2. Any decision taken by the Board of Management in respect of the matters specified in paragraph 1 without the agreement of the European Works Council shall be void.

3. If the European Works Council withholds its agreement or does not express its opinion within a reasonable period, agreement may be given by the court of arbitration mentioned in Article 128.

4. In respect of the decisions referred to in paragraph 1 above, employees' representative bodies set up in the various establishments shall exercise the right to participate, accorded by national law, only when the European Works Council is not competent to do so under Article 119, paragraph 2, first sentence.

Article 124

1. The Board of Management shall consult the European Works Council before making any decision concerning:

    (*a*) job evaluation;

    (*b*) rates of wages per job or for piece-work.

2. Article 123, paragraph 2 shall apply.

3. The Board of Management may make a decision without the opinion of the European Works Council where the latter does not inform the Board of its opinion within a reasonable time.

Article 125

1. The Board of Management shall also consult the European Works Council before making any decision relating to:

    (*a*) the closure or transfer of the undertaking or of substantial parts thereof;

    (*b*) substantial curtailment or extension of the activities of the undertaking;

    (*c*) substantial organizational changes within the undertaking;

    (*d*) establishment of long-term cooperation with other undertakings or the termination thereof.

2. In the cases specified in paragraph 1, the Supervisory Board shall not give the approval required under Article 66, paragraph 1 until the European Works Council has expressed its opinion, save where the European Works Council has not done so within a reasonable time.

Article 126

1. Consultation by the Board of Management with the European Works Council shall be in writing, setting out the reasons underlying a decision and the likely consequences of the decision from the point of view of the business and of the employees.

2. If the Board of Management disregards the recommendations contained in the European Works Council's opinion, it shall state its reasons for so doing.

Article 127

1. The European Works Council may, to the extent that it is competent, make collective agreements with the Board of Management of the S.E. in respect of the matters specified in Articles 123 and 124.

2. Collective agreements made by the European Works Council shall have priority over agreements made by the representative bodies referred to in Article 102.

Article 128

1. A court of arbitration shall be established for the settlement of disputes between the European Works Council and the Board of Management of the S.E.

2. The court of arbitration shall be composed of assessors, half of whom shall be appointed by the European Works Council and half by the Board of Management of the S.E., and an impartial chairman appointed by mutual agreement between the parties. In default of agreement as to appointment of the chairman or as to the assessors in general, they shall be appointed by the court within whose jurisdiction the registered office of the company is situate.

3. The members of the court of arbitration shall be subject to special obligations in the matter of professional secrecy.

4. Decisions of the court of arbitration shall be binding on both parties.

Article 129

1. A court of arbitration shall be established for the settlement of disputes between the European Works Council and the representative bodies referred to in Article 102.

2. Article 128, paragraphs 2, 3 and 4 shall apply.

Section Two: The Group Works Council

Article 130

1. A Group Works Council shall be formed in every S.E. which is the controlling company in a group having establishments in a number of Member States or whose dependent undertakings have establishments in a number of Member States, notwithstanding that such controlling S.E. is itself dependent on another company.

2. Other bodies which represent the common interests of employees vis-à-vis the Board of Management of the controlling S.E. may be formed in place of the Group Works Council. Such bodies shall have, in relation to the Board of Management of the controlling S.E., the same rights and obligations as the Group Works Council.

Article 131

The members of the Group Works Council shall be appointed by:

   (a) the European Works Councils in the companies within the group, where these are European companies in which a European Works Council must be formed pursuant to Article 100;

(b) the employees' representative bodies referred to in Article 102 in undertakings within the group, where these are companies incorporated under national law or are European companies in which it is not necessary to form a European Works Council.

Article 132

The representative bodies referred to in Article 131 shall appoint delegates to the Group Works Council from amongst their own members, in accordance with the following scale:

1 representative for each undertaking with less than 1,000 employees,

2 representatives for each undertaking with from 1,000 to 4,999 employees,

3 representatives for each undertaking with from 5,000 to 9,999 employees,

4 representatives for each undertaking with from 10,000 to 19,999 employees,

and an additional representative for every further 10,000 employees.

Article 133

Articles 111 to 118 shall apply to the operation of the Group Works Council.

Article 134

1. The Group Works Council shall be responsible for representing the interests of the employees of the undertakings within the group.

2. The Group Works Council shall be competent only in matters concerning a number of dependent undertakings or not less than one such undertaking and the controlling S.E. Its competence shall not extend to matters which form the subject of a collective agreement within the meaning of Section Four of this Title.

3. Articles 120 to 127 shall apply to the relationship between the Group Works Council and the Board of Management of the controlling S.E.

Article 135

1. The agreement of the European Works Council required under Article 123 shall be replaced by that of the Group Works Council where it is competent. Article 123, paragraph 4 shall apply to national representative bodies.

2. Collective agreements made by the Group Works Council shall have priority over those made by the European Works Councils or by the representative bodies referred to in Article 102.

Article 136

1. Courts of arbitration shall be established for the settlement of disputes between the Group Works Council and the Board of Management of the controlling S.E., or between the European Works Council in the group and the works council or representatives bodies referred to in Article 102 in the undertakings within the group.

2. Article 128, paragraphs 2, 3, 4 shall apply. The court which shall be competent to exercise the power conferred by Article 128, paragraph 2, second sentence, shall be determined by the law of the place in which the registered office of the controlling S.E. is situate.

Section Three: Representation of Employees
on the Supervisory Board

Article 137

1. The employees of the S.E. shall be represented on the Supervisory Board of the company. They shall appoint one member for every two appointed by the General Meeting. The Statutes may provide for a higher number of employees' representatives.

2. Where the number of employees' representatives on the Supervisory Board does not exceed three, at least one of them shall be a person who is not employed in an establishment of the S.E. Where the number of employees' representatives is four or more, at least two of them shall be persons who are not employed in an establishment of the S.E.

Article 138

1. Employees shall not be represented on the Supervisory Board if not less than two thirds of the employees of the S.E. so decide.

2. A decision to this effect may be taken only once during the terms of office of the Supervisory Board.

Article 139

1. The members of the representative bodies referred to in Article 102 shall elect representatives of the employees to the Supervisory Board. They shall not be bound by the decisions and instructions of the bodies of which they are members.

2. Each member shall have a number of votes equal to the number of employees in his establishment divided by the number of members of the representative body in that establishment. A fraction of a vote greater than one half shall be counted as a whole vote.

3. Election shall be by list.

4. The list of nominations must contain the names of as many candidates as there are posts to be filled on the Supervisory Board. An alternate shall be elected for each candidate.

5. The list of nominations shall take account of the matters specified in Article 137, paragraph 2. It shall include candidates of different nationalities in proportion to the number of employees in each of the Member States.

6. The list adopted shall be that which receives the most votes and at least one half of the votes polled.

7. If the majority required is not obtained on the first poll, a second poll shall be held. In this poll, voting shall take place only on the two lists which gained most votes during the first poll. The list adopted shall be that which receives the most votes.

Article 140

1. Lists of candidates may be submitted by the representative bodies referred to in Article 102, by the European Works Council, by the trade unions represented in the establishments of the S.E. and by the employees of the S.E. The Group Works Council may also submit lists of candidates for election to the Supervisory Board of an S.E. which is the controlling company of a group within the meaning of Article 223.

2. The lists of candidates submitted by employees shall be signed by not less than one tenth of the total number of employees in the S.E. or by not less than 100 employees of the S.E.

Article 141

1. The election shall be held during the two months following formation of the S.E.

2. Two months before expiration of the term of office of the Supervisory Board, elections shall be held to choose the employees' representatives for the following term.

Article 142

The Supervisory Board shall, notwithstanding that election of the employees' representatives shall not have taken place within the two months following formation of the S.E. or prior to commencement of a new term of office of the Supervisory Board, be entitled to exercise its powers through the members elected by the General Meeting, until such time as the employees' representatives shall be elected.

Article 143

1. Before the election, an electoral commission shall be appointed.

2. The electoral commission shall be responsible for preparing and holding the election and also for voting in pursuance of Article 138.

3. The electoral commission shall be composed of members of the representative bodies referred to in Article 102 in proportion to

the number of employees whom they represent. The number of such members shall not exceed twenty-five.

4. The members of the electoral commission shall not be bound by the decisions or instructions of the representative bodies of which they are members.

Article 144

The members of the Supervisory Board elected by the employees shall hold office for the same period as those appointed by the General Meeting. Articles 108 and 110 shall apply.

Article 145

Employees' representatives on the Supervisory Board shall have the same rights and duties as the other members of the Supervisory Board. They shall enjoy the same protection in the matter of dismissal as members of the European Works Council.

Section Four : Establishment of Conditions of Employment

Article 146

The conditions of employment which shall apply to the employees of the S.E. may be regulated by collective agreement made between the S.E. and the trade unions represented in its establishments.

Article 147

1. The conditions of employment governed by a collective agreement shall apply directly to and be binding on all employees of the S.E. who are members of a trade union which is party to that collective agreement.

2. It may be made a term of the contract of employment concluded between an S.E. and an employee to whom a collective agreement does not directly apply under the foregoing paragraph, that the conditions of employment contained in the collective agreement shall be incorporated in the contract.

TITLE VI: PREPARATION OF THE ANNUAL ACCOUNTS

Section One : General Provisions

Article 148

1. The annual accounts shall comprise the balance sheet, the profit and loss account, and the notes on the accounts. These shall constitute a composite whole.

2. The annual accounts shall be drawn up in accordance with regular and proper accounting principles.

3. They shall be presented clearly and accurately. Subject to the provisions on valuation and classification, they shall reflect as true and fair a view as possible of the company's assets, liabilities, financial position and results.

4. The methods of valuation and classification used in consecutive annual accounts, and particularly their manner of presentation, shall be consistent. Legitimate departures from these may be made in exceptional cases and must be duly explained and justified in the notes on the accounts.

Article 149

The provisions of Sections One to Six of this Title shall not apply to S.E.s the object of whose business is the making of loans (banks) or of contracts of insurance (insurance companies). The law of the Member State from which such companies are actually managed shall apply in place of those provisions.

Section Two : Classification of the Annual Accounts

SUBSECTION ONE : GENERAL PROVISIONS

Article 150

1. In both the balance sheet and the profit and loss account, the items specified in Subsections Two and Four of this Section shall always be shown separately. Items preceded by an Arabic numeral may be classified differently where the special nature of the undertaking so requires. A true and fair view must be reflected notwithstanding any different classification, which must in any event be explained in the notes on the accounts.

2. Balance sheet and the profit and loss account items preceded by an Arabic numeral which in relation to the size of the company are of minor importance may be lumped together.

3. Comparative figures for the previous financial year shall be shown in respect of each item in the balance sheet and the profit and loss account.

Article 151

Assets shall not be shown net of liabilities, nor income net of charges, or vice versa.

SUBSECTION TWO: BALANCE SHEET

Article 152

The balance sheet shall be drawn up either in the horizontal (Art. 153) or in the narrative (Art. 154) form of presentation.

Article 153

Horizontal form of presentation

The following items shall be shown on the assets side:

A. Costs of formation

B. Fixed assets

    I. Intangible assets:

        1. Research and development costs,

        2. Concessions, patents, licences, trade-marks and similar rights which:

            (*a*) were acquired for consideration and are not to be included under 3, or

            (*b*) were created by the company itself,

        3. " Derivativer Firmenwert ", " goodwill ", " fonds de commerce ", " avviamento ",

        4. Work in progress and prepayments on account of intangible assets.

    II. Tangible assets:

        1. Land and buildings,

        2. Industrial plant and machinery,

        3. Other plant and industrial and commercial equipment,

        4. Plant under construction and prepayments on account of tangible assets.

    III. Investments and other financial assets:

        1. Investments other than those included under B-III-2,

        2. Holdings in associated companies,

        3. Securities representing financial assets other than those included under B-III-1 and 2,

        4. Claims on companies in which the S.E. holds an investment,

        5. Claims on associated companies,

        6. Other claims.

C. Current assets:

    I. Stocks:

        1. Raw materials and auxiliary materials including fuel,

        2. Products in course of manufacture, including rejects,

        3. Finished products and goods for resale,

        4. Prepayments on account of stocks.

    II. Debtors:

    (Amounts becoming due and payable within one year shall be shown separately in each case.)

        1. Debtors (trade),

   2. Debtors (undertakings in which the S.E. holds an investment),
   3. Debtors (associated companies),
   4. Miscellaneous.

  III. Securities forming part of current assets and other liquid assets:
   1. Bills of exchange,
   2. Other securities forming part of current assets except cheques included under 3,
   3. Balances with banks and on post office current accounts, cheques and cash.

D. Pre-payments

E. Loss per balance sheet

The following items shall be shown on the liabilities side:

   I. Share capital:

   Different classes of shares, if any, shall be shown separately, stating the nominal amount of each share.

  II. Reserves:
   1. Balance on share premium account,
   2. Reserves arising on revaluation,
   3. Reserves for intangible assets,
   4. Statutory reserves,
   5. Free reserves.

 III. Depreciation not shown on the assets side:
   1. Depreciation of costs of formation,
   2. Depreciation of intangible assets,
   3. Depreciation of tangible assets,
   4. Depreciation of investments and other financial assets.

   (Items included under 2 to 4 should be broken down in the same way as the corresponding assets.)

  IV. Provision for depreciation, where the provision is not shown on the assets side:
   1. Of intangible assets,
   2. Of tangible assets,
   3. Of investments and other financial assets.

   (Items included under 1 to 3 should be broken down in the same way as the corresponding assets.)

V. Provisions for contingencies and charges:
  1. Pensions and similar commitments,
  2. Taxation (provision for future taxation being shown separately),
  3. Miscellaneous.

VI. Creditors:

(In respect of each of the following headings, debts becoming due and payable within one year and fully secured debts shall be shown separately.)
  1. Loans (convertible loans being shown separately),
  2. Bank borrowings,
  3. Prepayments on orders received,
  4. Suppliers of goods and services,
  5. Bills of exchange,
  6. Creditors (companies in which the S.E. holds an investment),
  7. Creditors (associated companies),
  8. Miscellaneous.

VII. Accruals.

VIII. Profit per balance sheet.

Article 154
Balance sheet in narrative form.

Article 155
1. Where an asset or a liability relates to more than one item in the balance sheet, this fact shall be stated, where it is necessary to a proper understanding of the balance sheet, against the item under which it is shown.

2. Investments in associated companies shall be shown only under the item which relates thereto.

Article 156
The following, unless required to be shown on the liabilities side, shall be set out separately at the end of the balance sheet or in the notes on the accounts:

1. Contingent liabilities on bills of exchange issued and negotiated, indemnities, guarantees and similar commitments,

2. Any financial obligations incurred for an amount exceeding 100,000 units of account and for a term exceeding one year.

Liabilities incurred towards associated companies are to be shown separately.

SUBSECTION THREE: PARTICULARS CONCERNING CERTAIN ITEMS IN THE BALANCE SHEET

Article 157

Costs of formation shall include, in particular, costs of incorporation and of issue of capital, expenses incurred on inauguration, expansion or reconstitution of the undertaking, and discounts.

Article 158

1. Whether a particular asset is to be classified as fixed or current shall depend upon its purpose.

2. Fixed assets shall comprise only those which are permanently used to enable the company to operate.

3. Where the classification of a fixed asset is in doubt, an indication of the item under which it has been included shall be given either in the balance sheet or in the notes on the accounts.

4. The balance sheet or the notes on the accounts shall indicate the changes in fixed assets that have taken place; using as starting point the purchase price or initial production cost of the replacement cost severally for each item of fixed assets, there shall be shown by way of total as at the date of the balance sheet, first, the assets acquired, assets disposed of, transfers and appreciations in value during the accounting period and, secondly, depreciation and provisions for depreciation. If depreciation and provisions therefor are shown in the balance sheet they may be entered either:

(a) on the assets side, or
(b) on the liabilities side.

5. Paragraph 4 shall equally apply to the treatment of costs of formation.

Article 159

Under research and development costs there shall be included only the research and development costs relating to particular products and processes.

Article 160

Under " Land and buildings " shall be included land, whether built on or not, and any buildings erected thereon including their fixtures.

Article 161

1. Investments for the purposes of this Title shall mean rights of participation, whether or not represented by scrip certificates, in other undertakings, which rights are intended, by establishing a permanent link with those undertakings, to promote the company's own business.

Ownership of 10 per cent. of the shares in the capital of a company limited by shares shall be deemed to constitute an investment.

2. Associated companies shall mean legally autonomous companies existing inside or outside the Member States which, in relation to the S.E., are dependent or controlling undertakings (Art. 6), undertakings forming part of the same group (Art. 223) or undertakings under the same management as the S.E. but in such manner that none of them is a dependent or controlling company.

Article 162

Under " Prepayments " there shall be shown, on the assets side, expenditure incurred during the accounting period but relating to a subsequent period.

Article 163

Provision in respect of intangible assets shall be the adjusting item for " Research and development costs " on the assets side and for the intangible assets referred to in Article 153 at B-I-2 (*b*).

Article 164

1. Under depreciation there shall be included all losses in value definitively sustained as at the date of the balance sheet.

2. Provisions for depreciation shall be the adjusting items for losses in value of assets which have not yet definitively been sustained but which are to be expected in the light of prudent valuation.

Article 165

Under " Provisions for contingencies and charges " there shall be included:

1. Debts whose origin, existence or amount is doubtful;
2. Losses which may arise from current operations;
3. Charges arising during the financial year but involving expenditure only in a subsequent year.

Article 166

Under " Accruals " there shall be shown, on the liabilities side, income received before the date of the balance sheet but attributable to a subsequent financial year.

SUBSECTION FOUR: CLASSIFICATION OF THE
PROFIT AND LOSS ACCOUNT

Article 167

The profit and loss account shall be prepared in accordance with one of the following methods.

Article 168

  I. Trading results (excluding income and expenditure, if any, included under II):

1. Net turnover,
2. Changes in stocks of finished and semi-finished products,
3. Other goods and services supplied by the undertaking to itself,
4. Other trading income arising out of the operations of the undertaking,
5. Raw materials and auxiliary materials including fuel,
6. Labour costs,
7. Depreciation of costs of formation,
8. Depreciation and provisions for depreciation of intangible and tangible assets,
9. Other trading costs,
10. Trading profit or loss.

 II. Financial results:

11. Income arising under agreements requiring transfer of profits, whether relating to the whole or part of the profits, income from associated undertakings being shown separately,
12. Income from trade investments, other than income shown under II-11, income from associated undertakings being shown separately,
13. Income from other securities held and from claims forming part of the financial assets, income from associated undertakings being shown separately,
14. Other interest and similar income, that from associated undertakings being shown separately,
15. Expenditure arising from absorption of losses,
16. Depreciation and provisions for depreciation of investments and other fixed financial assets,
17. Interest and similar charges, those arising in respect of associated undertakings being shown separately,
18. Financial profit or loss.

III. Non-recurring income and expenditure:

19. Non-recurring income
20. Non-recurring expenditure
21. Balance of non-recurring items
22. Subtotal

IV. Taxation:
    23. Taxation of profits
        (*a*) current
        (*b*) future
    24. Other taxes not included under I, II or III above
    25. Subtotal

  V. Set-off or transfer of profit or loss:
    26. Income arising as a result of set-off of losses
    27. Profits transferred under agreement requiring transfer of profits, whether relating to the whole or a part of the profits

  VI. Profit for the year/Loss for the year

  VII. Profit or loss brought forward from the previous year:
    28. Subtotal

VIII. Changes in reserves:
    29. Withdrawals from reserves
    30. Appropriation of profit for the year to reserves

  IX. Profit/Loss to balance sheet

Article 169

A. *Expenditure*

  I. Trading costs (excluding those, if any, included under II):
    1. Reduction in stocks of finished and semi-finished products
    2. Raw materials and auxiliary materials including fuel
    3. Labour costs
    4. Depreciation of costs of formation
    5. Depreciation and provisions for depreciation of intangible and tangible assets
    6. Other trading costs

  II. Financial expenditure:
    1. Expenditure arising from absorption of losses
    2. Depreciation and provisions for depreciation of investments and other fixed financial assets
    3. Interest and similar charges, those arising in respect of associated undertakings being shown separately

  III. Non-recurring expenditure

  IV. Taxation:
    1. Taxation of profits
        (*a*) current
        (*b*) future
    2. Other taxes not included under I, II or III above

V. Profits transferred under agreement requiring transfer of profits, whether relating to the whole or a part of the profits

VI. Profit:
1. Loss brought forward from the previous year
2. Appropriation of profit for the year to reserves
3. Profit to balance sheet

B. *Income*

I. Trading income (excluding income, if any, included under II):
1. Net turnover
2. Increase in stocks of finished and semi-finished products
3. Other goods and services supplied by the undertaking to itself
4. Other trading income

II. Financial income:
1. Income arising under agreements requiring transfer of profits, whether relating to the whole or a part of the profits, income from associated undertakings being shown separately,
2. Income from trade investments other than as shown under II-1, income from associated undertakings being shown separately,
3. Income from other securities held and from claims forming part of the financial assets, income from associated undertakings being shown separately,
4. Other interest and similar income, that from associated undertakings being shown separately

III. Non-recurring income

IV. Income arising as a result of set-off of losses

V. Losses:
1. Profit brought forward from the previous year
2. Withdrawals from reserves
3. Loss to balance sheet

Article 170

I. Trading results (excluding any income and expenditure, if any, shown under II):
1. Net turnover,
2. Production costs of goods and services supplied (including depreciation and provisions for depreciation),

3. Gross trading profit,
4. Distribution costs (including depreciation and provisions for depreciation),
5. General administration expenses (including depreciation and provisions for depreciation),
6. Other trading income,
7. Trading profit or loss.

II. Financial results:

8. Income arising under agreements requiring transfer of profits whether relating to the whole or a part of the profits, income from associated undertakings being shown separately,
9. Income from trade investments, other than income shown under II-8, income from associated undertakings being shown separately,
10. Income from other securities held and from claims forming part of the financial assets, income from associated undertakings being shown separately,
11. Other interest and similar income, that from associated undertakings being shown separately,
12. Expenditure arising from absorption of losses,
13. Depreciation and provisions for depreciation of investments and other fixed financial assets,
14. Interest and similar charges, those arising in respect of associated undertakings being shown separately,
15 Financial profit or loss.

III. Non-recurring income and expenditure:

16. Non-recurruing income,
17. Non-recurring expenditure,
18. Balance of non-recurring items,
19. Subtotal.

IV. Taxation:

20. Taxation of profits,
    (*a*) current,
    (*b*) future,
21. Other taxes not included under I, II or III above,
22. Subtotal.

V. Set-off or transfer of profit or loss:

23. Income arising as a result of set-off of losses,
24. Profits transferred under agreement requiring transfer of profits, whether relating to the whole or a part of the profits.

VI. Profit for the year/Loss for the year.

VII. Profit or loss brought forward from the previous year:

    25. Subtotal.

VIII. Changes in reserves:

    26. Withdrawals from reserves,

    27. Appropriation of profit for the year to reserves.

IX. Profit/Loss to balance sheet.

Article 171

A. *Expenditure*

I. Trading costs (excluding those, if any, included under II):

    1. Production costs of goods and services supplied (including depreciation and provisions for depreciation),

    2. Distribution costs (including depreciation and provisions for depreciation),

    3. General administration expenses (including depreciation and provisions for depreciation).

II. Financial expenditure:

    1. Expenditure arising from absorption of losses,

    2. Depreciation and provisions for depreciation of investments and other fixed financial assets,

    3. Interest and similar charges, those arising in respect of associated undertakings being shown separately.

III. Non-recurring expenditure.

IV. Taxation:

    1. Taxation of profits,

        (*a*) current,

        (*b*) future,

    2. Other taxes not included under I, II or III above.

V. Profits transferred under agreement requiring transfer of profits, whether relating to the whole or a part of the profits.

VI. Profits:

    1. Loss brought forward from the previous year,

    2. Appropriation of profit for the year to reserves,

    3. Profit to balance sheet.

B. *Income*

I. Trading income (excluding income, if any, included under II):

    1. Net turnover,

    2. Other trading income.

II. Financial income:

1. Income arising under agreements requiring transfer of profits, whether relating to the whole or a part of the profits, income from associated undertakings being shown separately,

2. Income from trade investments other than as shown under II-1, income from associated undertakings being shown separately,

3. Income from other securities held and from claims forming part of the financial assets, income from associated undertakings being shown separately,

4. Other interest and similar income, that from associated undertakings being shown separately.

III. Non-recurring income.

IV. Income arising as a result of set-off of losses.

V. Losses:

1. Profit brought forward from the previous year,

2. Withdrawals from reserves,

3. Loss to balance sheet.

Subsection Five: Particulars Concerning Certain Items in the Profit and Loss Account

Article 172

" Net turnover " shall comprise the receipts from sale of the products, goods and services which it is the company's normal business to supply, less any reductions in selling prices, value added tax and other taxes calculated on turnover.

Article 173

Under " Other goods and services supplied by the undertaking to itself " shall be shown all goods and services supplied by the undertaking and applied for its own internal use, where these are included in the assets, but excluding increases in stocks of finished and semi-finished products.

Article 174

Under " Expenditure arising as a result of absorption of losses " shall be shown losses incurred by other companies which the S.E. is committed to absorb.

Article 175

1. Under " Non-recurring income " and " Non-recurring expenditure " shall be shown income and expenditure which is attri-

butable to another financial year and income and expenditure arising otherwise than as a result of the company's normal activities.

2. If these items of income and expenditure are not unimportant for the purpose of assessing the results, they shall be shown as a separate item in the profit and loss account or in the notes on the accounts.

Article 176
Under " Taxation of profits " shall be shown the actual amount of tax payable in respect of the financial year and also, separately, the amount of any future tax liabilities.

Article 177
Under " Income arising from absorption of losses " shall be shown expenditure repayable by third parties pursuant to agreements for pooling of losses.

Article 178
Under "Appropriation of profit for the year to reserves " shall be shown the amount of profit for the year which the Board of Management and the Supervisory Board decide to appropriate to reserves in accordance with Article 217, paragraph 1.

Section Three : Evaluation of Items in the Annual Accounts

SUBSECTION ONE: GENERAL PRINCIPLES

Article 179
1. The following general principles shall be applied in evaluating items for purposes of the annual accounts:

(a) Only profits earned as at the date of the balance sheet shall be included; proper allowance shall, however, be made for all risks foreseeable at that date.

(b) Proper allowance shall be made for any items involving losses which come to light after the date of the balance sheet but before it has been finalized, where the same have arisen during the financial year to which the annual accounts relate.

(c) Proper allowance shall be made for any depreciation in value, irrespective of whether the financial year closes with a loss or a profit.

(d) All assets and liabilities shall be valued separately.

(e) The closing balance sheet relating to one financial year shall match up with the opening balance sheet relating to the following year.

2. Exceptions may be made in applying these general principles

where special circumstances so require. The exceptions, and the reasons therefor, shall be duly explained in the notes on the accounts.

Article 180

Articles 182 to 189 shall apply to the valuation of items comprised in the annual accounts.

Article 181

1. In place of the valuation rules referred to in Article 180, the replacement cost method of valuation may be used. The notes on the accounts shall specify the items which have been valued on this basis.

2. Where the replacement cost method of valuation is used the following rules shall apply:

(a) Differences arising as a result of the application of the replacement cost method of valuation in place of the valuation rules referred to in Article 180 shall be included under " Reserves arising on revaluation ".

(b) Revaluation reserves may be written back only if the amounts transferred thereto are no longer required for the purpose of replacement of assets. If no longer required for that purpose, they shall be written back. These amounts shall be added to the profit for the year or shall be deducted from the loss for the year. They shall be shown in the profit and loss account as a separate item.

(c) Subject to Article 41, revaluation reserves may be capitalized.

(d) The differences referred to in 2 (a) shall, in the notes on the accounts, be shown separately at least in respect of the following items:

    I. Balance sheet:

        (1) Fixed assets:

            (a) Intangible assets,

            (b) Tangible assets,

            (c) Trade investments and other fixed financial assets.

        (2) Current assets.

    II. Profit and loss account:

        (1) Depreciation of fixed assets:

            (a) Intangible assets,

            (b) Tangible assets,

            (c) Trade investments and other fixed financial assets.

        (2) Provisions for depreciation of fixed assets:

            (a) Intangible assets,

            (b) Tangible assets,

            (c) Trade investments and other fixed financial assets.

(*e*) Depreciation and provisions for depreciation shall be calculated annually on the basis of the replacement cost arrived at for the year in question.

(*f*) In addition, Articles 182 to 189 shall apply.

SUBSECTION TWO: VALUATION RULES

Article 182

1. (*a*) Items of fixed assets shall be shown in the balance sheet at purchase price or production cost after charging depreciation and making provision for depreciation.

(*b*) The purchase price or production cost of fixed assets having a working life limited in time shall be depreciated at rates which are in keeping with regular and proper accounting principles.

(*c*) (*aa*) Provision for unusual depreciation of items of fixed assets may be made whether or not their working life is limited in time, so that their value be shown at the lower figure attributable to them as at the date of the balance sheet or as accepted for tax purposes.

(*bb*) Special depreciation shall be charged if it is anticipated that the reduction in value will be permanent.

(*cc*) Such lower figure shall cease to apply when the circumstances on the basis of which the depreciation was charged or the provision for depreciation was made have ceased to obtain.

2. The purchase price shall be calculated by adding to the price paid the expenses incidental thereto.

3. (*a*) The production cost shall be calculated by adding to the purchase price of raw and auxiliary materials including fuel the manufacturing costs directly attributable to the product in question.

(*b*) A reasonable proportion of the manufacturing costs which are only indirectly attributable to the product in question may also be added to the production cost to the extent that they relate to the period of manufacture.

(*c*) Costs of distribution shall not be included in production cost.

4. (*a*) Interest on loans raised to finance the acquisition of fixed capital assets may be included in production cost to the extent that it relates to the period during which the acquisition was made; the inclusion of this interest element in the assets shall be mentioned in the notes on the accounts.

(*b*) Interest on own capital may be included in production cost; the reasons for including this element in the assets, and the amount of the interest, shall be indicated in the notes on the accounts.

Article 183

1. Where intangibles are brought in as assets, they shall be depreciated over the period of their useful economic life assessed with proper commercial caution.

2. A reserve shall be constituted of an amount equal to the research and development costs included under assets and to the value of the intangible assets referred to in Article 153, B-I-2 (*b*). Amounts withdrawn from such reserve shall form part of the profit for the year or be deducted from the loss for the year. They shall be shown in the profit and loss account as a separate item.

Article 184

Fixed assets as well as raw materials and auxiliary materials including fuel which are constantly being replaced may, notwithstanding Article 179, paragraph 1 (*d*), be shown on the assets side at a fixed quantity and value, if variations in the quantity, value and composition thereof are negligible.

Article 185

Where an S.E. holds an investment, within the meaning of Article 161, in excess of 50 per cent, that holding shall be shown at its true value.

Article 186

1. Current assets shall be valued at purchase price or production cost.

2. If the market price at the date of the balance sheet is lower than the purchase price or production cost, the lower value shall be used.

3. If the market price cannot be ascertained and the purchase price or production cost is higher than the value which ought to be imputed to the relevant assets at the date of the balance sheet, it is the latter value which shall be adopted.

4. Current assets may be shown at a lower value than that calculated in accordance with paragraphs 2 or 3 above:

   (*a*) if this is required, upon a reasonable commercial assessment, so that the valuation of these items does not have to be changed in the short term on account of fluctuations in value, or

   (*b*) if this is permitted for tax purposes.

5. Such lower value shall cease to apply when the circumstances on the basis of which it was adopted no longer obtain.

6. The definitions of purchase price and of production cost contained in Article 182, paragraphs 2 to 4, shall apply.

Article 187

Identical items of stocks which have been purchased at different prices may be valued at the balance sheet date either on the basis of weighted average prices or by the " First in first out " (Fifo) method or " Last in first out " (Lifo) method.

Article 188

1. Costs of formation shall be shown as a separate item in the balance sheet at purchase price or production cost.

2. They shall be duly depreciated over a five-year period. A different procedure may be adopted in exceptional cases if warranted by the circumstances.

3. Items included under this heading shall be explained in the notes on the accounts.

4. (*a*) Where debts or loans to be repaid exceed the principal, the difference may be capitalized under costs of formation as a separate item.

(*b*) The amount of the difference shall be written off not later than the time when repayment of the loan or debt is made.

Article 189

Provisions shall not exceed in amount the sums which a reasonable businessman would consider necessary.

Section Four : Contents of the Notes on the Accounts

Article 190

The notes on the accounts shall contain commentary on the balance sheet and profit and loss account in such manner as to give as true and fair a view as possible of the company's assets, liabilities, financial position and results.

Article 191

In addition to the information required under other Articles in this Statute, the notes on the accounts shall set out information in respect of the following matters in any event:

1. The principles of valuation applied to the various items in the accounts;

2. Any exceptions to the general principles set out in Articles 148, paragraph 4, and 179, which may affect comparison with the accounts as at the end of the previous year; any major differences which result must be quantified;

3. The names and registered offices of undertakings in which the S.E. holds not less than 10 per cent of the shares, together with the percentage holding in each case;

4. Any investments in the capital of the S.E. of which it has been notified in accordance with Article 47, paragraph 5, together with the names of the owners thereof;

5. Any group of companies to which the S.E. belongs either as a controlling company or as a dependent undertaking, or to which it has ceased to belong, together with an explanation of the circumstances; the S.E. must also state whether it is under common management with other companies without any of them being controlling companies or dependent undertakings;

6. The names of associated companies (Art. 161, par. 2), the legal and business relationship with each of them, and any events that have taken place in any of them which might materially affect the position of the S.E.;

7. Turnover, broken down according to products, operations and markets;

8. The composition of the labour force split up as between wage earners and salary earners, showing their age-groups and places of employment, average wages and salaries, and the amount of social security contributions during the financial year;

9. Total emoluments during the financial year paid to the Board of Management and the Supervisory Board, and to former members of the Board of Management or, in the event of death, to their dependants, with a breakdown of sums paid in respect of each category;

10. Value added tax and other taxes comprised in the trading results, financial results and non-recurring income and expenditure.

Article 192

In respect of the items specified in Article 191, paragraphs 3 and 6, the information required may be omitted where in the opinion of a reasonable businessman it could seriously prejudice the interests of the undertakings in question. Such omissions shall be mentioned in the notes on the accounts or in a document pursuant to Article 193.

Article 193

The information required to be given under Article 191, paragraphs 3 and 6, may be contained in a document which shall be filed with the European Commercial Register. Where the information is supplied in this manner, that fact shall be mentioned in the notes on the accounts.

Article 194

The notes on the accounts shall contain a proposal for appropriation of profit for the year.

Section Five : Contents of the Annual Report

Article 195

1. The annual report shall review the development of the company's business and position during the past financial year, having regard to the principles of regular and proper accounting.

2. In addition to the information required under other Articles in this Statute, the annual report shall set out information in respect of the following matters in any event:

    (*a*) Important events that have taken place since the end of the financial year;

    (*b*) The company's likely future development;

    (*c*) Proposed capital expenditure, the scale thereof and the amount of the expenses likely to be incurred in connection therewith.

Section Six : Preparation of Group Accounts

Article 196

1. If the S.E. is the controlling company in a group of companies, it shall, in respect of the group, draw up a consolidated balance sheet and a consolidated profit and loss account together with notes on the consolidated accounts and a consolidated annual report. The consolidated accounts, prepared as at the same date as the annual accounts of the S.E., shall relate to every undertaking which, in accordance with Article 223, is a member of the group.

2. If the S.E. is a dependent company within a group of companies, it shall, in respect of its own part of the group and where Article 227, paragraph 2, applies, draw up a part-consolidated balance sheet and a part-consolidated profit and loss account together with notes on the part-consolidated accounts and a part-consolidated annual report. Such accounts, which shall be prepared as at the same date as the annual accounts of the S.E., shall relate to the undertakings controlled through the S.E. Articles 197 to 202 shall apply to part-consolidated accounts and reports.

Article 197

1. (*a*) Consolidated accounts shall not relate to undertakings within the group where the effect would be to make the information contained in the consolidated accounts less meaningful.

(*b*) Consolidated accounts need not relate to undertakings within the group which are so small that the view reflected of the assets, liabilities, financial position and results of the group is not affected by omitting them.

2. (*a*) The reason for non-consolidation of the accounts of any undertaking within the group shall be stated in the notes on the accounts.

(*b*) The annual accounts of undertakings such as are referred to in paragraph 1 (*a*) shall be drawn up as at the date of the consolidated accounts and shall be annexed to the notes thereon.

Article 198

1. The consolidated accounts shall comprise the group balance sheet, the group profit and loss account and the notes on the accounts. These shall constitute a composite whole. They shall comply with regular and proper accounting principles.

2. Consolidated accounts shall be presented clearly and accurately. Subject to the provisions on presentation and valuation, they shall reflect as true and a fair view as possible of the group's assets, liabilities, financial position and results.

Article 199

The provisions of Section Two of this Title shall apply to the presentation of consolidated accounts subject to the following exceptions:

1. In the group balance sheet:

    (*a*) The amount of any differences as between the book value at the date of first consolidation of investment holdings in the capital of undertakings in the group, and the value thereof including reserves and profits, on subsequent valuation, shall be shown separately under one item entitled " Consolidation equalization account ";

    (*b*) Interests held by companies outside the group in the capital, reserves and profits of undertakings within the group shall be shown as a separate item;

    (*c*) Stocks may be grouped together under one global item.

2. In the group profit and loss account the following items may be lumped together:

(a) Article 168, items I-2 to 9;
(b) Article 169, items A-I-1 to 6 and B-I-2 to 4;
(c) Article 170, items I-2 to 6;
(d) Article 171, items A-I-1 to 3 and B-I-2.

Article 200

1. As the undertakings in a group constitute one economic unit, all assets and liabilities shall be incorporated in the group consolidated balance sheet at the values shown in the balance sheets of the undertakings within the group.

2. The annual accounts of undertakings to which consolidated accounts relate shall be prepared so far as possible in accordance with the same rules of valuation.

Article 201

1. In so far as the information contained in the notes on the consolidated accounts is important for the purpose of assessment thereof, Articles 191 to 193 shall apply.

2. The methods of consolidation and, in particular, the sources and composition of the consolidation equalization account and the non-elimination, if any, of profits on transactions between undertakings within the group shall be explained.

Article 202

Article 195 shall apply to the consolidated annual report.

Section Seven : Audit

Article 203

1. The annual accounts and, in so far as it reviews developments in the company's business and position during the past financial year, the annual report shall be audited by an independent auditor acting on his own responsibility.

2. Only persons who are suitably qualified and experienced may be appointed auditors. They shall have obtained their professional qualifications by satisfying the requirements for admission and by passing a legally organized examination and shall be persons authorized in a Member State to act as auditors of the annual accounts of *sociétés anonymes* whose shares are quoted on a stock exchange.

3. Auditors shall be completely independent of the S.E.

Article 204

1. The auditor shall be appointed by the General Meeting. In respect of the first financial year, the auditor may be appointed by the General Meetings of the founder companies.

2. He may not be removed by the General Meeting save where there are serious grounds for so doing. He shall be entitled to be present during discussions concerning his removal.

3. The auditor shall be entitled to withdraw from his contract where there are serious grounds for so doing.

Article 205

The auditor shall ascertain whether the accounting system and the annual accounts comply with this Statute and with the Statutes of the company and with the principles of regular and proper accounting.

Article 206

1. In carrying out his duties, the auditor shall be completely free to examine and check any documents and assets of the S.E.

2. He shall be entitled to require any explanation or information that he may consider necessary for the proper execution of his duties.

3. If the carrying out of his duties shall so require, he shall have the like rights in respect of associated undertakings.

4. The auditor may be assisted in his work by colleagues or specialists. They shall have the same rights as the auditor himself and shall act under his responsibility. The auditor and those who assist him shall keep secret all matters of professional confidence.

Article 207

1. If, on completion of his audit, the auditor has no objection to make in respect of the annual accounts, he shall certify them without qualification.

2. If he has any objection to make in respect of the annual accounts, he shall qualify his certificate as appropriate or withhold it altogether.

3. Any qualification or withholding of a certificate shall be expressly explained.

Article 208

1. The auditor shall, furthermore, present to the Supervisory Board a written report on the results of his audit.

2. The auditor shall also report any matters which he discovers in carrying out his duties and which might jeopardize the existence of the company or significantly affect its development, or which indicate serious infringements by the Board of Management otherwise than in respect of preparation of the accounts, of any of the provisions of this Statute or of the Statutes of the company.

Article 209

The provisions of Article 20 relating to the liability of auditors shall apply also to the liability of auditors of the annual accounts.

Article 210

The provisions of this Section shall apply to the audit of the consolidated accounts and report of a group of companies or of part of a group of companies.

*Section Eight : Approval of the Accounts and Report
Appropriation of Profits, Discharge of Directors, and Publication*

Article 211

The Board of Management shall, before the end of the first three months of each financial year, draw up the annual accounts and report for the previous financial year.

Article 212

The annual accounts and report shall be submitted by the Board of Management to the Supervisory Board. The auditor's report shall be annexed thereto.

Article 213

1. The annual accounts and report shall be settled by the Board of Management and the Supervisory Board in joint session but voting separately.

2. At the request of the chairman of the Supervisory Board, the auditors shall, in an advisory capacity, attend meetings of the Supervisory Board at which the annual accounts and report are settled.

Article 214

1. Failing agreement by the Supervisory Board and the Board of Management in the matter of approval of the annual accounts, the accounts shall be approved by the General Meeting, save where the disagreement between the Board of Management and the Supervisory Board relates only to appropriation of the profit.

2. The annual accounts and report prepared by the Board of Management, together with the Supervisory Board's comments which shall be contained in a document to be appended to the notes on the accounts, shall be laid before the General Meeting for its decision.

Article 215

Articles 211 to 214 shall apply to the approval of the consolidated accounts and report of a group of companies and of a part of a group of companies.

Article 216

1. At the General Meeting, duly convened in accordance with Article 84, there shall be presented in one document:

    (*a*) The annual accounts;

    (*b*) The auditors' certificate. If the certificate is qualified or a certificate has been withheld, this shall be mentioned and explained;

    (*c*) The annual report.

2. As from the date of the notice convening the General Meeting, the documents referred to in the preceding paragraph (annual documents) may forthwith be obtained from the company by any person free of charge. A statement to this effect shall appear in the notice.

3. The annual documents shall form the basis upon which the General Meeting will make its decision with respect to the appropriation of profit and the discharge of the members of the Board of Management and of the Supervisory Board.

4. Paragraphs 1 and 2 of this Article shall apply to the consolidated accounts and report of a group of companies and of a part of a group of companies.

Article 217

1. If the Board of Management and the Supervisory Board approve the annual accounts, they may appropriate part of the profit for the year, but not exceeding one half thereof, to reserves.

2. Failing agreement by the Supervisory Board and the Board of Management as to the amount or manner of appropriation of the profit for the year, the matter shall be resolved by the General Meeting.

3. In the event of such disagreement, the comments of the Supervisory Board shall set out its views in a document to be appended to the notes on the accounts.

4. The General Meeting shall determine the appropriation of the balance of profit shown in the balance sheet (paragraph 1) on the basis of the joint proposals of the Board of Management and of the Supervisory Board and, where requisite, the appropriation of profit for the year (paragraph 2) on the basis of the proposals of the Board of Management and of the views of the Supervisory Board referred to in the preceding paragraph.

Article 218

1. The General Meeting to which the annual documents are presented shall determine whether a discharge be given to the members of the Board of Management and of the Supervisory Board. A

separate vote shall be held in respect of the discharge of any particular member if one quarter of the shareholders represented shall so
require.

2. A discharge is a vote of confidence by the General Meeting. It
relates to all matters and acts apparent from the annual documents.

3. The General Meeting may not, after giving a discharge, resolve
to bring an action for liability against the Board of Management or
any of its members. The giving of a discharge shall not, however,
preclude the bringing of other actions against the Board of Management, the Supervisory Board of any of their members, or against the
company.

Article 219

1. Immediately after the General Meeting two copies of the document laid before it in accordance with Article 216, and of the Minutes
of the meeting, shall be filed in the European Commercial Register.

2. Notice of filing and, if appropriate, an announcement of any
declaration of dividend, shall forthwith be published by the Board of
Management in the company journals.

3. Paragraphs 1 and 2 of this Article shall apply to publication of
the annual documents of a group of companies or of a part of a
group of companies.

Section Nine : Legal Proceedings in Respect of the
Annual Accounts and Report

Article 220

1. One or more shareholders whose shares represent in total five
per cent of the share capital or a nominal value of 100,000 units of
account, or the representative of a body of debenture holders, may
apply, setting out their reasons, to the court within whose jurisdiction
the registered office is situate, if they consider that the presentation of
the annual accounts or of the report, in so far as it reviews developments in the company's business and position during the previous
financial year, does not comply with the requirements of this Statute,
provided that their objections have been recorded in the Minutes
of the General Meeting.

2. The application shall be made within three months, computed
from the date of filing required under Article 219, paragraph 1.

3. The court may call on one or more experts to assist it in reaching its decision. Articles 203 and 206 shall apply to these experts.

4. Evidence shall be heard in chambers in the presence of both
parties. The judgment of the court shall be published.

Article 221

1. Where the court upholds the application, it shall order precisely how the company is to rectify its annual accounts or its annual report. Such order may be of future application only.

2. Where the order of the court relates to the balance sheet or the profit and loss account for the year in respect of which the application is made, these shall be deemed to be invalid. The company shall then draw up a new balance sheet or profit and loss account, with due regard to the terms of the order, and shall submit the same to the General Meeting within the time-limit prescribed. The court may limit the consequences of the invalidity.

3. Where the order is of future application only, the court may subsequently, on application by the company, rescind the order if the circumstances have changed.

Article 222

The provisions of this Section shall apply to the consolidated accounts and report of a group of companies and of a part of a group of companies.

TITLE VII: GROUPS OF COMPANIES

Section One : Definition and Scope

Article 223

1. A controlling company and one or more undertakings controlled by it, whether existing within the Member States or not, shall constitute a group within the meaning of this Statute if all of them are under the sole management of the controlling company and if one of them is an S.E.

Each of them is an undertaking within the group.

2. Where an undertaking is controlled by another within the meaning of Article 6, there is a presumption that the controlling company and the controlled undertaking constitute a group.

3. Where all the shares of an undertaking formed under national law, being an undertaking within a group and having its registered office in a Member State, are held by an S.E., any provisions of national law which in these circumstances require the undertaking to be wound up shall not apply.

Article 224

1. Where the controlling company of a group is an S.E., Sections Three to Five of this Title shall apply to dependent undertakings whose registered offices are situate in the Member States and to their relationship with the controlling S.E.

2. Where an S.E. is a dependent undertaking, Sections Three to Five of this Title shall apply to the S.E. and to its relationship with the controlling company, whether the registered office of the controlling company is situate in the Member States or elsewhere.

Article 225

1. An S.E. may apply to the Court of Justice of the European Communities for a declaration as to whether it is an undertaking within a group within the meaning of this Statute.

An undertaking formed under national law may likewise apply to the Court of Justice for a declaration as to whether it is a dependent undertaking within a group controlled by an S.E.

2. Where the S.E. or the undertaking formed under national law makes no application for a declaration pursuant to paragraph 1, the following persons shall be entitled to apply:

(a) Shareholders who, if the undertaking were held to be dependent, would be outside shareholders and who hold between them either 5 per cent of the capital, after deducting the shares belonging to the undertaking held to be the controlling undertaking, if that be the case, or shares in the S.E. of a nominal value of not less than 50,000 units of account; or

(b) Creditors, where the undertaking which might be held to be a controlling company does not comply with the requirements of Article 239.

3. The Court of Justice shall give judgment after hearing evidence from the undertakings within the group. It shall, where appropriate, determine the date with effect from which the undertaking becomes an undertaking within the group.

4. Costs shall be a matter for decision by the Court of Justice.

Section Two : Publicity
Article 226

1. Where an S.E. becomes an undertaking within a group, it shall forthwith cause that fact to be registered in the European Commercial Register and to be announced in the company journals.

2. The same shall apply where an S.E. ceases to form part of a group.

Article 227

1. An S.E. which is a controlling company shall draw up consolidated annual accounts and a report in accordance with the provisions of Title VI.

2. An S.E. which is a dependent undertaking through which other undertakings are controlled shall, in accordance with the provisions of Title VI, draw up part-consolidated annual accounts and a report, save where the controlling company of the group itself draws up accounts in accordance with the provisions of Title VI relating to preparation of the accounts of groups of undertakings.

Section Three : Protection of Outside Shareholders

Article 228

1. Outside shareholders of a dependent undertaking having its registered office in the Member States may elect for:

(*a*) Payment in cash pursuant to Article 229, or

(*b*) Exchange of shares pursuant to Article 230.

2. Where the controlling company of a group has also undertaken, in accordance with Article 231, to make annual payments calculated in relation to the nominal value of each share, outside shareholders may elect instead to receive such payments.

Article 229

1. Where the controlling company of a group is an S.E. it shall make an offer to the outside shareholders to purchase for cash the shares held by them in a dependent undertaking whose registered office is situate within the Member States.

2. A controlling company incorporated under national law, whether its registered office is situate within the Member States or not, shall be subject to the like obligation in respect of the outside shareholders of an S.E. over which it has control.

Article 230

1. Where the controlling company of a group is an S.E. it shall, in addition to making an offer to purchase for cash the shares of outside shareholders in a dependent undertaking whose registered office is situate in the Member States, offer to exchange those shares for shares in the capital of the S.E.

2. The controlling company of a group, being a *société anonyme* incorporated under national law whose registered office is situate in the Member States, shall be subject to the like obligation in respect of the outside shareholders of a dependent S.E.

3. If, in the cases referred to in paragraphs 1 and 2, the controlling company of a group is in turn a dependent of an S.E. or of a *société anonyme* incorporated under national law whose registered office is situate in the Member States, it may offer to exchange the

shares of outside shareholders of an undertaking over which it has control not for shares in its own capital but for shares in the capital of the company by which it is itself controlled.

Article 231

The controlling company of a group, whether its registered office is situate in the Member States or not, may also undertake to compensate outside shareholders of a dependent undertaking whose registered office is situate in the Member States by paying them an annuity in compensation calculated in relation to the nominal value of their shares.

Article 232

1. A dependent undertaking whose registered office is situate in the Member States shall, immediately upon becoming a member of a group or being held by the Court of Justice to be a member of a group, appoint independent experts and instruct them to prepare a report concerning the amount of the payment in cash and, where necessary, the share exchange ratio that are appropriate.

Article 15, paragraph 2, shall apply to such experts.

2. The experts shall be entitled to obtain any information from the dependent undertaking and from the controlling company and to undertake any investigations that may be necessary.

Article 233

1. Upon completion of their investigations, the experts shall deliver their report to the dependent undertaking.

2. The dependent undertaking shall forthwith forward the report to the controlling company.

3. Within a reasonable period after receiving the report, the controlling company shall inform the dependent undertaking of its proposals concerning the amount of the payment in cash and, where necessary, the share exchange ratio, indicating at the same time whether it intends to make payment of annuities in compensation.

4. The management organs of the dependent undertaking shall prepare for the benefit of its shareholders a summary of the experts' report, setting out the results of the investigations undertaken and the main facts and circumstances on which the results are based. The said organs shall comment on the report and its conclusions. They may make proposals, stating their reasons, concerning the amount of the payment in cash and the share exchange ratio that they consider appropriate.

Article 234

1. The competent organ of management in the dependent under-taking shall within a reasonable period convene a General Meeting to decide on the amount of the payment in cash and, where necessary, the share exchange ratio.

2. The notice convening the meeting shall be accompanied by the controlling company's proposals concerning the amount of the payment in cash and, where appropriate, the share exchange ratio and, further, where appropriate, the amount of the annuity in compensation. Any proposals made by the organs of management shall also be sent to the shareholders.

3. There shall appear in the notice convening the meeting a note to the effect that shareholders are entitled to obtain free of charge on request a summary of the experts' report, the management organs' comments thereon and, if appropriate, a memorandum on the proposals made under paragraph 2.

Article 235

1. When the proposed cash offer and share exchange ratio are put to the vote, shares held by the controlling company or attributable to it in accordance with Article 6, paragraph 4, shall be disregarded.

2. A majority of three-quarters of the capital entitled to vote pursuant to paragraph 1 and represented at the General Meeting shall be required in order for the vote to be decisive. Non-voting shares shall be counted in calculating the majority. They shall carry the right to vote.

Article 236

1. If the General Meeting rejects the proposals of the controlling company, the amount of the payment in cash and, where appropriate, the share exchange ratio shall, on application by the controlling company, be determined, without right of appeal, by the court within whose jurisdiction the registered office is situate. Such application shall be made within one month of the decision of the General Meeting.

2. The same shall apply if the resolution of the General Meeting to accept the controlling company's proposals is challenged. The action brought for this purpose shall be in respect only of the question whether the proposed cash payment or share exchange ratio is equitable and shall lie only on the part of outside shareholders who voted against the resolution at the Meeting and caused their opposition to be recorded in the Minutes, and who hold between them not less than 20 per cent of the capital entitled to vote pursuant to Article 235.

3. The court may, at the expense of the dependent undertaking, appoint independent experts who satisfy the conditions prescribed by Article 5, paragraph 2. Article 232, paragraph 2, shall apply.

Article 237

1. The competent organ of management in the dependent undertaking shall give notice in the company journals of the amount of the payment in cash and of the ratio of exchange of shares within two months of the passing of the resolution by the General Meeting or, where Article 236 applies, within one month of the giving of judgment by the court. At the same time, it shall give notice in the company journals of any undertaking by the controlling company to pay annuities in compensation to outside shareholders pursuant to Article 231, and of the terms of such undertaking.

2. Every outside shareholder of the dependent undertaking shall be entitled to require payment in cash or, if appropriate, exchange of his shares within three months of publication of the final notice in the company journals.

3. The undertakings within the group shall be jointly and severally liable in respect of payment in cash. The controlling company shall be liable in respect of exchange of shares.

4. Where the controlling company has undertaken to pay annuities in compensation pursuant to Article 231, payment thereof shall be made to outside shareholders who have not exercised their right under paragraph 2.

Article 238

The provisions of this Section shall apply to dependent undertakings existing as *sociétés à responsabilité limitée*. References to outside shareholders and to the General Meeting shall be read as if there were substituted therefor references to outside members and the meeting respectively.

Section Four : Protection of Creditors

Article 239

1. A controlling company, whether its registered office is situate in the Member States or not, shall be jointly and severally liable for the obligations of a dependent undertaking whose registered office is situate in the Member States.

2. Proceedings may, however, be brought against the controlling company only where the creditor proves that he has endeavoured, and failed, to obtain payment of his debt from the dependent undertaking.

Section Five : Instructions

Article 240

Where the protection provided for in Section Three has been accorded in conformity with the procedure prescribed therein, the organ appointed to represent a dependent undertaking shall not refuse to carry out the instructions of its controlling company whose registered office is situate in the Member States on the grounds that they would be contrary to the interests of the dependent undertaking.

TITLE VIII: ALTERATION OF THE STATUTES

Article 241

Any alteration of the Statutes shall be effected by resolution of the General Meeting.

Article 242

1. The substance of a proposed alteration of the Statutes shall be specified in the agenda of the meeting issued under Article 84.

2. As soon as notice of the General Meeting has been given, the shareholders may apply to the company for the complete text of the proposed alteration to be supplied to them immediately and free of charge. A note to this effect shall appear in the notice of meeting.

3. The Board of Management shall set out in a report the reasons for its proposed alteration of the Statutes. Paragraph 2 shall also apply to the report.

Article 243

1. The General Meeting may be duly held only if not less than one half of the capital is represented. If the first notice of meeting fails to produce such quorum, a second notice shall be issued. The General Meeting may then be duly held irrespective of the amount of capital represented. A note to this effect shall appear in the notice of meeting.

2. Resolutions shall be duly passed if three quarters of the votes validly cast are in favour thereof.

3. The Statutes may impose more stringent requirements.

Article 244

1. The alteration of the Statutes shall be notified by the Board of Management to the Court of Justice of the European Communities for registration in the European Commercial Register.

2. The notification shall be accompanied by two authenticated copies of:

> (a) the Minutes of the General Meeting and of the annexes prescribed by Article 94, relating to the alteration of the Statutes;
>
> (b) the complete text of the Statutes as altered.

Article 245

1. The Court of Justice of the European Communities shall satisfy itself that the meeting was properly held, that the resolutions were validly passed and that where the capital has been increased it has been paid up in full, save where the increase is by way of creation of new capital within the meaning of Article 41, paragraph 3.

2. The Court of Justice of the European Communities shall refuse registration in the European Commercial Register where:

> (a) the resolution or the proceedings were not in accordance with the provisions of this Statute or of the Statutes of the company;
>
> (b) in the case of an increase of capital it does not appear from the auditors' report that payment up in full is certain or, in particular, that the value of subscriptions in kind is at least equal to the nominal value of the shares to be allotted in exchange.

Article 246

1. Where the Court of Justice finds no grounds for refusing or postponing registration, it shall order that the alteration of the Statutes be registered in the European Commercial Register and shall forward to the Registrar the notification and the annexed documents.

2. Notice of registration of the alteration shall be published in the company journals.

3. Until notice of registration of the alteration of the Statutes has been published in the company journals, the alteration shall not be relied on to defeat the claims of third parties unless the company proves that they had knowledge thereof.

TITLE IX: WINDING UP, LIQUIDATION, INSOLVENCY AND SIMILAR PROCEDURES

Section One : Winding Up

Article 247

An S.E. shall be wound up:

> (a) by resolution of the General Meeting;

(*b*) on expiration of the period for which the company was formed as specified in its Statutes;

(*c*) in the circumstances referred to in Article 249, paragraph 4; or

(*d*) on declaration of insolvency of the S.E.

Article 248

A resolution under paragraph (*a*) of Article 247 shall comply with the requirements relating to resolutions for alteration of the Statutes.

Article 249

1. If losses shown in the books reduce a company's net assets below half its share capital, the General Meeting convened for the purpose of considering the annual accounts pursuant to Article 84 shall decide whether the company should be wound up. Where this item is included in the agenda, the Board of Management shall expressly make known its opinion on the question of winding up in a special report approved by the Supervisory Board and referred to in the agenda. Any person entitled to attend the General Meeting may apply for a copy of this report to be sent to him free of charge fifteen days before the date of the meeting.

2. If it is decided not to wind up the company, its share capital shall be reduced within not more than two years from the date of the General Meeting referred to in paragraph 1 by an amount at least equal to the loss incurred, unless its net assets have in the meantime increased to an amount equal to not less than half of the capital. A reduction of the capital below the minimum level prescribed by Article 4 may be effected, however, only where an increase in the capital to the level prescribed by that Article is effected simultaneously. The Board of Management shall forthwith notify the European Commercial Register of the date on which the said two-year period will expire.

3. In each case the General Meeting shall pass its resolutions in accordance with the provisions which apply to alteration of the Statutes.

4. If a General Meeting has not been held, or if it has been unable within the period prescribed by paragraph 2 to pass valid resolutions either for winding up the company or for reducing its capital under the conditions hereinbefore contained, the company shall at the end of the two-year period prescribed by paragraph 2 automatically be dissolved.

Article 250

1. In the cases referred to in Article 247 (*b*) and (*c*), the Board of Management shall, for the purpose of registration, immediately notify the European Commercial Register of the winding up of the company and give notice in the company journals.

2. If the requirements of the preceding paragraph are not complied with before the expiration of two weeks following the winding up, any person concerned may apply to the court in whose jurisdiction the registered office is situate for an order that the winding up be registered in the European Commercial Register, and that notice be given at the company's expense.

Section Two : Liquidation

Article 251

1. Save in the event of a declaration of insolvency, winding up of the company shall be followed by liquidation which shall be carried out in accordance with the provisions of this Section.

2. Unless otherwise required by the provisions of this Section and in so far as the provisions thereof are not inconsistent with the purpose of the liquidation, S.E.s that are being wound up shall, until the liquidation is completed, continue to be subject to the same provisions as S.E.s which are not being wound up.

3. The provisions relating to the powers and duties of the members of the Board of Management shall, for purposes of the liquidation, apply to the liquidators. The liquidators shall be subject to control by the Supervisory Board.

Article 252

1. On winding up the powers of the Board of Management shall cease. The members of the current Board of Management shall carry out the liquidation unless other persons are appointed as liquidators by the General Meeting.

2. On the application of one or more shareholders holding between them either 5 per cent of the share capital or shares of a nominal value of 100,000 units of account, the court in whose jurisdiction the registered office is situate may, where serious grounds exist, remove the liquidators and appoint others in their place.

3. The General Meeting may at any time remove the liquidators and appoint others in their place.

4. The General Meeting shall determine the amount of the liquidators' fees. If the liquidators are appointed by the court under paragraph 2, the amount of their fees shall be determined by the court.

Article 253

Notice of the appointment or removal of liquidators shall be given to the European Commercial Register for the purpose of registration and be published in the company journals. Article 65 shall apply.

Article 254

The liquidators shall terminate work in progress, collect in the debts, convert the remaining assets into cash and pay off the creditors. If necessary for the purposes of the liquidation, they may enter into new commitments.

Article 255

1. Making specific reference to the winding up of the company, the liquidators shall invite the creditors to submit their claims. Notice for this purpose shall be published in the company journals on three occasions, with an interval of not less than two weeks between each.

2. Every creditor known to the company who has failed to present his claim within three months of the date of the final notice shall, in manner required by his national law, be invited in writing to do so.

3. Claims which are not presented within one year of the date of the final notice shall be extinguished. Express notice to this effect shall be given in the notices published pursuant to paragraph 1 and in the written invitation pursuant to paragraph 2.

Article 256

1. The liquidators shall lay before the General Meeting annual accounts in respect of their activities.

2. The provisions of the first seven Sections of Title VI concerning the preparation of accounts, of Article 218 concerning discharge of the members of the Board of Management and of the Supervisory Board, and of Article 219 concerning notices shall apply.

Article 257

1. Assets remaining after discharge of the liabilities shall be distributed amongst the shareholders in proportion to the nominal value of their shares.

2. Where a liability cannot be discharged for the time being, or is disputed, a distribution of assets may be made only if security is given in favour of the creditor or if the assets remaining after a partial distribution constitute adequate security.

Article 258

1. A complete or partial distribution of assets shall not be made until accounts prepared in accordance with Article 256, together with

a scheme of distribution drawn up after the end of the one-year period prescribed by Article 255, paragraph 3, have been presented to the General Meeting, and a further three months have elapsed after filing of the annual documents and scheme of distribution in the European Commercial Register during which no proceedings have been commenced in the court within whose jurisdiction the registered office is situate. The same shall apply where any such proceedings have been dismissed by the court.

2. Notwithstanding the provisions of Article 220, any person interested may bring such proceedings provided that they relate to the scheme of distribution.

Article 259

1. Upon completion of the liquidation the liquidators shall forthwith give notice thereof to the European Commercial Register for the purpose of registration and in the company journals.

2. If further action in respect of the liquidation shall thereafter become necessary, the court within whose jurisdiction the registered office is situate shall, on the application of the shareholders or of a creditor, renew the mandate of the former liquidators or appoint other liquidators.

Article 260

1. Following the liquidation, the books and records of the S.E. shall be lodged with the European Commercial Register for retention there for ten years.

2. The Court of Justice of the European Communities may authorize shareholders and creditors to examine such books and records.

Section Three : Insolvency and Similar Procedures

Article 261

An S.E. shall be subject to any Convention that may be concluded between the Member States in respect of insolvency, arrangements with creditors and similar procedures.

Article 262

For the purpose of application of the regulations relating to jurisdiction which are contained in any convention concluded between the Member States in respect of insolvency, arrangements with creditors and similar procedures, the business of an S.E. shall always be deemed to be carried on from the registered office specified in its Statutes.

Article 263

1. The syndic appointed upon the insolvency of an S.E. shall ensure that the order made at the commencement of insolvency proceedings is registered in the European Commercial Register before it is published in the Official Gazette of the European Communities and in the company journals. The entry in the Register shall include the particulars required by any convention concluded between the Member States in respect of insolvency, arrangements with creditors and similar procedures.

2. The syndic shall also notify the European Commercial Register of decisions made pursuant to any such convention.

TITLE X : CONVERSION

Article 264

1. By resolution of the General Meeting passed in like manner to a resolution for alteration of the Statutes, an S.E. may be converted into a *société anonyme* constituted under the laws of one of the Member States.

2. Conversion shall not be effected until three years after formation of the S.E.

3. The S.E. shall be converted into a company under the laws of the Member State in which its effective management is located.

Article 265

The reasons for the proposal to convert an S.E. into a *société anonyme* constituted under the laws of a Member State shall be set out in a report by the Board of Management. Article 242, paragraph 2 shall apply to such report.

Article 266

1. The resolution for conversion shall be notified by the Board of Management to the Court of Justice of the European Communities.

2. This notification shall be accompanied by:

(*a*) two authenticated copies of the Minutes of the General Meeting and, where they relate to the resolution for conversion, the annexes specified in Articles 94 and 265;

(*b*) the authenticated text of the Statutes as altered by the General Meeting.

3. The Court of Justice of the European Communities shall ascertain whether the resolution was validly passed.

4. If the resolution was passed in accordance with the provisions of this Statute and of the Statutes of the S.E., the Court of Justice of the European Communities shall return the documents mentioned in paragraph 2 to the S.E. together with a certificate that the resolution was validly passed.

Article 267

The company shall subsist as an S.E. until the day on which it acquires legal personality as a *société anonyme* constituted under national law.

Article 268

1. Immediately after acquiring legal personality as a *société anonyme* constituted under national law, the company shall send to the European Commercial Register one of the copies referred to in Article 266, paragraph 2 (*a*) together with one copy of the documents and supporting papers required under its national law for formation of *sociétés anonymes*, including the certificate that the requisite notices have appeared in the national publications.

2. The European Commercial Register shall register the conversion and give notice of the conversion in the Official Gazette of the European Communities, making due reference to the registration effected, filing of documents and giving of notices pursuant to the national law where the documents and supporting papers sent to the European Commercial Register are evidence thereof.

3. The conversion of the company shall not be relied on to defeat the claims of third parties until such time as notice of the conversion has been published in the Official Gazette of the European Communities.

TITLE XI: MERGER

Section One : Merger of European Companies

Article 269

1. An S.E. may, without being put into liquidation, merge with another S.E.:

(*a*) by formation of a new S.E. to which the whole of the assets and liabilities of the merging companies shall be transferred in exchange for shares in the new S.E.;

(*b*) by transfer to the acquiring S.E. in exchange for shares therein of the whole of the assets and liabilities of the S.E. acquired.

2. An S.E. in liquidation may be party to a merger by formation of a new S.E. or by acquisition of an S.E., provided that distribution

of the assets amongst the shareholders of the S.E. in liquidation has not begun.

Article 270

1. Merger by formation of a new S.E. shall require a resolution of the General Meeting of each S.E. passed in like manner to a resolution for alteration of the Statutes.

2. Sections One and Two of Title II of this Statute shall apply. For purposes of application of those Sections, references to the "auditors" shall be deleted and there shall be substituted therefor in each case a reference to the "auditors and the annual accounts."

Article 271

1. Merger by take-over shall require a resolution of the General Meeting of each S.E. passed in like manner to a resolution for alteration of the Statutes.

2. Sections One and Two of Title II of this Statute shall apply by analogy save where this Article and the following Articles otherwise provide. For purposes of application of those Sections, references to the "auditors" shall be deleted and there shall be substituted therefor in each case a reference to the "auditors of the annual accounts".

3. A merger by take-over shall be notified by the acquiring S.E. to the Court of Justice of the European Communities for registration in the European Commercial Register.

4. Notice of registration shall be published in the company journals of the merging companies.

5. The S.E. acquired shall cease to exist on the date of publication in the Official Gazette of the European Communities. With effect from that date the liability of the acquiring S.E. shall be substituted for that of the S.E. acquired.

Section Two : Merger of S.E.s with Sociétés Anonymes Incorporated under the Law of One of the Member States

Article 272

1. An S.E. may, without being put into liquidation, merge with a *société anonyme* incorporated under the law of one of the Member States:

(a) by formation of a new S.E., to which the whole of the assets and liabilities of the merging companies shall be transferred in exchange for shares in the new S.E.;

(b) by transfer to the acquiring S.E. in exchange for shares therein of the whole of the assets and liabilities of the S.E. acquired.

2. An S.E. in liquidation or a *société anonyme* incorporated under the law of one of the Member States and in liquidation may be party to a merger by formation of a new S.E. or to a merger by takeover of a *société anonyme* incorporated under the law of one of the Member States provided that distribution of the assets of the company in liquidation amongst its shareholders has not yet begun.

Article 273

Sections One and Two of Title II of this Statute shall apply to merger by formation of a new S.E. For purposes of application of those Sections, references to the " auditors " shall be deleted and there shall be substituted therefor in each case a reference to the " auditors of the annual accounts."

Article 274

1. Article 271 shall apply to merger by takeover of a *société anonyme* incorporated under the law of one of the Member States.

2. The merger shall be notified by the acquiring S.E. to the Court of Justice of the European Communities for registration in the European Commercial Register.

3. Notice of registration shall be published by the S.E. in its company journals. The *société anonyme* acquired shall procure notice of merger to be given in like manner to notice of dissolution of a company as prescribed by the law under which the *société anonyme* was incorporated.

4. The S.E. taken over shall cease to exist on the date of publication in the Official Gazette of the European Communities. With effect from that date the liability of the acquiring S.E. shall be substituted for that of he *société anonyme* acquired.

TITLE XII: TAXATION

Section One : Formation

Article 275

1. Where a European holding company within the meaning of Articles 2 and 3 is formed by *sociétés anonymes* incorporated under the law of one of the Member States or by European companies, allotment to the shareholders of those companies of shares in the European holding company in exchange for shares in those companies shall not give rise to any charge to tax.

2. Where such shares form part of the assets of an undertaking, the Member States may waive this rule if the shares in the European

holding company are not shown in the balance sheet for tax purposes of that undertaking at the same value at which the shares in the *sociétés anonymes* or in the European companies were shown.

Section Two : Tax Domicile

Article 276

1. For purposes of taxation, the S.E. shall be treated as resident in the Member State in which the centre of its effective management is located.

2. Action to remove any difficulties or doubts which arise in connection with the application of paragraph 1 shall be taken by Member States if a competent authority in a Member State shall consider it necessary or if the S.E. shall request it to do so.

3. The competent authorities in Member States may communicate with each other direct with a view to making an agreement for purposes of the preceding paragraph. The S.E. interested in or affected by such action, or its representative, shall at its request be allowed to give evidence.

4. In default of agreement in pursuance of paragraphs 2 and 3, each State concerned may refer the matter to the Court of Justice, whose decision shall be final. The S.E. shall be entitled to be heard.

5. For so long as the centre of effective management shall not definitively have been determined by such action as aforesaid, the liability of the S.E. for payment of tax shall at its request be deferred.

Article 277

Where an S.E., which for purposes of taxation has been resident in a Member State for not less than five years, transfers its effective management to another Member State, the State in which the centre of effective management was located prior to the transfer:

(a) shall not impose any charge to tax on any increase in value of the assets of the S.E., that is to say on the amount of the difference between the real value of those assets and the value thereof as shown in the balance sheet of the S.E. for tax purposes, where those assets are from an accounting point of view attributed at the same value to a permanent establishment of the S.E. in that State, and contribute towards the taxable income of that establishment;

(b) shall authorize any such permanent establishment as is referred to in (a) above to carry forward and retain free from liability to tax under general law any provisions and reserves created by the S.E. in that State and which are exempt in whole or in part from liability to tax;

    (*c*) shall permit such permanent establishment to carry forward and write off, in accordance with general law, losses incurred by the S.E. which have not yet been written off for tax purposes in that State;

    (*d*) shall from the date of transfer waive all right to impose any charge to tax in respect of the activities of the S.E. carried on outside its territory, if, for tax purposes, the S.E. includes such activities with those that it carries on in the State to which it transfers its centre of effective management. Where they are so included, paragraphs (*b*) and (*c*) above shall not apply if the provisions, reserves or losses therein referred to relate to activities carried on outside the territory of the State in which the centre of effective management was located prior to the transfer.

Section Three : Permanent Establishments and Subsidiaries

Article 278

1. Where an S.E. whose domicile for tax purposes is in a Member State has a permanent establishment in another Member State, only the latter Member State shall have the right to charge to tax the profits of that establishment.

2. If during any tax period the overall result of the operations of an S.E.'s permanent establishments in that State shows a loss, that loss shall be deductible from the taxable profits of the S.E. in the State in which it is resident for tax purposes.

3. Subsequent profits made by those permanent establishments shall constitute taxable income of the S.E. in the State in which it is resident for tax purposes up to an amount not exceeding the amount of the loss allowed by way of deduction under paragraph 2 above.

4. The amount of the loss deductible under paragraph 2 above and the amount of profit chargeable to tax under paragraph 3 above shall be determined in accordance with the law of the State in which the permanent establishment or establishments are located.

Article 279

The tax treatment of a permanent establishment maintained in a Member State by an S.E. which is resident for tax purposes in another Member State shall not result in a greater charge to tax for that permanent establishment than would arise in the case of a company carrying on a business of the same nature and being resident for tax purposes in that other State.

Article 280

1. The expression " permanent establishment " means a fixed place of business at which an S.E. carries on its activities in whole or in part.

2. The term " permanent establishment " includes in particular:

    (*a*) a seat of management;

    (*b*) a branch;

    (*c*) an office;

    (*d*) a factory;

    (*e*) a workshop;

    (*f*) a mine, quarry or any other site for extraction of natural resources;

    (*g*) work of construction or assembly carried on for more than twelve months.

3. Installations and warehouses falling within sub-paragraphs (*a*) to (*e*) below shall not be considered permanent establishments irrespective of whether one or all of the criteria specified therein are satisfied:

    (*a*) installations used solely for storage, display or delivery of goods owned by a company;

    (*b*) warehouses for goods owned by a company and maintained solely for the purpose of storage, display or delivery;

    (*c*) warehouses for goods owned by a company and maintained solely for the purpose of processing by another undertaking;

    (*d*) a fixed place of business used solely for the purpose of purchasing goods or collecting information for a company;

    (*e*) a fixed place of business used by a company solely for the purpose of promotion, supplying information, scientific research or similar preparatory or auxiliary activities.

4. A person acting in one Member State on behalf of a company in another Member State, other than an independent agent within the meaning of paragraph 5, shall be deemed to be a " permanent establishment " in the former State if in that State he enjoys and regularly exercises the right to make agreements in the name of the company, save where his activities are limited to the purchase of goods for the company.

5. A company in one Member State shall not be treated as having a permanent establishment in another Member State simply because it carries on its activities therein through a broker, a general agent or any other independent agent acting in the normal course of their activities.

6. The fact that a company in one Member State controls or is controlled by a company that is subject to the law of another Member State or that carries on its activities therein (whether through a permanent establishment or not) shall not be sufficient in itself to make either of those companies a permanent establishment of the other.

Article 281

1. Where an S.E. holds not less than 50 per cent of the capital of another company whose profits are chargeable to tax and whose operations in any tax period result in a loss, that loss shall be deductible, in proportion to the holding, from the profits chargeable to tax of the S.E. in the State in which the S.E. is resident for tax purposes.

2. A deduction made pursuant to paragraph 1 above shall be final if, under the law applicable to the company whose capital is held as aforesaid, the loss referred to in the said paragraph cannot be carried forward to other tax periods. Conversely, the subsequent profits of that company shall constitute taxable income of the S.E. in the State in which it is resident for tax purposes up to an amount not exceeding the amount of the loss allowed by way of deduction and *pro rata* to the capital held at the time those profits were earned.

3. Where the holding falls below 50 per cent, any loss deducted from the profits of the S.E. under paragraph 1 above during the preceding five tax periods shall, notwithstanding the provisions of paragraph 2, be added back to the taxable profits of that S.E.

4. Where such holding as is referred to in paragraph 1 above is in the capital of a company resident in a Member State, the amount of the loss deductible under paragraph 1 above and the amount of the subsequent profits taxable under paragraph 2 above shall be determined in accordance with the law of that contracting State.

TITLE XIII: OFFENCES

Article 282

1. The Member States shall introduce into their law appropriate provisions for creating the offences set out in the annex hereto.

2. Provisions of national law applicable to breach of regulations relating to companies shall not apply to breach of any of the provisions of this Statute.

TITLE XIV: FINAL PROVISIONS

Article 283

The Member States shall implement the requirements of Article 282 within six months of the making of this regulation.

Article 284

This regulation shall be binding in its entirety and directly applicable in each Member State.

It shall enter into force six months after publication in the Official Gazette of the European Communities.

ANNEX TO COUNCIL REGULATION No.
EMBODYING A STATUTE FOR EUROPEAN COMPANIES

The following persons shall be guilty of an offence and liable to punishment accordingly:

I. Any member, as such, of the Board of Management, of the Supervisory Board or of any other organ of management of a founder company who wilfully makes any false statement in or omits material facts from the report on formation, or the annexes thereto, in respect of:

(a) the amount of the share capital or the nominal value and number of the shares,

(b) the valuation of capital subscribed in kind or the source of such capital,

(c) the expenses incurred in connection with formation,

(d) the privileges and benefits granted to persons who took part in the formation of the company.

II. Any member, as such, of the Board of Management or of the Supervisory Board of an S.E. who wilfully makes any false statement or omits material facts with a view to registration of an increase or reduction in the share capital of an S.E.

III. Any person who wilfully issues any share before the nominal amount thereof has been fully paid up.

IV. Any person who, in order to exercise a right of vote at a General Meeting, wilfully makes use of shares of another person which he has obtained for that purpose by granting or promising special benefits or who, for that same purpose, transfers shares to another person in return for or in consideration of the promise of special benefits.

V. Any member of the Board of Management or of the Supervisory Board who wilfully makes any false statement in or omits material facts from the annual accounts, consolidated annual accounts, part-consolidated annual accounts or in the report, consolidated report or part-consolidated report.

VI. A member, as such, of the Board of Management or of the Supervisory Board who, by deliberate act or omission, causes false or incomplete information to be used in the preparation of the auditor's report.

VII. Any auditor who, as such auditor, wilfully prepares a false or incomplete auditor's report.

VIII. Any person to whom Article 82 applies and who in respect of the matters therein specified wilfully fails to carry out the formalities, apply for alteration or give notice as thereby required.

Text 8

A. *Convention on the Mutual Recognition of Companies and Legal Persons, signed on February 29, 1968*

Preamble

The High Contracting Parties to the Treaty establishing the European Economic Community,

Being desirous of implementing the provisions of Article 220 of the said Treaty concerning the mutual recognition of companies within the meaning of Article 58, second paragraph,

Whereas the mutual recognition of companies or firms within the meaning of Article 58, second paragraph, should be as liberal as possible, without prejudice to the application to companies of the other provisions of the Treaty,

Have decided to conclude the present Convention on the mutual recognition of companies and bodies corporate and have for this purpose nominated as plenipotentiaries:

His Majesty the King of the Belgians:
>   M. Pierre Harmel, Minister for Foreign Affairs;

The President of the Federal Republic of Germany:
>   M. Willy Brandt, Vice-Chancellor and Minister for Foreign Affairs;

The President of the French Republic:
>   M. Maurice Couve de Murville, Minister for Foreign Affairs;

The President of the Italian Republic:
>   M. Amintore Fanfani, Minister for Foreign Affairs;

His Royal Highness the Grand-Duke of Luxembourg:
>   M. Pierre Grégoire, Minister for Foreign Affairs;

Her Majesty the Queen of the Netherlands:
>   M. J. M. A. H. Luns, Minister for Foreign Affairs;

Who, meeting in the Council, having exchanged their Full Powers, found in good and due form,

Have agreed as follows:

CHAPTER I: RECOGNITION: SCOPE AND CONDITIONS

Article 1

Companies under civil or commercial law, including co-operative societies, established in accordance with the law of a Contracting

State which grants them the capacity of persons having rights and duties, and having their statutory registered office in the territories to which the present Convention applies, shall be recognized as of right.

Article 2

Bodies corporate under public or private law, other than the companies specified in Article 1, which fulfil the conditions stipulated in the said Article, which have as their main or accessory object an economic activity normally exercised for reward, and which, without infringing the law under which they were established, do in fact continuously exercise such activity, shall also be recognized as of right.

Article 3

Notwithstanding the foregoing, any Contracting State may declare that it will not apply the present Convention to any companies or bodies corporate specified in Articles 1 and 2 which have their real registered office outside the territories to which the present Convention applies, if such companies or bodies corporate have no genuine link with the economy of one of the said territories.

Article 4

Any Contracting State may also declare that it will apply any provisions of its own legislation which it deems essential, to the companies or bodies corporate specified in Articles 1 and 2 having their real registered offices on its territory, even if these have been established in accordance with the law of another Contracting State.

The suppletory provisions of the legislation of the State making such a declaration shall apply in only one of the following two cases:

(i) If the memorandum and articles of association so permit, if necessary by an express general reference to the law in accordance with which the company or body corporate has been established.

(ii) If, the memorandum and articles of association so permitting, the company or body corporate fails to show that it has actually exercised its activity for a reasonable time in the Contracting State in accordance with the law under which it was established.

Article 5

For the purpose of this Convention, the real registered office of a company or body corporate shall mean the place where its central administration is established.

CHAPTER II: RECOGNITION: EFFECTS

Article 6

Without prejudice to the application of Article 4, all companies or bodies corporate recognized by virtue of this Convention shall have the capacity accorded to them by the law under which they were established.

Article 7

Any State in which recognition is sought may refuse such companies or bodies corporate any rights and powers specified which it does not grant to companies or bodies corporate of a similar type which are governed by its own laws. However, the exercise of this power may not result in the withdrawal from such companies or bodies corporate of their capacity, as persons having rights and duties, to award contracts, or to accomplish other legal acts or to sue or be sued.

The companies or bodies corporate referred to in Articles 1 and 2 may not invoke the restrictions on their rights and powers specified in this Article.

Article 8

The capacity, rights and powers of a company recognized by virtue of this Convention may not be denied or restricted for the sole reason that the law in accordance with which it was established does not grant it the legal status of a body corporate.

CHAPTER III: PUBLIC POLICY

Article 9

In each Contracting State, the application of this Convention may only be waived when the company or body corporate invoking it contravenes by its object, its purpose or the activity which it actually exercises the principles or rules which the said State considers as being a matter of public policy as defined in private international law.

If the law under which a single proprietorship is established allows it to possess the status of a company, such company may not for that reason alone be considered by a Contracting State as conflicting with public policy as defined in private international law.

Article 10

Principles or rules contrary to the provisions of the Treaty establishing the European Economic Community may not be deemed a matter of public policy within the meaning of Article 9.

CHAPTER IV: FINAL PROVISIONS

Article 11

In relations between the Contracting States, this Convention shall apply notwithstanding any conflicting provisions concerning recognition of companies or bodies corporate contained in other conventions to which the Contracting States are or will be parties.

However, the present Convention shall be without prejudice:

(i) To those rules of municipal law

(ii) And to those provisions of international conventions

which are or will be in force and which provide for recognition in other cases or with wider effects, provided that such recognition or such effects are compatible with the Treaty establishing the European Economic Community.

Article 12

This Convention shall apply to the European territories of the Contracting States, to the French Overseas Departments and to the French Overseas Territories.

Any Contracting State may declare by notification to the Secretary-General of the Council of the European Communities that this Convention applies to the country or countries, or to the territory or territories indicated in the said declaration, whose international relations it governs.

Article 13

This Convention shall be ratified by the signatory States. The instruments of ratification shall be deposited with the Secretary-General of the Council of the European Communities.

Article 14

This Convention shall come into force on the first day of the third month following deposit of the instrument of ratification by the last signatory State to complete this formality.

Article 15

The declarations specified in Articles 3 and 4 must be made for each signatory State no later than the time when its instrument of ratification of this Convention is deposited. They shall take effect on the day this Convention comes into force. If the declaration specified in Article 12, second paragraph, is made no later than the time when the sixth instrument of ratification of this Convention is deposited, it shall take effect on the day this Convention comes into force; if the declaration is made at a later date, it shall take effect on the first day of the third month following receipt of its notification.

Any Contracting State may at any time withdraw either or both of the declarations made by virtue of Articles 3 and 4. The withdrawal shall take effect on the first day of the third month following the receipt of its notification by the Secretary-General of the Council of the European Communities. It shall be final.

Article 16

The Secretary-General of the Council of the European Communities shall notify the signatory States of:

(i) The deposit of every instrument of ratification;
(ii) The date of entry into force of this Convention;
(iii) The declarations and notifications received in pursuance of Articles 3, 4, 12, second paragraph, and 15, second paragraph;
(iv) The dates when these declarations and notifications take effect.

Article 17

This Convention shall be concluded for an indefinite period.

Article 18

Any Contracting State may request the revision of the present Convention. In this event, a revision conference shall be convened by the President of the Council of the European Communities.

Article 19

This Convention, drawn up in one original only, in German, French, Italian and Dutch, the four texts being equally authentic, shall be deposited in the archives of the Secretariat of the Council of the European Communities. The Secretary-General shall supply a certified true copy to the Government of each signatory State.

IN WITNESS WHEREOF, the undersigned plenipotentiaries have affixed their signatures to this Convention.

Done at Brussels, on the twenty-ninth day of February, nineteen hundred and sixty-eight.

For His Majesty the King of the Belgians,
Pierre Harmel.

For the President of the Federal Republic of Germany,
Willy Brandt.

For the President of the French Republic,
Maurice Couve de Murville.

For the President of the Italian Republic,
    Amintore Fanfani.
For His Royal Highness the Grand-Duke of Luxembourg,
    Pierre Grégoire.
For Her Majesty the Queen of the Netherlands,
    Joseph M. A. H. Luns.

Protocol

Upon signing the text of the Convention on the mutual recognition of companies and bodies corporate, the plenipotentiaries of the High Contracting Parties to the Treaty establishing the European Economic Community adopted the texts of the following three declarations:

JOINT DECLARATION NO. 1

The Governments of the Kingdom of Belgium, the Federal Republic of Germany, the French Republic, the Italian Republic, the Grand Duchy of Luxembourg and the Kingdom of the Netherlands,

Declare that Article 1 of this Convention applies to the *società semplice* in Italian law and the *vennootschap onder firma* in Netherlands law.

JOINT DECLARATION NO. 2

The Governments of the Kingdom of Belgium, the Federal Republic of Germany, the French Republic, the Italian Republic, the Grand Duchy of Luxembourg and the Kingdom of the Netherlands,

Declare themselves ready to engage, as may be necessary under association agreements, in negotiations with any Associated State of the European Economic Community with a view to the mutual recognition of companies and bodies corporate within the meaning of Articles 1 and 2 of the aforesaid Convention.

JOINT DECLARATION NO. 3

The Governments of the Kingdom of Belgium, the Federal Republic of Germany, the French Republic, the Italian Republic, the Grand Duchy of Luxembourg and the Kingdom of the Netherlands,

Being desirous of ensuring that the Convention is applied as effectively as possible,

Being anxious to prevent differences of interpretation from impairing the unity of the Convention,

Declare themselves ready to study ways and means of achieving these ends, notably by examining the possibility of conferring certain

powers on the Court of Justice of the European Communities, and, as appropriate, to negotiate an agreement to this effect.
[*Signed as before*]

B. *Protocol concerning the Interpretation by the Court of Justice of the Convention of February* 29, 1968 *on the Mutual Recognition of Companies and Legal Persons, signed on June* 3, 1971

The High Contracting Parties to the Treaty establishing the European Economic Community,

Having regard to the Joint Declaration No. 3 appearing in the Protocol annexed to the Convention on the Mutual Recognition of Companies and Legal Persons, signed at Brussels on 29 February 1968,

Have decided to conclude a Protocol bestowing powers on the Court of Justice of the European Communities to interpret the said Convention and to this end have designated as Plenipotentiaries:

His Majesty the King of the Belgians:
  Mr. Alfons Vranckx, Minister of Justice;

The President of the Federal Republic of Germany:
  Mr. Gerhard Jahn, Federal Minister of Justice;

The President of the French Republic:
  Mr. René Pleven, Keeper of the Seals, Minister of Justice;

The President of the Italian Republic:
  Mr. Erminio Pennacchini, Deputy State Secretary, Ministry of Justice and Pardons;

His Royal Highness the Grand Duke of Luxembourg:
  Mr. Eugène Schaus, Minister of Justice, Deputy Prime Minister;

Her Majesty the Queen of the Netherlands:
  Mr. C. H. F. Polak, Minister of Justice;

WHO, being met within the Council, having exchanged their Full Powers, found in good and due form,

Have agreed upon the following provisions:

Article 1

The Court of Justice of the European Communities shall have jurisdiction to give preliminary rulings concerning the interpretation of the Convention on the Mutual Recognition of Companies and Legal Persons and the Joint Declaration No. 1 appearing in the

Protocol annexed to that Convention, signed at Brussels on 29 February 1968, and concerning the interpretation of this Protocol.

Article 2

1. Where a question relating to the interpretation of the Convention and the other texts mentioned in Article 1 is raised before any court or tribunal of one of the Contracting States, that court or tribunal may, if it considers that a decision on the question is necessary to enable it to give judgment, request the Court of Justice to give a ruling thereas.

2. Where such a question is raised in a case pending before a court or tribunal of a member State, from whose decisions there is no possibility of appeal under internal law, that court or tribunal shall be bound to bring the matter before the Court of Justice.

Article 3

1. Except where this Protocol provides otherwise, the provisions of the Treaty establishing the European Economic Community and those of the Protocol on the Statute of the Court of Justice annexed thereto, which are applicable when the Court is required to give a preliminary ruling, shall apply also to the procedure for the interpretation of the Convention and the other texts mentioned in Article 1.

2. The Rules of Procedure of the Court of Justice shall be adapted and supplemented, as necessary, in conformity with Article 188 of the Treaty establishing the European Economic Community.

Article 4

This Protocol shall apply to the European territory of the Contracting States, to the French Overseas Departments and to the French Overseas Territories.

The Kingdom of the Netherlands may, at the time of signing or of ratifying this Protocol, or at any time subsequently, by notifying the Secretary-General of the Council of the European Communities, declare that this Protocol shall apply to Surinam and to the Netherlands Antilles.

Article 5

This Protocol shall be ratified by the Signatory States. The instruments of ratification shall be deposited with the Secretary-General of the Council of the European Communities.

Article 6

This Protocol shall come into force on the first day of the third month following the deposit of the instrument of ratification of the last Signatory State to complete this formality. However, its entry into force shall occur at the earliest at the same time as that of the Convention of 29 February 1968 on the Mutual Recognition of Companies and Legal Persons.

Article 7

The Secretary-General of the Council of the European Communities shall notify the Signatory States of:

(*a*) the deposit of any instrument of ratification;

(*b*) the date of entry into force of this Protocol;

(*c*) the declarations received pursuant to Article 4, second paragraph.

Article 8

This Protocol shall be concluded for an unlimited period.

Article 9

Each Contracting State may ask for this Protocol to be revised. In that event, a revision conference shall be convened by the President of the Council of the European Communities.

Article 10

This Protocol, drawn up in a single original in the German, French, Italian and Dutch languages, all four texts being equally authentic, shall be deposited in the archives of the Secretariat of the Council of the European Communities. The Secretary-General shall transmit a certified copy to the Government of each of the Signatory States.

IN WITNESS WHEREOF, the undersigned plenipotentiaries have affixed their signatures below this Protocol.

Done at Luxembourg on the third day of June in the year one thousand nine hundred and seventy-one.

Pour sa Majesté le Roi des Belges,

Voor Zijne Majesteit de Koning der Belgen,

    Alfons Vranckx

Für den Präsidenten der Bundesrepublik Deutschland,

    Gerhard Jahn

Pour le Président de la République Française,

    René Pleven

Per il Presidente della Repubblica Italiana,

    Erminio Pennacchini

Pour Son Altesse Royale le Grand-Duc de Luxembourg,
    Eugène Schaus
Voor Hare Majesteit de Koningin der Nederlanden,
    C. H. F. Polak

Joint Declaration

The Governments of the Kingdom of Belgium, the Federal
Republic of Germany, the French Republic, the Italian Republic, the
Grand Duchy of Luxembourg and the Kingdom of the Netherlands,

at the time of signing the Protocol concerning the interpretation
by the Court of Justice of the Convention of 29 February 1968 on
the Mutual Recognition of Companies and Legal Persons,

wishing to ensure that these provisions are applied as effectively
and as uniformly as possible,

declare that they are willing, in co-operation with the Court of
Justice, to organise an exchange of information on the decisions made
by the courts and tribunals mentioned in Article 2 (2) of the said
Protocol in application of the Convention of 29 February 1968 and
of the Joint Declaration No. 1 appearing in the Protocol annexed to
that Convention.

IN WITNESS WHEREOF, the undersigned plenipotentiaries have
affixed their signatures below this Protocol.

Done at Luxembourg on the third day of June in the year one
thousand nine hundred and seventy-one.

[*Signed as before*]

Text 9

Proposal for a Regulation of the Council on the
Control of Concentrations between Undertakings,
submitted by the Commission to the Council
on July 18, 1973

The Council of the European Communities,

Having regard to the Treaty establishing the European Economic Community and in particular to Articles 87 and 235 thereof;

Having regard to the proposal from the Commission;

Having regard to the Opinion of the European Parliament;

Having regard to the Opinion of the Economic and Social Committee;

Whereas, for the achievement of the objectives of the Treaty establishing the European Economic Community, Article 3 (f) requires the Community to institute " a system ensuring that competition in the Common Market is not distorted ";

Whereas analysis of market structures in the Community shows that the concentration process is becoming faster and that the degree of concentration is growing in such manner that the preservation of effective competition in the Common Market and the objective set out in Article 3 (f) could be jeopardized;

Whereas concentration must therefore be made subject to a systematic control arrangement;

Whereas the Treaty already provides some powers of action of the Community to this end;

Whereas Article 86 applies to concentrations effected by undertakings holding a dominant position in the Common Market or in a substantial part of it which strengthen such position to such an extent that the resulting degree of dominance would substantially restrict competition;

Whereas the power of action aforesaid extends only to such concentrations, as would result in only undertakings remaining in the market whose conduct depended on the undertaking which had effected the concentration; whereas it does not extend to the prevention of such concentrations;

Whereas additional powers of action must be provided for to make it possible to act against other concentrations which may distort competition in the Common Market and to establish arrangements for controlling them before they are effected;

Whereas under Article 235 of the Treaty the Community may give itself the powers of action necessary for the attainment of its objectives;

Whereas, to institute a system ensuring that competition in the Common Market is not distorted, it is necessary, in so far as trade between Member States may be affected, to submit to control arrangements such concentrations which give undertakings the power to prevent effective competition in the Common Market or in a substantial part of it, or which strengthen such a power;

Whereas the power to prevent effective competition must be appraised by reference, in particular, to the scope for choice available to suppliers and consumers, the economic and financial power of the undertakings concerned, the structure of the markets affected and supply and demand trends for the relevant goods or services;

Whereas concentrations which, by reason of the small significance of turnover and market share of the undertakings concerned, are not likely to impede the preservation of effective competition in the common market may be excluded from this Regulation;

Whereas it may be found necessary, for the purpose of reconciling objectives to be attained in the common interest of the Community, especially within the frame of Common policies, to exempt certain concentrations from incompatibility, under conditions and obligations to be determined case by case;

Whereas the Commission should be entitled to take decisions to prevent or terminate concentrations which are incompatible with the Common Market, decisions designed to re-establish conditions of effective competition and decisions declaring that a particular concentration may be considered to be compatible with the Common Market; whereas the Commission should be given exclusive jurisdiction in this matter, subject to review by the Court of Justice;

Whereas, to ensure effective supervision, prior notification of major concentrations and the suspension of concentrations by undertakings should be made obligatory;

Whereas a time-limit within which the Commission must commence proceedings in respect of a concentration notified to it and a time-limit within which it must give a final decision on the incompatibility of a concentration with the Common Market should be laid down;

Whereas undertakings concerned must be accorded the right to be heard by the Commission as soon as proceedings have commenced, and third parties showing a sufficient interest must be given the opportunity of submitting their comments;

Whereas the Commission must have the assistance of the Member States and must also be empowered to require information to be given and to carry out the necessary investigations in order to examine concentrations in the light of provisions of this Regulation;

Whereas compliance with this Regulation must be enforceable by means of fines and periodic penalty payments; whereas it is desirable to confer upon the Court of Justice, pursuant to Article 172, unlimited jurisdiction to that extent;

Whereas this Regulation should extend both to concentrations which constitute abuses of dominant positions and to concentrations which give the undertakings concerned the power to prevent effective competition in the Common Market; whereas it should therefore be stipulated that Regulations Nos. 17 and 1017/68 do no longer apply to concentrations from the date of entry into force of the present Regulation;

Has adopted this Regulation:

Article 1—Basic provisions

1. Any transaction which has the direct or indirect effect of bringing about a concentration between undertakings or groups of undertakings, at least one of which is established in the Common Market, whereby they acquire or enhance the power to hinder effective competition in the Common Market or in a substantial part thereof, is incompatible with the Common Market in so far as the concentration may affect trade between Member States. The power to hinder effective competition shall be appraised by reference in particular to the extent to which suppliers and consumers have a possibility of choice, to the economic and financial power of the undertakings concerned, to the structure of the markets affected, and to supply and demand trends for the relevant goods or services.

2. Paragraph 1 shall not apply where:
—the aggregate turnover of the undertakings participating in the concentration is less than 200 million units of account and
—the goods or services concerned by the concentration do not account in any Member State for more than 25 per cent. of the turnover in identical goods or services or in goods or services which, by reason of their characteristics, their price and the use for which they are intended, may be regarded as similar by the consumer.

3. Paragraph 1 may, however, be declared inapplicable to concentrations which are indispensable to the attainment of an objec-

tive which is given priority treatment in the common interest of the Community.

Article 2—Definition of concentration

1. The concentrations referred to in Article 1 are those whereby a person or an undertaking or a group of persons or undertakings, acquires control of one or several undertakings.

2. Control is constituted by rights or contracts which, either separately or jointly, and having regard to the considerations of fact or law involved, make it possible to determine how an undertaking shall operate, and particularly by:

(1) Ownership or the right to use all or part of the assets of an undertaking;

(2) Rights or contracts which confer power to influence the composition, voting or decisions of the organs of an undertaking;

(3) Rights or contracts which make it possible to manage the business of an undertaking;

(4) Contracts made with an undertaking concerning the computation or appropriation of its profits;

(5) Contracts made with an undertaking concerning the whole or an important part of supplies or outlets, where the duration of these contracts or the quantities to which they relate exceed what is usual in commercial contracts dealing with those matters.

3. Control is acquired by persons, undertakings or groups of persons or undertakings who:

(1) are holders of the rights or entitled to rights under the contracts concerned;

(2) while not being holders of such rights or entitled to rights under such contracts, have power to exercise the rights deriving therefrom;

(3) in a fiduciary capacity own assets of an undertaking or shares in an undertaking, and have power to exercise the rights attaching thereto.

4. Control of an undertaking is not constituted where, upon formation of an undertaking or increase of its capital, banks or financial institutions acquire shares in that undertaking with a view to selling them on the market, provided that they do not exercise voting rights in respect of those shares.

Article 3—Powers of decision of the Commission

1. When the Commission finds that a concentration is caught by Article 1 (1) and that the conditions laid down in Article 1 (3)

are not satisfied, it shall issue a decision declaring the concentration to be incompatible with the Common Market.

2. The decision by which the Commission declares a concentration to be incompatible within the meaning of paragraph 1 shall not automatically render null and void the legal transactions relating to such operation.

3. Where a concentration has already been put into effect, the Commission may require, by decision taken under paragraph 1 or by a separate decision, the undertakings, or assets acquired or concentrated to be separated or the cessation of common control or any other action that may be appropriate in order to restore conditions of effective competition.

4. When the Commission finds that a concentration is caught by Article 1 (1) and that the conditions laid down in Article 1 (3) are satisfied, it shall issue a decision declaring Article 1 (1) to be inapplicable; conditions and obligations may be attached thereto.

5. Subject to review by the Court of Justice, the Commission shall have sole power to take the decisions provided for in this Article.

Article 4—Prior notifications of concentrations

1. Concentrations shall be notified to the Commission before they are put into effect, where the aggregate turnover of the undertakings concerned is not less than one thousand million units of account.

2. Where concentrations proposed by an undertaking or a group of undertakings have already reached or exceeded the amounts referred to in paragraph 1, they shall be exempted from the obligation of prior notification, if the turnover of the undertaking the control of which they propose to acquire is less than 30 millions units of account.

3. The obligation to notify shall be discharged by the person or undertaking or the group of persons or undertakings which proposes to acquire control within the meaning of Article 2.

4. Concentrations which are not caught by paragraph 1 may nevertheless be notified to the Commission before they are put into effect.

Article 5—Detailed rules for calculating turnover and market shares

1. (*a*) The aggregate turnover specified in Articles 1 (2) and 4 (1) shall be obtained by adding together the turnover for the last financial year for all goods and services of:

(i) the undertakings participating in the concentration;
(ii) the undertakings and groups of undertakings which control the undertakings participating in the concentration within the meaning of Article 2;
(iii) the undertakings or groups of undertakings controlled within the meaning of Article 2 by the undertakings participating in the concentration.

(*b*) The market shares referred to in Article 1 (2) near those held in the last financial year by all the undertakings listed in sub-paragraph (*a*) above.

2. In place of turnover as specified in Articles 1 (2) and 4 (1) and in paragraph 1 of this Article, the following shall be used:
—for banking and financial institutions: one-tenth of their assets;
—for insurance companies: the value of the premiums received by them.

Article 6—Commencement of proceedings

1. Where the Commission considers that a concentration is likely to become the subject of a decision under Article 1 (1) or (3), it shall commence proceedings and so inform the undertakings in question and the competent authorities in the Member States.

2. As regards concentrations notified to it, the Commission shall commence proceedings within a period not exceeding three months unless the relevant undertakings agree to extend that period. The period of three months shall commence on the day following receipt of the notification, or if the information to be supplied with the notification is incomplete, on the day following the receipt of the complete information.

3. The Commission may commence proceedings after the expiry of the three months' period where the information supplied by the undertakings in the notification is false or misleading.

4. Without prejudice to paragraph 3 a concentration notified to the Commission shall be presumed to be compatible with the Common Market if the Commission does not commence proceedings before expiration of the period specified in paragraph 2.

Article 7—Suspension of the effecting of the concentration

1. Undertakings shall not put into effect a concentration notified to the Commission before the end of the time limit provided for in Article 6 (2) unless the Commission informs them before the end of the time limit that it is not necessary to commence proceedings.

2. Where the Commission commences proceedings it may by

decision require the undertakings to suspend the concentration until it has decided whether the concentration is compatible with the Common Market or has closed the proceedings.

Article 8—Communications of objections and hearings

1. Before taking decisions as provided for in Articles 3, 7, 13 and 14, the Commission shall give the undertakings concerned the opportunity of being heard on the matters to which the Commission has taken objection. The same opportunity shall be given to associations of undertakings concerned before decisions being taken as provided for in Articles 13 and 14.

2. If the Commission or the competent authorities of the Member States consider it necessary, the Commission may also hear other natural or legal persons. Applications to be heard on the part of such persons shall, where they show a sufficient interest, be granted.

3. Articles 2, 3, 4, 7, 8, 9, 10 and 11 of Regulation 99/63/EEC shall be applied.

Article 9—Closure of proceedings

If, after having commenced proceedings, the Commission considers that there are no grounds for action against a concentration, it shall close the proceedings and so inform the undertakings concerned and the competent authorities of the Member States.

Article 10—Requests for information

1. In carrying out the duties assigned to it by this Regulation, the Commission may obtain all necessary information from the governments and competent authorities of the Member States and from undertakings and associations of undertakings.

2. When sending a request for information to an undertaking or association of undertakings, the Commission shall at the same time forward a copy of the request to the competent authority of the Member State in whose territory the seat of the undertaking or association of undertakings is situated.

3. In its request the Commission shall state the legal basis and the purpose of the request and also the penalties provided for in Article 13 (1) (b) for supplying incorrect information.

4. The owners of the undertakings or their representatives and, in the case of legal persons, companies or firms, or of associations having no legal personality, the persons authorized to represent them by law or by their constitution, shall supply the information requested.

5. Where an undertaking or association of undertakings does not supply the information requested within the time limit fixed by the Commission, or supplies incomplete information, the Commission shall by decision require the information to be supplied. The decision shall specify what information is required, fix an appropriate time limit within which it is to be supplied and mention the penalties provided for in Article 13 (1) (b) and Article 14 (1) (a) and the right to have the decision reviewed by the Court of Justice.

6. The Commission shall at the same time forward a copy of its decision to the competent authority of the Member State in whose territory the seat of the undertaking or association of undertakings is situated.

Article 11—Investigations by the authorities of the Member States

1. At the request of the Commission, the competent authorities of the Member States shall undertake the investigations which the Commission considers to be necessary under Article 12 (1), or which it has ordered by decision pursuant to Article 12 (3). The officials of the competent authorities of the Member States responsible for conducting these investigations shall exercise their powers upon production of an authorization in writing issued by the competent authority of the Member State in whose territory the investigation is to be made. Such authorization shall specify the subject matter and purpose of the investigation.

2. If so requested by the Commission or by the competent authority of the Member State in whose territory the investigation is to be made, officials of the Commission may assist the officials of such authority in carrying out their duties.

Article 12—Investigating powers of the Commission

1. In carrying out the duties assigned to it by this Regulation, the Commission may undertake all necessary investigations into undertakings and associations of undertakings.

To this end the officials authorized by the Commission are empowered:

   (*a*) to examine the books and other business records;
   (*b*) to take or demand copies of or extracts from the books and business records;
   (*c*) to ask for oral explanations on the spot;
   (*d*) to enter any premises, land and means of transport of undertakings.

2. The officials of the Commission authorized to carry out these investigations shall exercise their powers upon production of an

authorization in writing specifying the subject matter and purpose of the investigation and the penalties provided for in Article 13 (1) (c) in cases where production of the required books or other business records is incomplete. In good time before the investigation, the Commission shall inform the competent authority of the Member State in whose territory the investigation is to be made of the investigation and of the identity of the authorized officials.

3. Undertakings and associations of undertakings shall submit to investigations ordered by decision of the Commission. The decision shall specify the subject matter and purpose of the investigation, appoint the date on which it is to begin and indicate the penalties provided for in Article 13 (1) (c) and Article 14 (1) (b) and the right to have the decision reviewed by the Court of Justice.

4. The Commission shall take decisions referred to in paragraph 3 after consultation with the competent authority of the Member State in whose territory the investigation is to be made.

5. Officials of the competent authority of the Member State in whose territory the investigation is to be made may, at the request of such authority or of the Commission, assist the officials of the Commission in carrying out their duties.

6. Where an undertaking opposes an investigation ordered pursuant to this Article, the Member State concerned shall afford the necessary assistance to the officials authorized by the Commission to enable them to make their investigation. Member States shall, after consultation with the Commission, take the necessary measures to this end before. . . .

Article 13—Fines

1. The Commission may by decision impose on undertakings and associations of undertakings fines of from 1,000 to 50,000 units of account where intentionally or negligently:

(*a*) they supply incorrect or misleading information in a notification pursuant to Article 4;

(*b*) they supply incorrect information in response to a request made pursuant to Article 10 or fail to supply information within the time-limit fixed by a decision taken pursuant to Article 10;

(*c*) they produce the required books or other business records in incomplete form during investigations under Article 11 or 12, or refuse to submit to an investigation ordered by decision taken pursuant to Article 12.

2. The Commission may by decision impose on natural or legal persons fines of from 1,000 to 1,000,000 units of account where,

either intentionally or negligently, they commit a breach of the obligation to notify under Article 4.

3. The Commission may by decision impose fines not exceeding 10 per cent. of the value of the re-organized assets where undertakings either intentionally or negligently, conclude an unlawful concentration before the end of the time-limit provided for in Article 6 (2) or in spite of a decision taken by the Commission under Articles 3 (1) or 7 (2).

Article 14—Periodic penalty payments

1. The Commission may by decision impose on undertakings or associations of undertakings periodic penalty payments up to 25,000 units of account for each day of the delay calculated from the date appointed by the decision, in order to compel them:

    (*a*) to supply complete and correct information which it has requested by decision taken pursuant to Article 10;

    (*b*) to submit to an investigation which it has ordered by decision taken pursuant to Article 12.

2. The Commission may by decision impose on such undertakings periodic penalty payments up to 50,000 units of account for each day of the delay, calculated from the day appointed by the decision, in order to compel them to apply the measures resulting from a decision taken pursuant to Article 3 (3).

Article 15—Review by the Court of Justice

The Court of Justice shall have unlimited jurisdiction within the meaning of Article 17 of the Treaty to review decisions whereby the Commission has fixed a fine or periodic penalty payment; it may cancel, reduce or increase the fine or periodic penalty payment imposed.

Article 16—Professional secrecy

1. Information acquired as a result of the application of Articles 10, 11 and 12 shall be used only for the purpose of the relevant request or investigation.

2. The Commission and the competent authorities of the Member States, their officials and other servants shall not disclose information acquired by them as a result of the application of this Regulation and of the kind covered by the obligation of professional secrecy.

3. The provisions of paragraphs 1 and 2 shall not prevent publication of general information or surveys which do not contain information relating to particular undertakings or associations of undertakings.

Article 17—Time-limits and publication of decisions

1. (*a*) Decisions under Article 3 (1) and (4) shall be taken within nine months following the date of commencement of proceedings, save where there is agreement with the relevant undertakings to extend that period.

   (*b*) The period of nine months shall not apply where the Commission is obliged to request information by decision taken pursuant to Article 10 or require an investigation by decision taken pursuant to Article 12.

2. The Commission shall publish the decisions which it takes pursuant to Article 3.

3. The publication shall state the names of the parties and the main content of the decision; it shall have regard to the legitimate interest of undertakings in the protection of their business secrets.

Article 18—Unit of account

For the purpose of this Regulation the unit of account shall be that used in drawing up the budget of the Community in accordance with Articles 207 and 209 of the Treaty.

Article 19—Liaison with the authorities of the Member States

1. The Commission shall forthwith transmit to the competent authorities of the Member States a copy of the notifications together with the most important documents lodged with the Commission pursuant to this Regulation.

2. The Commission shall carry out the procedure set out in this Regulation in close and constant co-operation with the competent authorities of the Member States; such authorities shall have the right to express their views upon that procedure, and in particular to request the Commission to commence proceedings under Article 86.

3. The Advisory Committee on Restrictive Practices and Monopolies shall be consulted prior to the taking of any decision under Articles 3, 13 and 14.

4. The Advisory Committee shall consist of officials having responsibility for restrictive practices and monopolies. Each Member State shall appoint an official to represent it; he may be replaced by another official where he is unable to act.

5. Consultation shall take place, at a meeting convened at the invitation of the Commission, not earlier than fourteen days following despatch of the invitation. A summary of the facts together with the most important documents and a preliminary draft of the decision to be taken, shall be sent with the invitation.

6. The Committee may deliver an opinion even if certain members are absent and unrepresented. The outcome of the consultation shall be annexed to the draft decision. The minutes shall not be published.

Article 20—Exclusive application of this Regulation

Regulation Nos. 17 and 1017 shall not apply to the concentrations covered by this Regulation.

Article 21—Implementing provisions

The Commission shall have power to adopt implementing provisions concerning the form, content and other details of notifications pursuant to Article 4 of this Regulation.

Article 22

This Regulation shall be binding in its entirety and directly applicable in all Member States.

This Regulation shall enter into force. . . .

Text 10

Draft Convention on the international merger of sociétés anonymes; Text drawn up by government experts pursuant to Article 220 third indent of the Treaty of Rome establishing the European Economic Community (1972).

PREAMBLE

The High Contracting Parties to the Treaty establishing the European Economic Community,

Guided by the wish to implement the provisions of Article 220 of the said Treaty which concerns the possibility of mergers between companies or firms governed by the laws of different countries,

Considering that the legal obstacles standing in the way of such operations should be removed without prejudice to the application to companies or firms of the other provisions of the Treaty,

Have decided to conclude the present Convention on the international merger of *sociétés anonymes* and for this purpose have appointed as their plenipotentiaries:

His Majesty the King of the Belgians:
———

The President of the Federal Republic of Germany:
———

The President of the French Republic:
———

The President of the Italian Republic:
———

His Royal Highness the Grand Duke of Luxembourg:
———

Her Majesty the Queen of the Netherlands:
———

WHO, meeting in the Council, and after exchanging their respective full powers, found in good and due form,

Have reached agreement on the following provisions:

CHAPTER I: FIELD OF APPLICATION

Article 1 [1]

1. Companies formed in accordance with the law of the different Contracting States may merge pursuant to the provisions of the present Convention provided they are accorded recognition in the Contracting States by virtue of the Convention of February 29, 1968, on the mutual recognition of companies and legal persons.

First variant: [2]

2. Where one of the merging companies is not accorded recognition in a Contracting State by virtue of Article 3 or Article 9 of the Convention on the mutual recognition of companies and legal persons, the present Convention shall not apply if one of the merging companies or the new company has its seat in the territory of the said State.

3. If none of the merging companies nor the new company has its seat in the territory of the State which, by virtue of Article 3 or Article 9 of the Convention of February 29, 1968, does not accord recognition to one of such companies, the merger shall not be effective with respect to that State.

Second variant: [3]

2. Where one of the merging companies is not accorded recognition in a Contracting State by virtue of Article 3 or Article 9 of the Convention on the mutual recognition of companies and legal persons, the present Convention shall not apply if one of the merging companies or the new company has its seat in the territory of the said State.

Article 2

Companies within the meaning of Article 1 are:
— *la société anonyme—de naamloze vennootschap* of Belgian law,
— *die Aktiengesellschaft* of German law,
— *la société anonyme* of French law,

---

[1] The Belgian delegation has made a general reservation with respect to the whole of the problem raised by the definition of the field of application of the Convention.

    The French delegation has proposed a text limiting the field of application of the Convention in cases where the decision-making centre of one of the companies is located outside the Community.

    The delegations considered that the problem involved one of economic policy to be examined in the Council.

[2] The German, French and Italian delegations favour this variant.

[3] The Belgian, Luxembourg and Netherlands delegations favour this variant. The German delegation might possibly endorse it as well.

— *la société anonyme* of Luxembourg law,
— *de naamloze vennootschap* of Netherlands law.

Article 3 [4]

The merger may occur either by acquisition of one [or several] company[ies] by another in accordance with Chapter II, or by the formation of a new company in accordance with Chapter III of the present Convention.

CHAPTER II: MERGER BY ACQUISITION

Section 1 : Definition of merger by acquisition

Article 4

Merger by acquisition is the operation whereby one company transfers to another, by winding up but without implementation of the liquidation procedure, the whole of its assets and liabilities by allotting to the shareholders of the company acquired shares in the acquiring company and, where applicable, by payment in cash of a balance not exceeding ten per cent. of the nominal value of the shares allotted or, in the absence of a nominal value, of their book value.

Article 5

1. The provisions of the present chapter shall also be applicable where one of the companies holds all or part of the shares of the other.

2. However, where the acquiring company holds all the shares of the company acquired, the provisions of Article 8, paragraph 1 (b) and (c) shall not be applicable. In this case:

(a) the report provided for in Article 11 shall be prepared only for the acquiring company;

(b) each of the reports provided for in Article 12 shall be prepared in accordance with such text but shall be submitted solely to the shareholders of the acquiring company.

Article 6

Merger by acquisition may also take place in respect of a company acquired in liquidation where the law applicable to such company so permits and provided that the company acquired has not yet commenced distributing its assets among its shareholders.

---

[4] The words between square brackets were proposed by the Italian delegation; this proposal did not meet with the approval of the other delegations.

Section 2: Preparation of the merger

Article 7

1. The organs of the merging companies which, according to the law applicable to each of the companies, are duly authorized in the case of mergers, shall prepare a merger plan in writing.

2. This plan shall take the form of a notarial deed where the law applicable to one of the merging companies so requires.

3. Where, by virtue of the law applicable to one of the companies, a contract has to be drawn up prior to the decisions of the general meetings, such contract shall constitute the merger plan within the meaning of the present Convention.

Article 8

1. The merger plan shall include as a minimum:
    (a) the name, legal form and seat of the merging companies;
    (b) the share exchange ratio and, where applicable, the amount of the cash payment;
    (c) the procedure for the allotment of the shares in the acquiring company and the date from which such shares entitle participation in the profits;
    (d) the date from which the operations of the company acquired are deemed to be effected on behalf of the acquiring company;
    (e) the rights which are accorded by the acquiring company to shareholders having special rights and to holders of securities other than shares, or the measures proposed in respect of them.

2. The merger plan shall in addition state that the merger is subject to the approval of the merger plan by the competent organs defined in Article 16.

Article 9

To be annexed to the merger plan are:
    (a) the up-to-date statutes of the merging companies;
    (b) the balance sheets, profit and loss accounts and annual reports of the merging companies for the last three financial years;
    (c) an interim statement of accounts as at the first day of the second month preceding the date of the merger plan where the last balance sheet relates to a financial year which ended more than six months prior to that date;

(d) the reports of the competent organs of the merging companies as provided for in Article 11;

(e) the experts' reports as provided for in Article 12.

Article 10

The interim statement of accounts provided for in Article 9 (c) shall be drawn up in accordance with the same methods and shall be presented in the same way as the last annual balance sheet. However,

(a) no new actual inventory shall be drawn up,

(b) the valuations appearing in the last balance sheet shall be amended only in the light of movements in book entries; but account shall be taken:

— of interim depreciations and reserves,

— of substantial changes in actual values not reflected in book entries.

Article 11

The organs of each of the merging companies, authorized according to the law respectively applicable to them, shall prepare a detailed report explaining and justifying, from the legal and economic point of view, the merger plan and in particular the share exchange ratio.

Article 12 [5]

1. At least one expert shall be appointed to each of the merging companies. The same person may be appointed only to one company.

2. Such experts shall be independent and, according to the law applicable to the company to which they are appointed, qualified to undertake the legally prescribed examination of the annual accounts of such company.

3. The method of appointment of the experts shall be determined by the law of the company to which they are appointed. They may be the persons responsible for examining the annual accounts where such persons fulfil the conditions of paragraph 2 of the present Article.

4. The experts shall examine the merger plan and prepare a report for the shareholders. The object and contents of such report shall be determined, for each company, by the law applicable to that company, but the experts shall in any event state whether, in their opinion, the exchange ratio is justified or not.

---

[5] The Belgian delegation expressed a reservation on this text. See appendix to the Chairman's report.

5. The declaration referred to in the preceding paragraph shall be supported at the least by the following matters:

  (a) the relative net assets of the companies on the basis of actual values;

  (b) the relative earnings of the companies, taking account of future prospects;

  (c) the valuation criteria in respect of net assets and earnings.

6. The report shall in addition indicate special evaluation difficulties, if any.

7. Each expert shall be entitled to obtain from the merging companies all useful information and documents and to undertake any necessary verification.

Article 13

1. In each of the Contracting States to whose laws the merging companies are subject, notice of the merger plan shall be published, at least one month prior to the date for which the general meeting is convened, in the national gazette designated for the publication of amendments to the statutes. The publication of the notice shall take place according to the provisions of the law applicable to each of the companies.

2. Such notice shall contain the matters stipulated in Article 8. It shall in addition state the disclosure arrangements provided for in Articles 14 and 15, the right of consultation and the right to obtain copies granted by such provisions as well as the right of the creditors to request the giving of a security pursuant to Articles 18 to 21.

Article 14

1. The merger plan, as well as the annexes referred to in Article 9 (a), (b) and (c), shall be deposited on the date of the convening of the general meeting which has to vote on the merger plan and in any event at least one month prior to the date of such meeting, in the file opened in the name of each of the merging companies in accordance with the law applicable to it.

2. A copy in full or in part of the documents referred to in paragraph 1 shall be obtainable simply upon request; the cost of such copy may not exceed the applicable administrative costs.

Article 15

1. From the time of the convening of the general meeting which is to vote on the merger plan, and in any event during the period of one month before the date of the meeting, each share-

holder shall be entitled to examine, at the registered office, the merger plan and the annexes referred to in Article 9.

2. A copy in full or in part of the documents referred to in paragraph 1 shall be obtainable by all shareholders, without charge and simply upon request.

Section 3 : Merger decision

Article 16

1. The merger shall require the approval of the general meeting of each of the merging companies.

2. Where, according to the provisions of the law of the State to which one of the companies is subject, a merger contract is to be prepared subsequent to the decisions of the general meetings, such provisions shall be applied.

3. The provisions of the law to which each of the companies is subject, concerning intervention in the merger decision by shareholders having special rights or holders of securities other than shares, shall be applicable.

Article 17

1. The convening, composition and holding of general meetings as well as the quorum and majority conditions shall be governed, for each of the merging companies, by the provisions of the law applicable to it in the case of mergers or, failing this, to amendments to the statutes.

2. The law of the company acquired or its statutes may lay down special majority or quorum conditions for mergers governed by the present Convention. However, in no event may such requirement be:

— either a majority exceeding three quarters of the votes cast at the general meeting and a quorum exceeding one half of the shares with voting rights upon a first convening and one quarter of such shares upon a second convening;

— or, if the law makes no provision for a quorum, a majority exceeding three quarters of the votes cast and four fifths of the registered share capital represented at the meeting taking the decision.

Section 4 : Protection of creditors

Article 18

1. Creditors other than debenture holders of the company acquired whose claim precedes the publication of the notice of the

merger plan concerning this company may, within thirty days of such publication, require the granting of a security.

2. Failing agreement within eight days of receipt of the creditor's request by the company, the court shall postpone the entry into effect of the merger until the granting of the security as ordered by it or until the rejection of the application. The court shall reject the request if the creditor already disposes of an adequate security or if one of the merging companies establishes that the acquiring company is manifestly solvent.

3. The company shall be exempt from granting a security if the debt, even if it has not matured, is repaid either prior to the decision of the court or not later than one month of such decision.

Article 19

1. The creditors other than debenture holders of the company acquired whose claim precedes the fulfilment of the disclosure formalities referred to in Article 27 may, within three months of the completion of these formalities, require the granting of a security by the acquiring company. However, the creditors who were entitled to require a security from the company acquired in pursuance of Article 18 may not avail themselves of the provisions of the present Article.

2. Failing agreement within eight days of receipt by the company of the creditor's request, the court may order the granting of a security. Should the company fail to grant such security within one month of the court's decision the claim shall be immediately enforceable. The court may reject the application where the creditor already disposes of a sufficient security or where it is established that the acquiring company is manifestly solvent.

3. The company is exempt from giving a security where the debt, even if it has not matured, is repaid either prior to the court's decision or not later than one month of such decision.

4. The application of the present Article shall in no way prejudice the effects of the merger.

Article 20

Without prejudice to the rules relating to the collective exercise of their rights, Articles 18 and 19 shall be applied to the debenture holders of the company acquired, unless the merger has been approved by a general meeting of debenture holders or, if the law governing the company acquired contains no provision for such a meeting or does not grant it the power to approve the merger, by the debenture holders individually.

Article 21

Each Contracting State may declare:

    (a) that it will apply only Article 19 to the creditors, whether debenture holders or otherwise;

    (b) that it will apply to the creditors, whether debenture holders or otherwise of the acquiring company, where the latter is subject to its laws, the same provisions as to the creditors of the company acquired.

Article 22

The provisions of the law, concerning the protection of shareholders with special rights or bearers of securities other than shares, to which each of the merging companies is subject, shall be applicable.

    Section 5 : Provisions on the question of participation [6]

See Annexe to the Chairman's report.

    Section 6 : Control and disclosure of the merger

Article 23

1. Where the law applicable to one of the merging companies makes provision, in the event of a merger, for a preventive control of legality, judicial or administrative, the provisions relating to such control shall apply to such company according to the law to which it is subject.

2. Where the law does not provide for a preventive control and where such control does not apply to all the legal acts necessary for the merger, then the minutes of the general meetings which decide on the merger and, where applicable, the merger contract subsequent to such general meetings, shall be drawn up and certified by notarial deed.

Article 24

1. If the control referred to in Article 23, paragraph 1 is prescribed for each of the merging companies, it shall relate solely:

    (a) as regards each company, to the legal acts and formalities required of it and to the absence of a judicial decision of postponement taken by virtue of Article 18;

    (b) furthermore, as regards the acquiring company, to the merger plan within the meaning of Article 7.

---

[6] The Italian delegation is opposed to the introduction into the Convention of provisions on this subject.

2. If the control is not prescribed for each of the merging companies it shall be concerned solely with the legal acts and formalities required of the company [companies] subjected [7] to such control and with the absence of a judicial decision of postponement taken by virtue of Article 18. As to the other company [the other companies],[7] the notary shall verify and certify solely:

— the existence and legality of the legal acts and formalities required of the company for which he is acting and of the merger plan within the meaning of Article 7;

— the absence of a judicial decision of postponement taken by virtue of Article 18.

3. Where the law of one of the merging companies prescribes the conclusion of a merger contract after the approval of the merger by the companies in question, the control or, where applicable, the verification by notary provided for in the previous paragraph shall relate solely:

(a) as to the company of which the law requires this contract, to the legal acts and formalities required of such company;

(b) as to the other company, to the legal acts and formalities required of it and in addition, if the law to which such company is subject provides for a control subsequent to the merger contract, to such contract;

(c) as to each company, to the absence of a judicial decision of postponement taken by virtue of Article 18.

In the case provided for in the present paragraph, the control or verification of the merger plan within the meaning of Article 7 shall be effected in the State where the control or verification formalities are completed in the first place.

Article 25

1. Where a control is necessary both as regards the acquiring company and the company acquired, this shall be carried out first of all on the acquiring company and the control necessary on the company acquired may proceed only if proof is provided that the necessary control formalities have been carried out on the acquiring company.

2. Where the control is only required either in respect of the company acquired or in respect of the acquiring company, it can take place only upon production of the notarial deed recording the decision by the general meeting of the other company approving the merger.

---

[7] The words between square brackets take account of the reservation expressed by the Italian delegation with respect to Article 3.

3. The provisions of paragraph 1 above are not applicable in cases where the law of the company acquired prescribes the conclusion of a merger contract after approval of the merger by the companies in question and where the law of the acquiring company requires a control of the merger subsequent to the conclusion of such contract.

Article 26

1. Where the conclusion of a merger contract is not prescribed by the law of one of the merging companies or where the merger contract prescribed by one of such laws was concluded before the general meetings decided upon it, the merger shall take effect on one of the following dates:

   (a) on the date of the notarial deed recording the decision of the general meeting either of the company acquired or of the acquiring company whichever is the last to approve the merger where neither of these companies is subject to control;

   (b) on the date of completion, with regard to the company acquired, of the control formalities where such control is necessary both for the acquiring company and for the company acquired;

   (c) on the date of completion of the control formalities either with regard to the company acquired or with regard to the acquiring company, where such control is necessary only in case of such companies.

2. Where the merger contract prescribed by the law of one of the merging companies was concluded after the approval of the merger by the companies in question, the merger shall take effect on the date of conclusion of the merger contract; however, where the merger requires a control of one of the merging companies and where such control occurs only after the conclusion of the merger contract, the merger shall take effect only on the date of completion of the control formalities of the company acquired or, where no control is necessary of the latter, on the date of completion of the control formalities of the acquiring company.

Article 27

1. The procedures for disclosure shall be determined in respect of each of the merging companies by the law applicable to it.

2. Apart from the matters prescribed for each of the companies by the law applicable to it, the disclosure shall mention the place and date of performance of the disclosure formalities laid down in Articles 13 and 14.

3. The acquiring company may itself undertake the disclosure formalities relating to the company acquired.

Article 28

Subject to the application of Article 31, the merger may be invoked against third-parties under the conditions laid down in the provisions of the law to which each of the companies is subject, on the invoking of mergers against third-parties or, in the absence of such provisions, on amendments to the statutes.

Section 7 : Effects of the merger

Article 29

Subject to the provisions of Article 31, a merger shall automatically entail the universal transfer, both as between the company acquired and the acquiring company and as regards third parties, of the whole of the capital (assets and liabilities) of the company acquired to the acquiring company.

Article 30 [8]

1. The employment contracts concluded by the company acquired shall be automatically transferred to the acquiring company. In his relations with the acquiring company, the employee retains the seniority acquired in the service of the company acquired; the legal effects of such seniority shall be determined by the employment contract and by the law applicable to such contract.

2. Where the dismissal or resignation of the employee, caused by his refusal to exercise his activity in a country other than that in which he exercised it prior to the merger, takes effect by virtue of the law applicable to the employment contract prior to the merger, the termination of such contract shall be deemed to have occurred by the action of the employer.

---

[8] All the delegations have approved the contents of this Article but only four delegations are in favour of retaining it in the Convention.

The Belgian delegation considers that it should not appear because social questions should be settled as a whole and because the solutions given by this text could prejudge those which might be adopted in the framework of the activities undertaken by the Commission on the social problems of international concentrations.

The Luxembourg delegation shares the point of view of the Belgian delegation.

The Italian delegation considers that this Article should be supplemented by two provisions :

(a) one, for a special indemnity for employees affected by a decision to transfer the place of work,

(b) the other, for a period of reflection additional to the period of notice for employees to whom proposals are made in respect of a substantial change in their employment contract.

This proposal did not meet with the approval of the other delegations.

3. However, the previous paragraph shall not be applicable if the employee has given an undertaking, in his employment contract with the company acquired to work, if need be, in the country where he is requested to exercise his activity, unless such undertaking is invalidated by virtue of the law governing the employment contract.

4. Paragraph 2 shall also be applicable when the merger entails any other substantial change to the employment contract.

Article 31

1. Where the law applicable to certain assets brought in by the company acquired requires special formalities, in the event of merger, to enable the transfer to be invoked against third parties, then such formalities shall be carried out in accordance with and their effect as well as the consequences of non-compliance shall be determined by such law.

2. The acquiring company may itself undertake such formalities.

Article 32

The issue of the shares of the acquiring company and of certificates representing such shares as well as, where applicable, of the cash adjustment, shall take place pursuant to the law applicable to the company acquired in the event of merger, or in accordance with the provisions of the merger plan insofar as such provisions are compatible with such law.

Section 8 : Liability and Nullity

Article 33

Any liability which may be incurred by reason of the merger operations shall be governed, in respect of each of the merging companies, by the law applicable to it in the event of merger.

Article 34

Without prejudice to the provisions of Article 35, the conditions for and the effects of nullity of the acts leading to the merger shall be governed, in respect of each of the merging companies, by the law applicable to it in the event of merger.

Article 35

After the date fixed in Article 26, the nullity of the merger may no longer be established or pronounced, except for lack of judicial or administrative control or certification in due legal form.

However, if in one of such cases the law applicable to the acquiring company excludes the nullity of the merger or subjects it to special conditions, such law shall be applicable.

Article 36

The civil sanctions other than nullity of the merger which may arise where nullity cannot be established or pronounced in application of the present Convention shall be determined by the law applicable to the acquiring company in case of merger. However, when the action for the granting of such sanctions is brought by the shareholders, the creditors or the contracting partners of the company acquired, such sanctions shall be determined by the law governing the company acquired applicable in case of merger.

Article 37

The nullity of the merger provided for in Article 35 may no longer be established or pronounced where it is still possible to eliminate the cause thereof and where regularization occurs in the time-limit fixed by the court.

Article 38

An action for nullity may no longer be brought after the expiry of a period of six months from the date on which the merger may be invoked against the party seeking the nullity.

Article 39

1. The decision establishing or pronouncing the nullity of the merger shall be published in the States where the seat of the companies having merged was located.

2. The procedure for and the effects of this publication shall be governed by the provisions of the law to which each of the companies is subject, on the invoking against third parties of amendments to the statutes.

3. Opposition by third parties, should the law of the State where the decision was pronounced so provide, is no longer admissible after the expiry of a period of six months from the performance of the disclosure formalities set out in the preceding paragraphs.

Article 40

1. The decision establishing or pronouncing the nullity of the merger shall not of itself affect the validity of the commitments entered into by the acquiring company or of those assumed towards it prior to the disclosure referred to in Article 39.

2. The companies which have taken part in the merger shall bear joint and several liability for the commitments of the acquiring company referred to in the previous paragraph.

CHAPTER III: MERGER BY FORMATION OF A NEW COMPANY

Section 1: Definition of a Merger by Formation of a New Company

Article 41

Merger by formation of a new company is the operation whereby several companies transfer to a company which they form by winding up but without implementation of the liquidation procedure, the whole of their capital (assets and liabilities) by allotting to their shareholders shares in the new company and, where applicable, by payment in cash of a balance not exceeding ten per cent. of the nominal value of the shares allotted or, in the absence of a nominal value, of their book value.

Article 42

1. The provisions of the present chapter shall also be applicable where one of the companies holds all or part of the shares of another.

2. However, where one of the merging companies holds all the shares of another, the report provided for in Article 11 shall be prepared only for the first company. In the same case, each of the reports provided for in Article 12 shall be prepared in accordance with such text but shall be submitted solely to the shareholders of the company which holds all the shares of the other company.

Article 43

Merger by formation of a new company may also take place where the companies which cease to exist are in liquidation if the laws respectively applicable to such companies so permit and provided that they have not yet commenced distributing their assets among their shareholders.

Section 2: Provisions of Chapter II Applicable to Merger by Formation of a New Company

Article 44

1. Articles 7 to 20, 21 (a), 22, 23, 24 (with the exception of paragraph 1, (b)), 29, [30], 31 and 32,[9] of Chapter II of the present

[9] This list will possibly have to be supplemented, taking account of the texts of Chapter II, Section 5.

Convention shall be applicable to merger by formation of a new company. For such application, the expressions "merging companies" or "company acquired," refer to the companies which cease to exist, and the expression "acquiring company" refers to the new company.

2. Article 8, paragraph 1, (a) shall likewise be applicable to the new company.

3. For the application of Articles 9, (a), 14 and 15, the draft statutes of the new company shall be added to the statutes of the companies which cease to exist.

4. For the application of Article 19, the reference to Article 27 shall be replaced by a reference to Article 48.

Section 3 : Special Provisions

Article 45

1. The merger plan or the draft statutes of the new company shall state the names of the members of the organs of the new company whose appointment, according to the law of the country of the registered office of such company, is to be decided either by the general meeting or the companies which themselves cease to exist.

2. The merger plan and the draft statutes of the new company shall be approved by the general meetings of each of the companies which cease to exist.

Article 46

The new company shall be formed and the disclosure of its formation shall be ensured in accordance with the provisions of the law of the country of its registered office which apply to the formation of companies as the result of a merger or, failing such provisions pursuant to the general law on the formation of companies.

Article 47

The merger shall take effect on the date on which the new company acquires legal personality.

Article 48

1. The procedure for the disclosure of the merger shall be determined in respect of each of the companies which cease to exist by the law applicable to it.

2. Apart from the matter presented for each of the companies which cease to exist and for the new company by the law applicable to them, the disclosure shall mention the place and date of

performance of the disclosure formalities laid down in Articles 13 and 14.

3. The new company may itself undertake the disclosure formalities relating to the companies which cease to exist.

Article 49

Subject to the application of Article 31, the merger may be invoked against third parties under the conditions laid down in the provisions of the law to which each of the companies which cease to exist and the new company are subject on the invoking of mergers against third parties or, in the absence of such provisions, on amendments to the statutes.

Article 50

Any liability which may be incurred by reason of the merger operations shall be governed, in respect of each of the companies which cease to exist, by the law applicable to it in the event of merger and for the new company by the law applicable in the event of formation of a company in the country of its registered office.

Article 51

The conditions for and the effects of nullity of the acts leading to the merger shall be governed, in respect of each of the companies which cease to exist, by the law applicable to it in the event of merger.

Article 52

1. The nullity of the new company shall be governed by the law of the country of its registered office applicable on the formation of a company.

2. The nullity of the merger may take place only if the new company is annulled.

CHAPTER IV: GENERAL PROVISIONS

Article 53

The decisions taken by the judicial or administrative authorities of a Contracting State in the exercise of the preventive control of legality provided for in Articles 23 and 24 shall be recognised in the other Contracting States in accordance with the provisions of the Convention of September 27, 1968, on jurisdiction and the enforcement of civil and commercial judgments.

Article 54

1. The persons who shall have the power to draw up the notarial deeds referred to in the present Convention shall be those authorized to draw up such deeds in the territory of the State to whose laws the company to which they relate is subject.

2. The deeds relating to several companies jointly may be drawn up by the persons authorized in one of the States to whose laws such companies are respectively subject.

3. The national provisions relating to the territorial authority of persons to draw up notarial deeds shall remain unaffected.

Article 55

The notarial and the deeds of a judicial or administrative authority drawn up in connection with a merger shall be exempt from authentication and any other similar formality.

Article 56

The present Convention shall not affect national and Community merger control provisions other than the preventive control of legality laid down in Articles 23 and 24. However, the nullity of a merger, even if it is provided for by the law under which such control has taken place, can be established or pronounced only in accordance with Articles 35 and 52, paragraph 2.

CHAPTER V: INTERPRETATION OF THE CONVENTION BY THE COURT OF JUSTICE OF THE EUROPEAN COMMUNITIES

Article 57

The Court of Justice of the European Communities shall have jurisdiction to give preliminary rulings on the interpretation of the present Convention.

Article 58

1. Where a question relating to the interpretation of the present Convention is raised before a court or tribunal of one of the Contracting States, that court or tribunal may, if it considers that a decision on the question is necessary to enable it to give judgment, request the Court of Justice to give a ruling thereon.

2. Where any such question is raised in a case pending before a national court or tribunal against whose decisions there is no judicial remedy under national law, that court or tribunal shall bring the matter before the Court of Justice.

Article 59

1. Insofar as the present Convention does not provide otherwise, the provisions of the Treaty establishing the European Economic Community and those of the annexed Protocol on the Statute of the Court of Justice, which are applicable where the Court is called upon to give preliminary rulings, shall likewise apply to the interpretation procedure under the present Convention.

2. The rules of procedure of the Court of Justice shall be adapted and supplemented if necessary in accordance with Article 188 of the Treaty establishing the European Economic Community.

Article 60 [10]

1. The relevant authority of a Contracting State may request the Court of Justice to give a ruling on a question of interpretation of the present Convention if the decisions given by courts or tribunals of such State are at variance with the interpretation given either by the Court of Justice, or by a decision of a court or tribunal of another Contracting State [referred to in Article 58, paragraph 2, or which has decided on appeal]. The provisions of the present paragraph shall apply only to decisions having the force of law.

2. The interpretation given by the Court of Justice following such request shall not affect the decisions in respect of which the interpretation was requested.

3. The *Procureur Général* with the Courts of Cassation of the Contracting States or any other body designated by a Contracting State shall be able to refer to the Court of Justice a request for interpretation in pursuance of paragraph 1.

4. The Registrar of the Court of Justice shall notify the Contracting States, the Commission and the Council of the European Communities of such request; within a period of two months from this notification, they shall be entitled to submit to the Court statements of case or written observations.

5. The procedure provided for in the present Article shall give rise neither to the giving nor to the refund of costs or expenses.

[10] The German, Belgian and Italian delegations are in favour of the text between square brackets. The French, Luxembourg and Dutch delegations prefer to delete it, but the Dutch delegation is prepared to fall in with the decisions of the majority.

The German delegation has formulated two reservations:

    (a) it reserves the right to revert to this text at the time of the Council discussions,

    (b) it has pointed out that the adoption of this Article should not prejudge the solution to be adopted in future conventions.

CHAPTER VI: FINAL PROVISIONS

Article 61

1. In the relations between the Contracting States the present Convention shall be applicable notwithstanding any provisions to the contrary on the international merger of *sociétés anonymes* by shares arising under different national laws contained in other conventions to which Contracting States are or may become party.

2. However, the present Convention shall not affect:
— either the rules of domestic law,
— or the provisions of international convention which are or which may come into force and which provide, in other cases, for the possibility of international mergers, provided that such rules or provisions are compatible with the Treaty establishing the European Economic Community.

Article 62

The present Convention shall apply to the European territory of the Contracting States, to the French overseas departments and to the French overseas territories. The Kingdom of the Netherlands may, at the time of signing or of ratifying the present Convention or at any time thereafter, by notice to the Secretary-General of the Council of the European Communities, declare that the present Convention shall apply to Surinam and the Netherlands Antilles.

Article 63

The present Convention shall be ratified by the signatory States. The instruments of ratification shall be deposited with the Secretary-General of the Council of the European Communities.

Article 64

The present Convention shall enter into force on the first day of the third month following the deposit of the instrument of ratification by the last signatory State to undertake this formality.

Article 65

1. The declarations provided for in Article 21 may be made on the date of signature of the Convention or at any date thereafter.

The declarations made not later than the time of deposit of the instrument of ratification shall take effect on the date of entry into force of the Convention.

The declaration made subsequently shall take effect on the first day of the third month following their receipt by the Secretary-General of the Council of the European Communities.

2. Any Contracting State may at any time withdraw its declarations or any one of them.

This withdrawal shall take effect on the first day of the third month following their receipt by the Secretary-General of the Council of the European Communities. It shall be final.

3. The declarations and their withdrawal shall be without effect on mergers the plans for which were published previously according to Article 13.

Article 66

The Secretary-General of the Council of the European Communities shall notify the signatory States of:

(a) the deposit of every instrument of ratification,

(b) the date of entry into force of the present Convention,

(c) the declarations and notifications received in pursuance of Articles 21, 62 and 65,

(d) the dates where such declarations and notifications take effect.

Article 67

The present Convention is concluded for an unlimited period.

Article 68

Any contracting State may request the revision of the present Convention. In this event, a revision conference shall be convened by the President of the Council of the European Communities.

Article 69

The present Convention, drafted in a single copy, in the German, French, Italian and Dutch languages, all four texts being equally authentic, shall be deposited in the archives of the Secretariat of the Council of the European Communities. The Secretary-General shall transmit a certified copy to each of the Governments of the Signatory States.

Joint Declarations

The High Contracting Parties to the Treaty establishing the European Economic Community, on the occasion of the signature of the Convention on the international merger of *sociétés anonymes*, have approved the text of the following declarations:

Joint Declaration No. 1[11]

The Governments of the Kingdom of Belgium, the Federal Republic of Germany, the French Republic, the Italian Republic, the Grand Duchy of Luxembourg and the Kingdom of the Netherlands,

Wishing to ensure the protection of employees' rights in the event of international mergers of companies,

Aware of the fact that the need for this protection is felt not only on the occasion of international mergers of companies, but also in all cases of international concentration operations, whatever form they assume,

Desirous of guaranteeing employees effective protection without prejudicing any more favourable provisions from which they benefit under the law applicable to them,

Note with satisfaction that the Commission of the European Communities has decided to set up for this purpose a working-group to study the questions raised in this area by international concentration operations with a view to the drawing up of a legal instrument regulating these matters.

Joint Declaration No. 2

The Governments of the Kingdom of Belgium, the Federal Republic of Germany, the French Republic, the Italian Republic, the Grand Dutchy of Luxembourg and the Kingdom of the Netherlands,

Desirous of ensuring as effective and uniform an application as possible of the provisions of the present Convention,

Declare their willingness to organise, in conjunction with the Court of Justice, an exchange of information on the decisions taken in application of the present Convention by the courts and tribunals referred to in Article 58, paragraph 2.

Joint Declaration No. 3

The Governments of the Kingdom of Belgium, the Federal Republic of Germany, the French Republic, the Italian Republic, the Grand Duchy of Luxembourg and the Kingdom of the Netherlands,

Aware that the problem of international mergers of companies raises not only strictly legal questions but also questions concerning the tax treatment of such mergers,

---

[11] Four delegations are in favour of this text. The German and Dutch delegations, on the other hand, are opposed to it.

Convinced that the absence of a solution in this field may prove an obstacle to the implementation of international mergers of companies and consequently may prevent the Convention from attaining its objectives,

Declare that the solution to the problems of a tax nature referred to in the second paragraph is an indispensable condition for the effective application of the present Convention, and

Therefore undertake to contribute to the very rapid adoption, in the framework of the European Communities, of the necessary measures in this respect.

INDEX